THE SOVIET BUDGET

How much does the Soviet Union spend on defence, economic development, social welfare, education? How does it finance the enormous scale of its expenditures under all these heads? What typical sequences are disclosed, and how do they mesh with other types of behaviour in the Soviet economy? Can one even believe the official figures? If so, what do they tell us? If not, in which directions may they need to be corrected? Has the degree of secretiveness varied over time? (Evidence is adduced to show that it has.) What are the branch and territorial components of the budget, and how are they put together, under which pressures and within which timescale? What is the budget's legal status, and how is it affected by legislative procedures? Based largely on an intensive analysis of quantitative series built up over a very long period, the investigation contributes to understanding the Soviet economy from an angle made possible by no other approach. Students of that economy, academic economists, specialists in international affairs and not least among them foreign offices, should be very interested both in the methods of analysis and in the conclusions.

Dr Raymond Hutchings is Senior Editor of ABSEES (Abstracts, Soviet and East European Series) and Project-Secretary for the United Kingdom for a multilingual economics dictionary. His career has included both diplomatic and academic appointments. A member of the research cadre of the British Foreign Service from 1952 to 1968, he served as Second Secretary in the Moscow Embassy from 1957 to 1959 and has visited the USSR another four times, most recently in 1971 when he was included in the retaliatory ban imposed by the Soviet government. In the academic world, he has held research posts at the Australian National University, 1964–8, Harvard University, 1972–3 and the Royal Institute of International Affairs, 1968–71, and teaching posts at the University of Southern California, 1962, the University of Maryland, 1961–2 and 1972, Pennsylvania State University, 1973, and the University of Texas at Austin, 1976, the last three posts with the status of visiting professor. He has made lecture tours in North America in most years from 1973 onwards.

He is the author of *Soviet Economic Development*, *Seasonal Influences in Soviet Industry* and *Soviet Science, Technology, Design* and of numerous articles and reviews, mainly about Soviet affairs.

THE SOVIET BUDGET

Raymond Hutchings

State University of New York Press
Albany

First published in U.S.A. by
State University of New York Press, Albany

For information, address State University of New York Press,
State University Plaza, Albany, N.Y., 12246

Library of Congress Cataloging in Publication Data

Hutchings, Raymond.
  The Soviet budget.

  Bibliography: p. 193
  Includes index.
  1. Budget—Soviet Union.   2. Soviet Union—
Appropriations and expenditures.   I. Title.
HJ2129.H87   1983   354.470072′2   82–19526
ISBN 0–87395–696–6
ISBN 0–87395–697–4 (pbk.)

Contents

List of Tables and Figures

FIGURES

Preface

I am concerned that our understanding of the Soviet budget should be enlarged within an integrated perspective of Soviet affairs, and hope the present book has made some progress in that direction.

Its writing was not supported by any grant, fund or institute of Russian or Soviet studies. The interest shown in my work by *Osteuropa-Wirtschaft* (editor: Franz-Lothar Altmann) is thankfully acknowledged. I am most grateful to more than three score universities, research and governmental institutions, mainly in North America, which over the past quarter century and particularly during the past decade have invited me to speak on various Soviet topics. I am greatly obliged to the National Foreign Assessment Center, and to other institutions and individuals, who have forwarded me material, often without my asking for it. Chatham House put up with my exorbitant demands on their lending facilities, and allowed me to carry off ancient copies of *Pravda* which still, on their yellowing tatters, preserved unreproduced data of bygone budgets. Via an unrelated enterprise, various fashion designers and craft shops unwittingly subsidised the time-consuming analysis. Thanks are otherwise due chiefly to my Hermes typewriter, my son's Casio calculator, my tax consultant, and of course to my wife Karen, not only for useful comments but for her vital contribution to our personal finances.

Croydon, England,   R.H.
November 1981

Glossary

DEF	'defence' (*oborona*) appropriation
dfp	deductions from profits
FNE	finance of national economy
FYP	five-year plan
Nar. khoz.	*Narodnoye khozyaystvo* (= National Economy − opening of title of annual statistical handbook)
PP	payments out of profits
SCM	social and cultural measures
sovnarkhoz	regional economic council (these were set up in 1957 and abolished in 1965)
TT	turnover tax (Russian: *nalog s oborota*)

PART I
The Economic, Institutional and Historical Setting

1 Introduction and Methods of Study

THE PHYSICAL SETTING

Snow muffles Moscow's streets, but inside the Great Kremlin Palace it is excessively warm and light. A mass of energetic-looking people are arriving. All have put on their best clothes; many wear medals, which especially commemorate some feat of labour. At ten o'clock, members of the Politburo enter the chamber, taking their places on a stepped stage facing the Supreme Soviet delegates who stand up as a mark of respect. Everyone claps. The agenda is quickly confirmed, by unanimous vote of course, and soon the Chairman of the State Planning Commission mounts the rostrum. The delegates settle down. Lenin in his niche advances a left arm and left leg. Now it is the turn of the Minister of Finance. The words drone on. We are surely in the world of Palmerston with his five-and-a-half hour speeches, perhaps a modern version of 'Civis Romanus Sum', only this is a land empire and one of no mean proportions, ten hours' difference between Brest-Litovsk and the Bering Strait. . . . Within two to three days the Budget Law has been promulgated, the delegates are dispersing. A swift and impressively orchestrated routine!

IMPORTANCE OF THE SUBJECT

Some 300 billion roubles have been rapidly voted: a huge sum far beyond one's capacity to grasp, but scarcely anyone on Earth will be left completely unaffected.

International affairs are still gripped by the opposition between East and West. This has various dimensions, but economics figures in all of them. The portion of a gross national product that is directly within the control of the respective governments engaged in that opposition must in that case particularly attract our attention. In financial terms, this means concentrating on the national budgets. The Soviet budget, since it appertains to one of the superpower antagonists, must be one of the topics studied. Moreover, it is fascinating in its own right.

AVAILABLE LITERATURE

There is no recent book in English on this subject. *The Development of the Soviet Budgetary System*, a valuable survey by R. W. Davies, was published in 1958. It has not been brought up to date. Another classic work is *Soviet Taxation*, by Franklyn D. Holzman, published in 1955. Two books in German by Günter Hedtkamp are more recent. His *Das sowjetische Finanzsystem* (1974) is primarily a history and factual record. In contrast are partial but penetrating studies, such as those by William T. Lee on Soviet defence spending. There are also articles by Lee and others (including the present writer) on budgetary topics; spending on defence is their most common focus. The subject has naturally attracted the expert attention of the National Foreign Assessment Center (for instance, its booklet *The Soviet State Budget since 1965*). A chapter in *The Soviet Economic System* (Nove, 1980) is useful; problems of interpretation are admitted, though detailed explorations are not undertaken. *Soviet Economic Development* (Hutchings, 1971, and its Second Edition, 1982) employed analytical methods which are exercised further in the present book. Most recently Igor Birman has produced the remarkable *Secret Incomes of the Soviet State Budget* (Birman, 1981). As this book appeared when the present one was already finished, it was not possible here to take its findings fully into consideration, but these – to the extent that they are compatible – appear to be, on the whole, complementary to those of the present book, just as Birman's examination solely of revenues is complementary to the emphasis in this one upon budget expenditures.

The literature in Russian is more voluminous, in particular from theoretical standpoints; however, the angle of view of Soviet authors is different and narrower. Publicisation of the budget is rather recent. Even in the USSR it is not claimed that Russia was the motherland of published budgets, an honour which is assigned to Britain (Piskotin, 1971, pp. 284–5). Annual budgets began to be published in Tsarist Russia only after 1861, following disclosures by émigrés of the unpublished figures, with detailed estimates being published from 1863 onwards (Hutchings, 1971a, p. 18; Piskotin, 1971, p. 285). Soviet writers claim that more is published now about the budget than before: the practice of Tsarist governments being contrasted with what they call the 'openness' (*glasnost'*) of Soviet budgets — beginning with that of 1918 (Piskotin, 1971, pp. 285–6). Soviet researchers must of course adopt a public stance which is basically approving of current practices, though they may go on to make criticisms in detail.

Moreover, with some qualifications Soviet published works do not set out to analyse, let alone solve, the mysteries in understanding and interpretation of the budget which are bound to strike an outsider. The budget enshrines relationships and quantities which either it is not the aim of Soviet commentators to uncover, or at any rate the censorship will foreclose any attempt to reach such an objective.

It is therefore left to scholars who are not Soviet citizens to carry out researches whose investigative content is both serious and open-ended. Even so, less work has been done than might have been expected. For this, there is a fundamental reason: many Western Sovietologists doubt that deep study of the budget is worthwhile, because in their view it is simply too easy for the Soviet government to offer data which are falsified or misleading in other ways; hence they think it more likely to lead to reliable results if they focus on aspects of the economy, the data relating to which enjoy in their view greater credibility.

That there are grounds for caution in this regard, must be readily admitted. For the Soviet national budget (talking now of the national budget rather than of provincial or local budgets) is bound to register a kind of panoramic view of the economy (or at any rate of that fraction of it which is directly regulated by the budget, which in the USSR is an unusually large fraction); it might therefore be compared with a panorama from a very tall building. Panoramic views of this nature in the USSR encompassing habited places are not vouchsafed to foreigners; even their amateur photography from an overflying aircraft is strictly forbidden. A map would provide comparable information, but large-scale undistorted maps of inhabited places are also unavailable. If the authorities are so careful not to grant views of the terrain, must one not be wary of accepting at their face value budgetary data which, if correct and complete, would provide a comparable overview of the economy? The inevitably affirmative answer necessary reduces the value of any investigation of the subject; but surely not to zero. An economy is an interconnected whole; even partial understanding of the budgetary scene must assist our comprehension. Naturally, to understand the economy completely, study of the budget will be insufficient; the present short book will, however, be justified if it does something towards reaching that goal.

As regards the alleged arbitrariness of budget quantities: this could scarcely apply to the bricks which make up the whole pyramid, so in principle arbitrariness could be exorcised, if only one could pursue the analysis in enough detail. The possibility exists in principle only: the 'budget' actually containing about 55 000 lesser budgets, research into any significant fraction of them by a single individual would be impossible even if all information were available – which it most certainly is not. Spot-checks may accomplish something, but tracing back the budget to its grass roots is less practicable for revenues than for expenditures (local authorities not being permitted to levy taxes on their own initiative), while the all-union section of the budget comprises a large block whose sub-divisions are not shown continuously.

The key to the problem is indeed whether information is correct and sufficient. Such information has to be obtained almost entirely from Soviet official sources, and any reservations about the veracity or completeness of Soviet information are consequently likely to apply in this field. For instance, particular years are under-reported, such as 1964, a year for which no forecast of budget spending on industry has been made public. (See below, Chapter 7.) As has been shown elsewhere, particular years are under-reported in Soviet economic statistics generally (Hutchings, 1982, pp. 36–7).

Current procedures for publication of the annual budget are regulated by the law of 30 October 1959, according to which, 'The law on the state budget of the USSR is published for the general information.' Analogous requirements are contained in the legislation of union and autonomous republics. These requirements are claimed to be strictly observed (Piskotin, 1971, p. 286). In turn, the legislation of union and autonomous republics envisages 'publication for the general information' of all budgetary decisions of local Soviets at all levels. Reports are carried of sessions of the Soviets. But due to the restricted scope of published indices, the general public is unable to gain a full appreciation of revenues and expenditures, as Piskotin admits (p. 287). Despite the constraints imposed by the 'conditions of struggle between the two opposing systems – socialism and capitalism', in his opinion it would be possible to make a substantial increase in the number of published indices. He adds two more observations which are of some interest. It would be 'extremely important from both an economic and a political viewpoint' to construct standardised forms for stating the volumes of expenditures in individual republics both from the union budget and from the budget of that republic (Piskotin, 1971, p. 115). While he does not say outright that such material should be published, this is presumably his meaning. He also proposes the confirmation of budget allocations to particular branches of the economy (engineering, coal-mining, agriculture etc.), rather than simply the total sum for finance of the national economy. From the standpoint of a domestic economist, let alone of a foreign one, these recommendations which appear to aim at a modest enlargement of the quantity of published information seem far from unreasonable.

The principal sources for the budget of the whole USSR for individual years are: the finance minister's speech when he presents the budget to the Supreme Soviet of the USSR (as mentioned in the second paragraph of this chapter); co-reports and debates within that body; the finance minister's 'closing word'; and the budget law. All these appear in *Pravda* and *Izvestiya*. An article on the budget is normally published in the monthly *Finansy SSSR* under the name of the minister of finance or of his deputy-minister in January of the year to which the budget applies. Summarised results appear in the annual statistical handbooks which usually are published about nine months after the end of the year to which the latest included totals refer. Except in abnormal circumstances, such as the Second World War (even then, information on an annual basis appeared retrospectively), all the above-mentioned sources recur annually. With the exception of the *Finansy SSSR* article, analogous sources are available for each of the republic budgets.

From 1938 to 1960, with one short break in 1948, the post of Minister of Finance of the USSR was held by Arseniy Grigor'evich Zverev. The present writer had the pleasure of conversing with him briefly in 1957. Bulky, affable, and modest in manner considering the enormous sums with which he regularly dealt, Zverev presided over the release of a far from abundant amount of budgetary information. Advancing to a professorial chair, he later published two books about the Soviet financing and pricing system; unfortunately, they shed no further light on his extremely long period at the summit of the financial pyramid, but his quite readable memoirs, *Zapiski ministra* (Zverev, 1973) do contain some revealing insights. Zverev was succeeded by V. F. Garbuzov, whose published writings are so far confined to his speeches, articles in *Finansy SSSR*, and other contributions to period-icals. On the whole, since Garbuzov took over, the quantity of pub-lished information about the budget has diminished further; notably, the release of any total for defence spending (*oborona*) that differed from the forecast for the same year was soon suppressed. On the other hand, fuller information *is* now provided about forecast *non-budget* expenditure.

In the statistical annuals, too, the budget is inconspicuous. The postwar series of these annuals started with the 1955 handbook, but until 1956 the budget did not even get a mention. In the 1977 handbook, out of 586 pages of tables the budget occupies only 5 – a rather typical proportion. With some exceptions – including the entire military-industrial complex – the prominence of items in these handbooks bears some relation to their importance, so the lack of prominence of the budget conveys some suggestion that it is regarded as not very important. On the other hand, financial matters are perhaps seen as peripheral in surveys which consist primarily of physical totals. Statistical material which focuses on the budgets appears infrequently, and concentrates on the scene at the local level.

Other Soviet literature relating to the budget can be divided into books primarily from an economic standpoint and books primarily from a legal standpoint. Rovinskiy, Plotnikov and Allakhverdyan are among writers who belong to the first category, while Piskotin and Bescherevnykh are among writers belonging to the second category.

Soviet economists have focused on the national budget, while not analysing as they deserve the 'essence, role and meaning' of republic and local budgets (Bobrovnikov, 1977, p. 3). This may seem curious considering the greater relative abundance of information about lower level budgets, but can probably be explained by the greater intrinsic importance of the national budget; the present book indeed shares the same predilection. Moreover, distinctive features of the budgetary system are most readily displayed at the national level, while aspects such as defence spending can only be illuminated there. However, some Soviet economists have spoken out in favour of the provision of a larger volume of relevant regional data (Piskotin, 1971, p. 115).

Remarks by Soviet economists of an interpretative nature about the budget, or which shed light on official data going much beyond what those data supply directly, are rare. Potentially the most important is a claim by Ya.G. Liberman that the budget is in reality inflated by not less than 20 per cent, because plants transmit certain funds to the budget and then receive them back again (Liberman, 1970, p. 270; see also below, Chapter 6).

The present writer has found Soviet works written from a legal-economic standpoint to be on the whole more useful for study even of the economics of the budget than the works of Soviet economists, though one might have anticipated the contrary. The former group of writers seem less inhibited in expressing their opinions, perhaps because they are less continuously aware than the economists of the security issues. If one might expect the economists to construct and analyse budgetary series, such exercises as a rule are conspicuous by their absence. The legal-economic approach elucidates which bodies are entrusted with specific tasks of budget composition and implementation, and it may go further in drawing attention to deviations from the legal letter. Naturally, this approach suffers also from certain limitations, especially as it embodies here the central fiction that approval of the budget depends in reality on members of the Supreme Soviet, when it depends in fact on the decision of the Central Committee of the Communist Party, or more exactly and directly on its Politburo. A main virtue of the legal-economic approach is that it pays heed to the budget's organic structure, through focusing on the circumstances and procedures of inclusion within the national budget of a congeries of lesser budgets, thus emphasising one dimension of the enquiry; while the study of quantitative series which is the approach chiefly adopted in this book enables it to be extended over time.

METHODS OF STUDY

Regarding what specific methods were used: basically the attempt was made to compare everything with everything else. Time would not permit a complete coverage, so choices, based on past experience and on hypotheses as to how the budget is made up, had to be made. These hypotheses essentially were only three: (1) budget figures are accepted as true in the first instance, (2) the budget is an integrated whole, and (3) study of a quantitative series stretching over a number of years will reveal more than study of a single year in isolation. Stress is laid particularly on (3).

As regards (1), it should be made clear that not all figures in the budget are regarded as both true and comprehensive. As will be concluded in Chapter 9, the figures for defence spending at any rate in recent years must be incomplete. But without an initial assumption that veracity was sufficient to make the analysis worthwhile one would never begin it. Falsification involves an effort and a possibility of deceiving friends as well as adversaries, so one may expect that it will be minimised. Belief in (2) is simply an extension to the budgetary sphere of the assumption of a unitary system that is normally made when studying the USSR. As regards (3), something has been said already; further analysis seems to vindicate strongly the truth of the hypothesis.

The information released about the budget of any single year being obviously inadequate and often pointing in no definite direction, any student in depth of the Soviet budget is compelled to enlarge his field of view to encompass quantitative changes over time, and consequently is likely to look for patterns in such changes; it is thus surprising that this step when taken in 1962 (Hutchings, *The ASTE Bulletin*, Fall 1962) was apparently a novel one. These, and later, efforts seeming to have yielded some useful results, the present book adopts a similar approach. Study of the budget over a span of years allows us not merely to trace it over a historical period: it greatly deepens our understanding of interrelationships both between budget components, and between budget and plan. As a further bonus, the patterns detected in such comparisons strengthen confidence (up to a point) in the validity of budget data, or (what is hardly less valuable) alternatively delineate areas where credibility has to be suspended.

Quantitative analysis of the budget is founded on a search for regularities in budget behaviour, and for interruptions in such regularities or deviations from them. If, for instance, budget quantities are found to alter non-randomly during periods of the same duration of the five-year plans, and it is possible to imagine what mechanism could give rise to that result, this may be interpreted as probably signifying a genuine (non-random) connection between the budget and the five-year plan. This perhaps cannot be strictly proved, but if illustrated with sufficient regularity it becomes very probable; anyone who disagrees can then be saddled with the burden of finding reasons for not believing in the postulated connection. If in this field one might have to be content with a limited result, given the importance of the theme that would not necessarily be a trivial accomplishment.

Although it was expected that various patterns would be found in the data, the final results went well beyond expectations.

The types of comparison will become clear in subsequent chapters; at this point, only some introductory remarks are warranted. In the first place, one must recognise that a problem of understanding the budget really exists. Even this requires a little experiment, the budget's exterior envelope being smooth and relatively simple. Two main sources of revenue – turnover tax and payments out of profits; three main spending clauses – finance of national economy, social and cultural measures, and defence: what could be simpler? The problems accumulate when one seeks to probe into, or to interrelate, these large and ill-defined elements; particularly, those comprising expenditures.

Yet one must examine revenues as well as expenditures. If that seems an obvious recommendation, it is one that has not always been heeded. Apart from the fact that revenues supply the wherewithal for expenditures, one must be alive to any possibility that the presentation of the budget has been adjusted to show the two sides in balance when this is not in fact the case.

It is desirable to make separate analyses of the union and the republic sections of the budget. As a rule the out-turn of both sections is reported in the statistical annual. The results are usually appreciably different from the forecast totals both in absolute terms and relative to each other; see in this connection Chapter 6 below. Frequently when the union section is underspent the republic section is overspent and vice versa. In effect the budget is divided into two parts with dissimilar behavioural characteristics. Consequently, whereas combining the parts tends to blur any regularities of behaviour, separating them makes the regularities reappear.

The summation of sub-items, and comparison of the total then obtained with the explicitly reported total for that whole category of sub-items, is a basic recourse. Such a comparison will often reveal a gap, which may even be very big. Soviet statistics often do not summate. Is this because items are being deliberately kept secret, or would the gap be filled with trivialities which are not itemised to spare the reader a cumbersome amount of detail? A more diligent search of available sources can sometimes achieve at least a partial answer to the question, while changes in the size of the gap over a period of years, especially any abrupt changes for which no reason can be at once assigned, may suggest other clues. It must be remembered that changes in large aggregates are smoothed out by comparison with changes in their constituent elements, a result which is probably desired by the authorities as it then becomes much harder to glimpse specific interactions.

For studying the budget over a long time-span, a considerable database is essential. Some of the principal series which it is possible to assemble are reproduced in Appendices 1 and 2. As is characteristic of Soviet statistics, the degree of detail is extremely uneven. For instance, as a rule expenditures are shown in more detail than revenues. Alternative breakdowns of principal items are usually conceivable and sometimes offered, but perhaps not simultaneously; for example, finance of national economy is often divided into industry, agriculture and other, or is divisible (approximately) into capital and non-capital expenditures; but the two breakdowns are never supplied for the *same* year, which surely cannot be accidental. The quantity of information provided about the whole finance of national economy clause has varied erratically.

Similarly, the sums allotted to industry or to other branches of the economy are revealed only for certain years, and with little or no component breakdown. Let us say that there are four possible categories: forecast budget spending (a), actual budget spending (b), forecast total spending (c), and actual total spending (d). Taking first industry, that is to say manufacturing and mining: from 1953 to 1981 inclusive information relating to these categories is available for the following numbers of years: (a) 25, (b) 16, (c) 23, (d) 13. Years for which all four categories of information are given number only 6 (1962, 1965, 1966, 1968, 1969, 1970). (This summary result is based on Table 7.4 and Appendix III, below). As regards spending on branches other than industry, the situation is similar or worse.

As regards revenues, one very interesting gap is the fact that totals are never forecast for turnover tax or for deductions from profits; the only forecast total is of 'revenues from state and co-operative enterprises and organisations'. For example, in 1958 that total should have been 57.03 bn; in 1975, 189.67 bn. Presumably the intention is to preserve flexibility in the eventual division of the total revenue as between its various elements. These two principal revenue sources currently account for less than two-thirds of the total stated revenue, and the composition of the remainder is by no means fully clear.

The procedures of composition, debate and legislation in regard to the budget leave many questions unanswered (as explored in Chapter 4). What is disclosed is essentially only the culmination of a lengthy procedure.

It can be presumed that the gaps and inconsistencies primarily reflect official concern for Soviet security interests, but the cloaking of security-sensitive data cannot be the only principle followed: it is also necessary to consider guidance of economists and public opinion within the Soviet Union, her allies or imaginable adversaries. Doubtless it is also preferred to keep secret the finances of the Communist Party and of leading Party and government members, or these may be subsumed under national security interests. Another reason for reticence may reside in the fact that Soviet statistics tend to report output in more detail than input. The budget has, of course, two sides – revenue and expenditure – in an approximate balance. In this connection, reticence may also be encouraged by the methods employed to arrive at a balance, or the 'global' balancing of revenues and expenditures could possibly conceal substantial imbalances or obscurities within their components.

Some support for a view that it is the balancing aspect that is especially sensitive can be found in the fact that 'in 1953 and 1954 . . . certain benefits from tax reductions and increases in government buying prices were recorded as an increase in expenditure' (Hutchings, 1971a, p. 196). (In 1955 the sums were withdrawn and the practice has not been revived.) Though higher buying prices would be properly stated as expenditures, tax reductions clearly count as reductions in revenues. Their inclusion as budget *expenditures* exhibited sensitivity to the budget total (making this as large as possible) overmastering exactitude in their allocation to the correct side of the accounts. It must then be added that it was not very long before the misallocation was corrected. One might, however, speculate that some analogous sleight-of-hand helps to account for some present-day residues (cf. National Foreign Assessment Center, 1977, p. 23).

In any case, what is viewed as security-sensitive may change, so that it is by no means necessary to assume that security-consciousness must result in the blacking-out of all information of interest, apart from the fact that we are interested also in much information which is not security-sensitive, and if we recall besides that the Soviet authorities themselves, being unpractised in the analysis of their system from outside, may well misconceive what can actually be accomplished in this direction.

In this book, rouble amounts are where possible given to the two decimal points after the billion (1000 million) digit, that is to the nearest 10 million roubles. Forecast spending is usually given in original sources to the nearest 1000 roubles, but in a global study such as the present one this extra precision would multiply fruitlessly the number of digits, and hence is ignored. Actual spending is reported in original sources to the nearest 1 million roubles in respect of social and cultural measures (hereafter often abbreviated SCM), but – so far as the whole USSR is concerned – only to the nearest 100 million roubles for finance of national economy (FNE) or defence (DEF) in the statistical annuals *Narodnoye khozyaystvo SSSR v 19 . . g.*, whereas actual republic FNE is reported in the statistical annuals of that republic to the nearest million roubles. Thus, by assembling data from each of the fifteen republics individually it would be possible to build up the FNE all-USSR total to the nearest million roubles. This has not been done, as such a laborious procedure would not be justified by an incremental precision insignificant by comparison with the frequent lack of clarity in the content or meaning of the totals.

Tables in the book thus frequently show actual totals less precisely than forecast ones, but the difference is less marked than in original sources. Given the decision to go for a two-digit precision after the billion digit wherever possible and to rely primarily on the all-union annuals, actual FNE and DEF are sometimes reported less precisely than actual SCM.

Considering the relatively small differences between less precise and more precise amounts, the unequal precision of the original sources is probably not due directly to any official intention to conceal divergences of actual from forecast sums. Indeed, as regards DEF that result is achieved far more effectively by not reporting *any* divergence (from 1963 onwards). More probably the inequality in exactitude is due to a not-caring attitude, another illustration of which is the fact that after the 'heavy' rouble (equal to 10 of the previous roubles) was introduced in 1961 all budget totals continued to be quoted to the same number of decimal points as before, so that in actuality the degree of exactitude was reduced by nine-tenths; there is no sign in published material that this lower precision has aroused objection, or indeed even has been noticed! All rouble amounts are expressed in this book in post-1961 values.

The quantitative series are based on official sources. Where – as is frequently the case – each figure in a series is drawn from a handbook or article of a different year, to cite detailed sources would be complicated and not proportionately helpful to the reader, so the easier way out has been chosen of referring more simply to 'annual statistical handbooks', 'annual articles in *Finansy SSSR*' or 'budget speeches and laws'. As a rule, one should look for the handbook or article of the year cited, while 'budget speeches and laws' can be found normally in *Pravda* or *Izvestiya* of the day after the date of delivery or promulgation. The dates of budget laws for the years 1950–81 inclusive are indicated in Table 4.1.

2 The Budget's Place in the Economic and Financial System

MAIN FACTS OF THE SOVIET FINANCIAL SYSTEM

It is easier to describe budget quantities, or the procedures for adopting the budget, than to say precisely what the Soviet budget itself actually is. We might state that the budget is the financial dimension of the annual economic plan, but from one angle this belittles the budget's status (because there is a process of interaction in the composition of the physical and financial dimensions) while from another it exaggerates it (as the authorities also envisage revenues and expenditures which are not included within the budget). It would also be correct to describe the budget as the most flexible instrument of financial management in the hands of the authorities, but then it must be made clear that all its instruments are in some degree flexible, and all are interrelated: in particular, the banking system and the system of price-formation are needed to support the budgetary system, and vice versa, while the political system upholds everything.

The more fundamental fact is that the Soviet economy is 'planned', but then what precisely should be understood in this connection by 'planned' would take volumes to expound, and no full definition can be attempted here. It will be understood that systematic efforts are devoted to planning in advance both the general development of the economy (over periods of different length) but also its short-period functioning. (Probably a fairly sizeable 'second economy' effectively escapes direct or detailed planning, yet this too must be greatly influenced by the planning system.)

The unified financial plan: budget and non-budget financing

Given the existence of non-budgetary financing, which also is envisaged by the authorities, the size of the budget is not rigidly determined. As Nove has pointed out, the distinction between investment which is financed out of budget grant, or out of retained profits, is not a fundamental one (Nove, 1980, pp. 235–6). For the state is at liberty to make higher grants depend on larger in-payments by enterprises, or of course to reduce the size of both out-payments and in-payments. In fact, one may go further. Over time, the budget might grow simply as a result of enlarging the payments on both sides of the account. Unless one were aware of what was happening, one would see as an actual growth what would really be a fictitious one. This will be examined further, later in this book.

The budget provides only a part (though a major part) of the funds destined for spending on the economy and on 'social and cultural measures'. Logically, then, attention ought to be focused in the first place on a broader unified financial plan. That was indeed the trend in 1930–1 (one of the main formative periods of the financial system), but from 1932 onwards attention has been focused on the budget (Davies, 1958, pp. 152–5). Remaining parts of any unified financial plan which may exist at present can be traced only indirectly, and often with even less consistency and detail than in the case of the budget proper. A main reason for this may well be the different degree and manner of control over parts of the financial plan which are *not* included within the budget. This has been Davies's opinion (pp. 153 and 155). The lack of systematic elaboration of the non-budgetary parts of the unified financial plan cloaks that document with an extra veil of secrecy, as is probably the intention. However, it is also true that the 'unified financial plan' has to be more flexible than the budget proper. (See for example the section on budget implementation in Chapter 4).

Since any 'unified financial plan' can only be composed at the very highest levels of financial management, we might expect the subject to be treated primarily in official treatises emanating from these levels. Actually (and if this is surprising it is also refreshing as it shows how personal initiative and idiosyncrasy are still generated in this highly structured system) while the subject is barely touched on in official treatises it has been the subject of a doctoral dissertation by A. M. Lyando, who argued that the place and role of the 'unified financial plan' should be increased as regards both the USSR as a whole and its constituent republics (Barkovskiy and Kartashova, 1966, p. 16). An author is rather liable to reach a conclusion that the importance of his chosen topic has been understated by others, but *why* had the topic been left in such obscurity? Barkovskiy and Kartashova observed that Lyando made an 'unexpected about-turn' (p. 17): having just recommended there should be a special examination of ways to combine budget funds and credits within a single generalising document, he then remarked that it 'would be possible not to dwell on this question'. Might the *volte-face* have resulted from a warning from the security authorities that the subject must not be pursued further? One can only speculate, but it seems quite likely. No actual 'unified financial plan' is available to analyse, apart from a statement of the revenue balance in 1960 (Kaser, 1970, p. 163), which showed budget revenue to be 79.4 per cent of total revenue. The minister of finance in 1981, comparing the budget with the 'total volume of the financial resources of the state', found that in 1971–5 the budget comprised 65.0 per cent of this larger total, in 1976–80 65.9 per cent (Garbuzov, 1981, p. 5). The relative share of budget revenue therefore declined from 1970 to 1971–5, but since then has, if anything, risen slightly.

Currently, the financing of capital investment is said to be carried out basically by enterprises' own funds, and only exceptionally, when the period over which such financing is to be redeemed exceeds five years, by budget allocations (Bobrovnikov, 1977, pp. 86–7). Yet in practice budget allocations still finance the larger part of investments.

If one neglects non-budget financing, the budget can be understood as the state financial plan, consisting of estimates of mutually (and approximately) balancing revenues and expenditures, and as a monetary fund for covering state expenditures; while in this respect no different from other legislative measures, annual budgets require to be legally enacted, in the case of the budget of the USSR by its Supreme Soviet. Until then, the budget is strictly speaking merely a 'project' (Bescherevnykh, 1976, p. 15).

Relative importance and status of physical and financial planning

Plans are drawn up in both physical and value terms, and in principle the two should match. The possibility of a clash between physical and financial plans obviously exists (for example Lavrov, 1955, p. 43) and can only be overcome by referring repeatedly from the one to the other. At the summit, this requires joint consideration of plan and budget by the Supreme Soviet, and analogously at lower levels. The necessarily intimate link seems to contradict the rather limited attention paid by Western Sovietologists to the budget by comparison with the attention they have devoted to economic planning in physical terms. It would seem that someone must be mistaken: either plan and budget are not actually so intimately linked, or Sovietologists have been misguided in not treating them as if they were. This problem was indeed one of the starting-points of the present book.

The problem of a potential (or actual) clash between two systems of quantification is not confined to a socialist system. Capitalist business firms also draw up plans in both physical and value terms, which quite conceivably may not match each other. Indeed inflation (or deflation, though that scarcely occurs nowadays) is bound to have the result that fulfilment of a value plan diverges from that of an associated plan in physical volume. However, if one goes to higher levels and ignores the major role in practice of governments in all countries in the management of economies, it may be argued that the question of which measurement system is paramount confronts the higher direction of a 'planned' economy but not any higher direction of an 'unplanned' one – as by hypothesis, in the latter case no higher direction exists. Apart from that imaginary limiting case, in a situation of rising (or falling) prices it will be prudent to supplement planning by volume with planning by value, and the more emphasis is paid to value considerations, the better spending should then be controlled. This seems to be a very elementary step, yet it is one that has been taken only recently in the planning of public expenditure in the United Kingdom. As the Chancellor of the Exchequer told the House of Commons in 1981:

> We have decided to make a major shift in the planning and control of spending from volume to cash. . . . This change to taking decisions in terms of cash will make a major contribution to improving financial management, and will do much to support our other efforts to increase cost consciousness and accountability throughout the public sector (*Daily Telegraph*, 11 March 1981).

In the Soviet economy, simultaneous planning by volume and value is less necessary in taking inflation into account, as the rate of rise of prices has been much lower than in market economies; however, it is hardly less necessary in regard to maximising the exploitation of limited resources.

Soviet economic planning, and the connection between plan and budget, would appear to provide an extra safeguard that the budget is drawn up in an optimum way. However, the connection between the two does not exclude specific features on either side. Although compiled on the basis of the economic plan, the budget contains a number of provisions which are independent of it − such as revenues from the agricultural tax, most administrative spending, and expenditure on pensions to mention only a few items.

The annual procedures for presenting both plan and budget to the Supreme Soviet suggest that the physical plans are in a formal sense pre-eminent. For example, the speech by the Chairman of Gosplan always precedes that of the Minister of Finance. However, the precedence tells us little about the actual relationship between physical and financial quantities. One or the other speech must come first! What distinguishes the Soviet economy from many others is that it is 'planned', not that it has an annual budget; one would then expect the plan to be presented first, to emphasise that difference. Moreover, the fact that the budget follows immediately after the presentation of physical plans suggests that the financial plans if not completely equal in status to the physical plans are at any rate very nearly equal. The posts of Chairman of Gosplan and Minister of Finance have both been held by their incumbents for very long periods, which suggests that *both* are key-posts in the governmental system.

Whether the relationship between plan and budget would emerge as closer than at present appears if both were made available for publication in much greater detail than they actually are has to remain conjectural as long as there is no opportunity to make that comparison. Yet if such a relationship would *not* emerge at many points, the simultaneous consideration of both documents by bodies such as the Supreme Soviet would be pointless. The probability begins to arise that in assuming a relatively minor role for the budget some observers have been mistaken, although it may be conceded that the Soviet Union has not entirely thrown off a reluctance to treat monetary matters as not less important than physical quantities. It may be noted also that communist ideology asserts that with the transition to 'Communism' commodity relations, and therefore also monetary relations, will disappear, and consequently will cease to exist in budgetary form, whereas planning will continue and indeed its role will be intensified (Bescherevnykh, 1976, p. 19). Thus in an ideological perspective the budget has a temporary place in the Soviet economic system, whereas planning has a permanent place. However, this theoretical difference has in practice little or no impact. There is no trace of any 'withering away' of either commodity or monetary relations.

There exist long-term plans, but not long-term budgets. The budgetary cycle recommences each year, and of course a budget cannot be simply a copy of the budget of the year before. The difference in envisaged duration would appear to settle any question of whether the plan or the budget is primary, at any rate for years following the first year of a long-term plan, were there not also some question firstly of the reality of the long-term economic plans. This matter has been debated elsewhere, following a very interesting presentation by Kyril Fitzlyon (Fitzlyon, 1969, pp. 164–92; cf. Hutchings, 1973b, pp. 253–62). Apparently, the immediate post-war five-year plans had become less 'real', and from about 1968 onwards there has been a drive to make them more 'real'. To the extent that this is achieved, and as long as there is no comparable introduction of long-term financial planning, the primacy of physical plans over financial ones should be intensified. Perhaps having themselves drawn the same conclusion, but being naturally protagonists of a financial approach, some Soviet financial experts have argued a need for a long-term financial plan, on the grounds of the growing importance of profitability in the planning of the economy and in view of the need to create conditions facilitating the planned and constant growth of budget revenues. In this matter, it has been alleged, the needs of the moment tend to overcome those of the remoter future, with the result that measures which would assure a larger growth of revenues, although in the more distant future, are neglected. Among measures of this kind we find an allusion to tourism, for instance along the northern coast of the Black Sea (Piskotin, 1971, pp. 23–4). It is interesting to find a Soviet expert advocating long-term financial planning, on the grounds rather similar to those adduced by the advocates of long-term planning within market economies.

Moreover, while it is possible to query the reality of long-term physical plans, certain allusions suggest that long-term financial plans or targets of an embryonic nature have been entirely absent. Thus, according to Ya. G. Liberman, budget growth has been 'artificially inflated, spurred on by a growth percentage established earlier' (Liberman, 1970, pp. 269–70).

If forecasts of budget revenues or expenditures are in fact drawn up for several years ahead, such forecasts are scarcely ever made public. However, the Ministry of Finance worked out its 'own' five-year plan coterminous with the 5th Five-Year Plan (Zverev, 1973, p. 249). Garbuzov (just appointed as minister) in 1961 disclosed his estimate of the budget in 1965: he said that this would be 110 bn roubles (*Pravda*, 30 September 1961). Actually, the budget in 1965 amounted to Rs 102.3 bn of revenues, Rs 101.6 bn of expenditures (*Nar. khoz. SSSR v 1965 g.*, 1966, p. 781). Given that the 1961 totals were respectively 78.0 bn and 76.3 bn, this is not a very impressive degree of accuracy: actual growth (as regards revenues) proving to be 31.2 per cent, when he had implied 41.0 per cent. It is conceivable that Garbuzov was making the forecast for effect rather than as an accurate prediction; he would not expect any Soviet citizen who was not authorised to do so to look at the figures critically, and he offered a rounded figure which was, however, not so 'round' as 100 billion roubles which in the upshot would have been a sounder forecast. If Garbuzov's estimate is (as it appears) legitimate material for analysis, the actual 1965 total fell short of expectation by an appreciable margin. One major reason for this could be the shift towards financing by loan which was embodied in the 1965 reform, although it has been implemented only very slowly. Other reasons can be imagined; for instance, the performance of the whole economy may have fallen short of expectation. The question is complicated by the fact that in 1962–5 the annual growth of the budget accelerated, and began to exceed the annual expenditure targets, as is examined further in Chapter 6. This deviation is opposite to that implied by the comparison of actual growth with Garbuzov's forecast; the contrast tends to suggest that decisions were shortly taken which Garbuzov as late as 30 September 1961 had not envisaged. In any case, it can be concluded that if any long-term financial plan existed at that time, it was not implemented very precisely.

If the budget is secondary in status it perhaps becomes harder to account for the limited effects of inflation in the Soviet economy in the post-war period regarded as a whole. The argument here is that the financial system, of which the budget is a prominent part, has been constructed and implemented so as to produce that result. Certainly, signs of inflationary pressure have been multiplying, and in particular the authorities have on their hands a serious problem of the overhang of savings bank deposits (See Chapter 11). Yet there is doubt in regard to the impact of inflation in the Soviet economy, whereas a number of economies experience inflation about which there is no doubt whatever. The Soviet Union apparently has been rather successful in curbing many, though not all, inflationary effects. This is most probably not mainly due to the financial system but to other features of Soviet society, notably the lack of trade union pressure for higher wage settlements. Still, the financial system must surely receive some part of whatever praise should be due, given that in the 1930s the trade unions were no less firmly controlled whereas inflationary pressure was much more marked. If then the financial system can hardly be denied some share of the credit, the same must apply to the budgetary system which is a prominent element in the financial system.

Perhaps the secret of Soviet success in avoiding the worst effects of inflation might reside in some unusually potent and effective theory of public finance, which empowers the financial authorities to control reliably the monetary circulation and the price level? We might then expect to hear about such a tool, which also might substantially help the governments of market or semi-market economies, struggling to contain inflationary pressures without resorting to measures which also have the effect of crippling their economies. But no such theory has been proclaimed.

Closer control over monetary circulation can be identified in one important dimension, namely the administrative-geographical one. Bogdanova points out that Gosbank economists participate in work at the *rayon* level in compiling plans of main directions of development of the *rayon*, so that plans should make the maximum contribution to tying together the monetary incomes and expenditures of the public (Bogdanova, 1970, p. 85). Interesting here is the direction of the influence to be exerted by the Gosbank over plans of physical production: if financial aspects always took a back seat, the direction of influence would always run from monetary circulation to physical plans.

Perhaps, however, the decisive element in the situation is the stifling of alternative power centres, which makes the Soviet system so much easier to control than a market or semi-market economy. One might from that angle even conclude that a minister of finance is a virtual fixture not because the post is so difficult that only a genius can fill it but mainly because he is not required to take any decision that is not of a routine nature. That would seem to be an unfair conclusion from Zverev's memoirs, which illustrate their author's very active management and intervention in a large number of fields, but many of these were concerned with considerations of efficiency and accountancy rather than with the budgetary steering of the economy; the budget being only one of the matters (although the chief one) for which the Minister of Finance had responsibility.

Budgetary decisions will only be rational if the financial plan has been conceived correctly, more correctly indeed than the physical plan. What can be said about the probable correctness of decisions taken in regard to the Soviet economy on the basis of value considerations?

Value judgements must be founded on prices, and the complaint is an old one that Soviet prices do not reflect value relationships. Given that prices are fixed from above, not automatically as the conjunction of supply and demand but (in theory, at any rate) taking into account a variety of considerations, the inaccurate reflection of values is not surprising. Given this lack of correspondence, the case would be strengthened for allowing physical quantities to overrule financial plans. In practice, implementation of physical plans not infrequently involves infringement of financial provisions; for instance, investment projects may perpetuate large cost overruns. This has always happened – allusions to it were as common in the 1920s as they are today – and of course it is not solely a phenomenon of the Soviet economy; it occurs also in economies which claim to reflect values more accurately, though especially within their state-owned sectors where respect for value is attenuated. In the USSR, if the phenomenon cannot be cured it also does not pass unnoticed. For the moment, the financial plans bend in the direction of accommodating the physical reality. More generally, in every socialist system – the Soviet economy despite its individual features in this respect fully qualifies as socialist – financial (including monetary) frameworks bend if that is necessitated by physical output plans, or perhaps by some other objective, such as of maintaining full employment (although that aspect is bedevilled by propaganda issues). Financial overruns are still seen as a defect, and if they continue or are aggravated, compensatory action will eventually follow; it would therefore be incorrect to conclude that the physical plans are simply getting away with it.

In Soviet circumstances then, which have the upper hand? If one insists on a plain answer, it must be the physical plans. The budget should reflect trends and pressures which are manifested in the composition and implementation of economic plans. For example it should be possible to find reflections of investment policy or of policies concerning defence and social and cultural measures, at least in broad terms. This is indeed the case although various obstacles are encountered which, however, may be partly circumvented through the study of quantitative series.

A study of this nature is facilitated by the fact that the financial system has been comparatively stable; since 1930–1 – when major changes were made – it has been preserved without essential change. Evidently, this regime has accumulated a large inertia, perhaps because it benefits officialdom or the Party, and this inertia outweighs any continuing disadvantages. The financial system is clearly not envisaged by the leadership as suitable for frequent manipulation – in contrast to the planning system, the higher levels of the business hierarchy, and even (under Khrushchev) the structure of the Communist Party.

If this is true of the financial system as a whole, it is almost equally true of the budgetary system. This has been slightly more changeable than the total financial system. The division into categories of expenditures and revenues permits complex permutations.

FURTHER EXPLANATION OF FEATURES OF FINANCIAL SYSTEM

The budget is drawn up in current roubles, but prices are never indicated. Naturally, price inequalities may distort the comparative size of totals, either relative to each other or by comparison with a previous total. But as noted above, the post-war impact of inflation in the Soviet economy appears to have been somewhat limited. Ames asserts that 'virtually nothing is known about Soviet decisions on price changes' (Ames, 1965, p. 161). There is actually no *simple* statement of principle in price-formation, the problem being bedevilled by the complexity of the criteria which are supposed to be taken into account, and which make prices in a mathematical sense over-determined. Where so many criteria are involved it would not be surprising if a price, once arrived at, were to show extreme stability, and this is indeed a main characteristic of Soviet prices. If any change is made, it is likely to be large and abrupt. This is well shown also in prices in Eastern Europe, where (as in Poland) large and abrupt price changes can even be fraught with political dangers. The fact that rates of turnover tax (one of the main items of revenue) are not published hardly helps the authorities in this connection, since any change in any case affect retail prices, to which consumers *are* sensitive. Consequently, the price lever which at first sight might seem a flexible instrument at the disposal of the Soviet financial authorities does not in fact exhibit much of that quality. However, this stability is a virtue from the angle of tracing budgetary series over time.

A substantial fraction of total revenues is raised from turnover tax, and the total volume of revenues from that source depends (other things being equal) on levels of prices; while another large fraction is raised from payments out of profits, concerning which one might say the same. Price levels are therefore a governing influence upon budget revenues. Although retail prices are on the whole very stable, price changes are announced from time to time. The announcement is never synchronised with the annual budget, perhaps with popular psychology in mind: price reductions may be thought to complement the spiritual uplift of springtime or the agreeable warmth of summer to counteract the shock of price increases. The effect in any case is to appear to dissociate price changes from budget policy.

The lack of allusion to tax rates may suggest that raising revenues plays a minor role in the Soviet economic system. Taxation policy does not exert many of the indirect effects that characterise a market economy, or at any rate such effects are less widespread. Nevertheless, raising revenue plays a more important part in the management of this economy than one would gather from the limited publicity it receives. Both in the task of matching incomes, disposable to be spent on goods on sale, with the availability of such goods, and with that of ensuring full (but not overfull) employment of resources in authorised directions, it plays an essential part. Timely and sufficient payment of revenues into the budget closes a circuit which, if left open, would both signify and multiply disorder. If official accounts are truthful, the two sides of the budget have been in balance with normally a slight surplus of revenue (to the extent that this is not offset by additions to credits). If they are not truthful, the systemic problems are probably much more serious.

Are revenues taken as the datum to which expenditures have to be adjusted, or is it the other way round – or something in between? The answer probably varies at different periods and even at different times within a five-year plan. It is likely that, in the earlier stages of Soviet industrialisation, revenues were called on to make the main effort of adjustment, whereas at the present time this effort is distributed more evenly. The purse-strings are probably held less tightly than usual in the final year of a five-year plan so far as spending on the economy is concerned, but more tightly for some competing item. The accelerated growth of the budget in recent years suggests that ways have now been found to expand revenues, though on the other hand a shrinkage of the surplus betokens that revenues are under increasing pressure. Likewise, the more centralised management of revenues than that of expenditures argues considerable attention to the level of revenues. But in any case: 'balancing the budget' is a phrase never heard in high-level public statements. Perhaps many years later a more obscure source may allude to difficulties overcome in a particular year (see below, p. 66).

It is a bedrock of the Soviet financial system that it contains only one bank, the Gosbank (apart from specialised banks for investment and foreign trade), and that the Gosbank enforces strong and universal controls, each enterprise being required to have an account with it. Furthermore, the Gosbank is intimately linked with the budgetary system, being the recipient and reservoir of budget funds, although decisions connected with the national finances are the preserve of the Ministry of Finance (Hutchings, 1971a, p. 168).

Another peculiarity of the Soviet financial system is an enforced separation between two types of money: cash is virtually limited entirely to the consumer sector, payment by draft virtually entirely to the producer sector. The use of cash by state organisations is restricted to the payment of wages, buying agricultural products, and other small sums. Existing barriers on spending cash by budget-financed bodies date from the period of goods deficit and in the view of Piskotin (for example) they had clearly outlived their usefulness. A *rayon* may spend only up to 2000 roubles a month, yet (for example) to furnish a club with armchairs costs 5000–6000 roubles; co-operatives have the furniture in stock, but are only permitted to sell it for cash. In practice, illegal ways will be found to circumvent such restrictions (Piskotin, 1971, pp. 306–7, citing proceedings of the Tatar Supreme Soviet in 1967). Private citizens do not usually possess cheque accounts. Thus, for either sector the choice between the two forms of money is lacking or very limited.

Major differences between the Soviet monetary system and that of a market economy are the differentiation in the former of velocities of circulation and the much closer control exercised over the velocity of circulation especially in the socialist sector. The latter is superficially at variance with the rarity or absence of allusion in Soviet texts to velocity or circulation, even where the analysis would require it to be mentioned (for example Chernomordik, 1936, p. 311). The velocity of circulation within a recent period is evidently a state secret; thus, Gusakov examines only the experience of the 1920s and 1930s, long before the date of his own book (Gusakov, 1974, pp. 172–202), although in one reported instance new cash put into circulation was supposed to make 12 circuits per quarter (Zverev, 1973, p. 258). While the circulation of drafts is very rapid, that of cash is much slower, in part because individuals retain in their pockets or savings accounts substantial sums as long as they do not find commodities which they want, so as to be able to buy them when they *are* found (see also Chapter 11).

Payments by draft having to be made through the Gosbank whereas cash may be paid direct, payment by draft is inherently much the more controllable of the two forms. Although the connection of payment by draft with the socialist sector and of payment by cash with the private sector is in some degree historically determined, one of its roots being the unfamiliarity of the public with non-cash payments and another a predisposition that wages should be paid in a tangible and familiar form, this identification hints at a much more acute need to control payments by socialist organisations than by individuals. It is implied that the cash sector of the economy is relatively well controlled. This conclusion is made less certain by the paucity of data relative to cash circulation: as Garvy points out, most of the significant data generated within the monetary system are not published. The USSR has not joined any of the international monetary and financial organisations, such as the IMF, which would involve reporting obligations which she has been unwilling to accept (Garvy, 1977, p. 151). One reason (though probably not a decisive one) may be the existence of a fairly substantial 'second economy', which must be supported almost exclusively by cash payments.

The difference in the speed of circulation of drafts and of cash has an approximate analogy in two different frequencies of in-payments of taxes into the exchequer: either daily or 4–6 times a year. Entertainment tax (*nalog so zrelishch*) is normally paid the following day. The most important fixed payments, and also turnover tax, are paid daily (turnover tax on the third day after completion of the turnover). By contrast, income taxes from plants are paid four times a year, from collective farms five times (including a final settlement based on the actual results of the year's activity), while payments by individuals are made monthly (out of wages) or 2–4 times a year (on notification from financial bodies) (Tsypkin, 1973, pp. 63–4).

INVESTMENT IMPLICATIONS

A Soviet enterprise is provided with a sum of working capital which is called its 'own', but this is purposely made insufficient to cover all its needs at all seasons of the year, and it must apply to the Gosbank for the remainder. As regards funds for development, these are now supposed to come primarily from enterprises' 'profits', but the budget still provides a substantial proportion. The deliberately arranged shortage of 'own' funds within the socialist sector, whereas surplus funds are held by individuals, is a potent source of imbalance. If the two barriers were lifted — the ban on using private funds for investment, and the related enforced separation between drafts and cash — funds would presumably flow from the private (consumer) (cash) sector into the socialist (producer) (draft) sector. This is proved not only by the existing disparities between quantities of money in the two sectors (relative to need) and in their circulation velocities, but by the emergence of condominiums for building apartments for which the populace is willing to provide the funds (Pallot and Shaw, 1981, p. 193). Conceivable openings for financing larger investments to produce the things that people want, while simultaneously mopping up the vast accumulation of surplus purchasing power (see below, Chapter 11), have gained the attention of some Soviet economists, but for the present to move any further in that direction is regarded as too radical a departure from traditional practices; it would indeed gnaw at the foundations of a centrally planned economy.

The circulation problem amounts to a vicious circle. The bigger the disparity in quantities of funds and velocities of circulation as between the public and private sectors, the more pressures must mount to enable funds to flow from the overfull sector to the underfull one; yet to resist that pressure, the more strictly the sectors must be kept separate, a separation which in turn, as time passes, will intensify the disparity.

While the ban on private investment lasts, as it must on ideological grounds, the investment rate must remain lower than it would otherwise be, while the share of the budget in total investment must remain higher. The budget as a whole must also be larger than it would be otherwise. More exactly: while decentralised pressure within the socialist sector tends to raise the investment rate to an even higher level than is demanded by centrally approved plans of economic and military aggrandizement, the refusal of any significant opportunity to private investors tends to lower that rate. As long as living standards remained low while perspectives of economic development were relatively simple, decentralised pressure to raise the investment rate was overwhelmingly preponderant, that is the net result was unquestionably to increase the investment rate. As living standards have risen and as, concomitantly, to raise them still further demands more flexible and diversified efforts, the prohibition on private investment is exerting a more important and irksome restraint. Preservation of the barrier against private investment, in conjunction with the aim of keeping up the total volume of investment, as well as a large total of non-investment expenditure, thus necessitates a relatively large budget.

3   Budget Structure

THE BUDGET AND THE PRINCIPLE OF CENTRALISATION

Essentially the Soviet Union has only one unified budget, which is sub-divided for administrative convenience, as will be explored shortly in some detail. Why such unity? Answers can be offered on various planes of sophistication, or indeed prejudice. One might reply: 'The USSR is a totalitarian state, so naturally that is how it is.' That might not be wrong, but we will not find Soviet writers saying it. The 'official' Soviet explanation is contained in clause (*stat'ya*) 2 of the Budget Law of 30 October 1959; having referred to the state structure of the USSR it goes on: 'In accordance with this the state budget of the USSR unites the union budget and the state budgets of the union republics.' This, however, is not a sufficient reason, if indeed it is *any* reason. Piskotin argues that the state structure of the USSR actually determined the existence of the union budget and of republic budgets, but not their *unified* existence. To explain that, he is in no doubt that the real reason is to be found in the socialist system of the economy of the USSR (Piskotin, 1971, p. 71). But 'socialism' being a word with numerous shades of meaning, we must go further, and will hardly be mistaken in reaching the conclusion that the decisive feature is the centralised character of the Soviet economic system.

As its name suggests the Soviet Union is a federal state, made up of fifteen union republics; but since unlike the United States or Australia it has no federal territory, all budget revenues and expenditures are gathered, or disbursed, on the territory of one republic or another. Nevertheless, the budget is constructed on a centralised basis. Expressed in ideological language, this is an aspect of 'democratic centralism'. So far as the budget is concerned, centralisation rests on four pillars: the budget of each lower-level organ is included within that of a higher-level one (so that the national budget is necessarily inclusive of all budgets); each higher-level budget fixes the total amount of lower-level budgets for units included within its jurisdiction; lower-level budgets are forbidden to reduce their planned revenues or expenditures; and contributions are made from higher-level budgets to the revenues of lower-level ones.

All budgets formally on the same level, for instance all republic budgets, enjoy identical rights. The republic budgets in turn contain the budgets of autonomous republics (ASSRs) and those of all lower-level public organisations down to and including local (*mestnyye*) budgets. Their proportion of the republic budget varies, depending on the year of observation and on the republic's constitutional structure. For example, in 1977 the budgets of ASSRs and of lower-level organisations comprised 36.3 per cent of the RSFSR budget (Bobrovnikov, 1977, p. 39). The extent of dependence of lower upon higher levels is shown by the fact that union and autonomous republics meet less than half their expenditures from their own revenues (Piskotin, 1971, p. 101). The bedrock here is the large role assigned to the union (federal) budget, although its percentage share has been somewhat variable.

'The budget' embraces all budgets of public authorities and state organisations. Every territorial administration is both entitled and required to have its own budget. All allusions also suggest that it can have only *one* budget that is exclusive to itself, yet that has not been found to be stipulated explicitly, though it is implied by the formulation that each republic, territory and so on has 'its budget', in the singular (Lavrov, 1961, p. 25) and by Piskotin's statement that the system and quantity of local budgets is determined by the territorial-administrative structure of the union republics (Piskotin, 1971, p. 129). More exactly, the number of budgets equals the number of administrative units singly and in their normal (geographical and hierarchical) groupings. Consequently, over time the number of budgets changes in accordance with developments in the territorial-administrative division of the USSR: increases or reductions in the number of separate units, reclassification of their status, and also changes in their grouping. Although the 15 republics are stable units, at lower levels over any appreciable period of time substantial changes take place. Between 1960 and 1967, for instance, the number of local budgets of different categories (reflecting corresponding changes in the territorial-administrative structure) altered in a manner which clearly reflected the continuing process of urbanisation (see Table 3.1). At the same time, there was also taking place a certain consolidation, which continued for some years but has now been reversed: as reported in

TABLE 3.1 *Numbers of budgets of different categories*

Types of budgets	1960	1967
Territory, oblast and circuit	136	121
City	1 682	1 888
Rayon	3 888	3 374*
Workers' settlement	2 956	3 460
Rural	43 704	40 229
Total	52 366	49 072

* Including 415 'town' rayons.

SOURCES *Mestnyye byudzhety SSSR* (1960) p. 3; Piskotin (1971) p. 129.

1970 there were some 48 000 independent budgets (Voluyskiy, 1970, p. 105), whereas by 1981 their number had risen to 51 000 (Garbuzov, 1981, p. 4). As regions subordinate to republics also had combined budgets which included the budgets of units subordinate to themselves, the total number of budgets at any one time is somewhat larger than the number of independent budgets; this larger total is not reported systematically, but would be in the region of 55 000.

'The budget' can be measured also by the quantities of funds which it handles. The revenue forecast for 1981 is 298.4 bn roubles, expenditure very slightly less at 298.2 bn. These are record totals, but while from official angles this is meritorious there is nothing surprising about it, budget totals having grown continuously since 1955. The population of the USSR being estimated at 266.6 million on 1 January 1981, at the present time the annual budget amounts to about 1100 roubles per Soviet man, woman or child. Comparative figures for some past decennial dates are: 1940, 93 roubles; 1950, 237; 1960, 363; 1970, 648. (Those figures are based on revenue totals, and on the population at 1 January of the same year.) Thus, since 1940 the *per capita* budget has increased about twelvefold. While there are insuperable difficulties in arriving at an exact exchange rate, 1100 roubles are equivalent to something like 1500 US dollars. This is a significant sum per head, which when multiplied by 266.6 million is transformed into an immense total!

These totals must be in current prices (although this is not stated explicitly); thus they include no allowance for price changes. No official published index is available for deflating this series. An official index of state *retail* prices on individual items of popular consumption, which lists 1940 as 100, has been standing at 139 since 1970. The immobility of this series is suspicious, and it does not take into account replacement of items by new items of higher quality but also of higher price; the limited coverage is also noteworthy. Budget expenditure would usually not be at retail prices. For what it is worth, this deflator applied to budgetary spending would reduce the *per capita* rise since 1940 to about 8½-fold.

Dividing both forecast revenues and population in 1981 by 50 000 – the approximate number of budgets – we would obtain an 'average' budget with revenues of about 6 million roubles and encompassing some 5300 souls. The immense total is therefore not necessarily incompatible with a more human scale. But however large or small a budget may be, because of its structured inclusion within the national budget and dependence to a large extent on subventions from above it is not something that belongs to that unit or locality as its very own.

One of the more striking manifestations of centralisation is the fact that only the budget of the USSR has the right to levy taxes – whether these be all-union, republic or local. The attribution to the highest organs of state power and state administration of the right to decide taxes and revenues was embodied in Article 14, paragraph L of the 1936 Constitution of the USSR (Tsypkin, 1973, pp. 18–19), though the Constitution of 1977 modified this wording, replacing 'Union, republic and local budgets' by 'the USSR State Budget' (Sharlet, 1978, p. 98). Budgets at all lower levels have the right to their 'own' revenue sources, but these are nominated from above and they cover only a fraction of the given unit's total expenditures. In 1967, for example, this fraction was on average 41.3 per cent (Piskotin, p. 73). The rest is provided in the form of deductions (transfers) from turnover tax or other all-union taxes and revenues, or as subsidies from the union budget. The same principle applies to local budgets relative to republic ones, the proportion raised from local revenues being in this case even smaller. For instance, in Belorussia in 1968 only 19.9 per cent of the expenditures of local budgets was covered by local revenues (Piskotin, p. 74).

There is consequently a large difference between the revenues and the expenditures of republic and local budgets. The revenues of republics include sums which will be transferred to local budgets and will figure among *their* expenditures (Gozulov, p. 398). In 1949, for instance, revenues of republic budgets amounted to 7.744 bn roubles but their expenditures amounted to 2.834 bn, while revenues of local budgets were 1.499 bn roubles but their expenditures totalled 6.409 bn. The proportion received from higher levels by lower ones rose between

TABLE 3.2   *Sources of local revenues*

	1940	1950	1958
Revenues from plants, organisations and properties subordinated to councils of ministers of Autonomous Soviet Socialist Republics and local soviets	19.5	10.8	21.0
Local taxes and duties (*sbory*), income tax from co-operatives and others	21.7	14.2	13.1
Transfers from state taxes and non-tax revenues	49.1	67.8	51.2
Other revenues	4.7	3.0	4.5
Subsidies and funds received from republic budgets	4.7	4.2	10.1
Total	99.7	100.0	99.9

SOURCE *Mestryye byudzhety SSSR* (Moscow, 1960) p. 3.

1940 and 1950, but it declined from 1950 to 1958 when the proportion remained slightly above the 1940 levels (see Table 3.2).

The bias of these arrangements is intriguing. It is perhaps the opposite of what one might expect. Would not a centralised, totalitarian system seek to centralise expenditure but to decentralise revenue-gathering? That arrangement would presumably maximise revenue-gathering, while keeping expenditure under more immediate control.

The fact that permission is not given to lower-level budgets to levy taxes expresses of course an intention to hold down revenue gathering by lower levels. But over and above this, revenue-gathering and spending by lower levels which otherwise would have taken place will be inhibited. Would not such decentralised tendencies conflict with the presumed propensities of a centralised and authoritarian system to maximise revenues and expenditures?

The system certainly presupposes a fully or almost fully socialised economy, for otherwise the architects of the system would not want to hold back local authorities from taxing the life out of the non-socialised sector – which was, of course, one of the methods employed for squeezing out the private sector from the Soviet economy.

Given that condition, the system complements other arrangements in the economy for holding down expenditures. One of the most powerful tendencies in this economy, as well as one of the longest-lived and hardest for the authorities to overcome, is the tendency towards over-investment. This has its origin basically in the fact that over a long period grants were essentially free of charge to the organisation receiving the investment, which also was under great pressure to expand its output. The controlling and restricting bias of the financial system emerges as one of the mechanisms for restraining this tendency. The same lever could of course be employed to prevent other kinds of expenditure of which the government or Party disapproved.

Centralised revenue devolution seems an excellent lever in the hands of central governments which do not command other means of influencing local authorities. This is indeed one of the bases of public finances in the United Kingdom. In Soviet circumstances, on the other hand, that lever might seem superfluous. Yet the risk of unbridled spending by local authorities is by no means hypothetical. The problem has evoked concern recently in Britain, where local authorities may levy higher rates to cover higher expenditures, although the electors may eventually turn them out of office. As regards the USSR 'parochialism' (*mestnichestvo*) has been a familiar charge. In the 1920s its effects, for instance a proliferation of investments in small plants to produce window glass (Hutchings, 1958, pp. 336–7), were manifest. In 1926/27 the budgets of all republics except the RSFSR were in deficit, although receiving the maximum deductions from direct taxes, owing to too sharp an increase in expenditure, especially on FNE (Bescherevnykh, 1976, p. 79). Curbing local authority cowboys in this matter was a prerequisite for accomplishing industrialisation governed by ordered priorities.

More generally, the economic life of persons and institutions is usually controlled by the incomes they receive: 'Who pays the piper calls the tune.' But local authorities cannot be abolished, or if in individual cases their powers might be taken over by superior levels, this is not practical on any wide scale – and in the USSR, nearly fifty thousand authorities might need to be reined in! The law or the KGB might punish offenders, but the one is too cumbersome, the other too crude and arbitrary. And the offenders would have to be caught first. It would be using a knife to chop a bacterium. What is required is a built-in fiscal control – which is furnished by conditional revenue devolution.

This structure nourishes certain inherent tendencies. Lower level budgets must be interested in the fulfilment or over-fulfilment of revenue plans by higher level organs within whose jurisdiction they are and from which they expect to receive subventions – though how precisely they could influence what happens is not clear. On the other hand, they are not interested, or are only weakly interested, in increasing their 'own' revenues. Hence there should be an inherent tendency towards intensifying still further centralisation as regards fund-gathering, but towards intensifying still further decentralisation of spending. Thus dispersed initiatives are likely to strengthen the characteristic already built into the system for revenue-collecting and disbursement to be performed by different levels.

The fact that a budget surplus is always forecast suggests that the total is pitched at a level that is high enough to tolerate achieving in practice a slightly lower level; however, the forecast surplus now falling well short of the actual one, the eventual total must be affected by more complicated influences (see pp. 88–90 and 137–8).

In an economy which lacks substantial reserves of productive capacity, it is not possible to accumulate financial surpluses that correspond to real values. However, as seen by the Soviet financial authorities, the sums remain on the books and so can still be drawn on. Thus, accumulated surpluses from pre-war years were one of the sources of financing the growth of defence spending during the Second World War (Vaynshteyn, 1957, p. 51; cf. Hutchings, 1971a, p. 169). According to a more recent statement, the budget surplus increases the credit resources of the Gosbank and the Stroybank (this latter finances construction) and may also augment the FNE clause (Garetovskiy, 1978, p. 18).

The centralising features endow the whole system with a marked degree of unity. The system seems tailor-made for an economy which it is intended to make manoeuvrable at the command of the centre (cf. Piskotin, p. 75). To a large extent this is indeed the case. If the economy were decentralised in other ways yet the budget structure remained unchanged, that structure would exert a centralising effect. This probably occurred during the *sovnarkhozy* period (1957–65) and contributed towards the revocation of that system. Although we shall see that in some distinctive respects the actual performance of the budget is less centralised than its form, on the whole the disbursement of funds is one of the channels through which a centralising effect is exerted. The budget accumulates resources for spending on defence, and other 'all-union' purposes such as transport and certain industries regarded as of national importance. It transfers funds from consumption to production. Though also important, the decentralising influences are not comparable in magnitude with the centralising ones. To be included here are some expenditures on social and cultural measures, and any diversion of resources to poorer or more outlying regions for reasons not connected with their national importance.

Revenues

There are two main revenue sources, turnover tax (TT) and payments out of profits (PP). TT and PP usually together comprise about two-thirds of what are stated to be total revenues (see Table 10.13). Taxes on the population in 1970 brought in 8.8 per cent of total revenues (Piskotin, p. 157). Some other items, such as customs duties, entertainment tax and various local taxes (see above, Table 3.2) have been mentioned, but a substantial gap is left between the total of itemised revenues and what is stated to be the revenue total.

Rates of turnover tax are not normally published: they evidently belong to the corpus of economic information that is regarded as confidential; as if their revelation might jeopardise national security, or arouse unrest or disquiet. Formally, grounds for differentiating TT are said to be: the technical level of production organisation; the purchasing method and the quality of the raw materials; transportation costs; the quality and assortment of production; and the profitability of different types of production (Suchkov, 1945, pp. 15–16). Social grounds, for instance dissuasion of alcohol drinking, play some part although the attitude of those drawing up the Soviet budget, as of those drawing up other budgets whose revenues set much store on alcoholic drinks, is inevitably ambiguous. TT is levied at higher rates on obsolete products. It helps to finance the introduction of new products by light industry (Garetovskiy, 1978, pp. 51–2).

On the whole, rates of taxation in the USSR are very high, as was established by Holzman who concluded that 'No other nation has ever levied as high a rate of taxation as the Soviet Union' (Holzman, 1955, p. 307).

One sometimes meets references to 'other' accounts or receipts. For instance, Vaynshteyn mentions current accounts of the Gosbank (the repository of budgetary funds) which hold 'extra-budget (special) funds, and also current accounts for holding budgetary funds of organisations and persons which do not have the right of credit disposal' (accounts nos 155, 154 and 156); also with division (*razdel*) X: 'other accounts, in which are reflected special transactions (*raschety*) with the Ministry of Finances of the USSR' (Vaynshteyn, 1957, p. 61). 'Special' funds may, for instance, cover house repairs, or the current costs of museums, exhibitions, lecture halls, libraries or picture galleries which are financed by admission charges or subscription (Vaynshteyn, 1957, p. 93). (Holzman (1955, p. 221) too refers to 'other' receipts, though without other explanation).

Expenditures

The redistributive function of the budget is very important. Certain branches of the economy have been regularly donors, others regularly receivers. As reported in 1970, donor branches of industry were, above all, engineering, light industry and the food industry; 'receiving' branches included oil-refining, coal-mining, chemicals, electric power and electrification (Piskotin, p. 231). The emphasis here on providing subsidies to energy-producing branches, even before the global energy crisis which erupted in 1973, is noteworthy. The comparatively high profitability of engineering in general is interesting, and at first sight unexpected since the price of many capital goods have been kept artificially low, to encourage the introduction of improved technical equipment. Some engineering (including defence-related) branches of industry were nevertheless achieving relatively high rates of profitability (Sitaryan, 1968, p. 43). Successive price reforms have considerably reduced intersectoral redistribution.

Funds for redistribution consist largely of turnover tax, which historically (apart from a 10 per cent levy on producer goods for supervisory purposes) has been paid by the consumer goods industries, not by producer goods or by agriculture. Consequently, regions characteristically are either predominantly payers or predominantly receivers of turnover tax (Piskotin, pp. 80–1).

FNE which is derived from the budget and from the resources of plants and organisations consists of: capital investment; operational expenses not included in costs; scientific research for productive purposes; training of cadres; formation of state reserves, and certain other expenditures (Massarygin, 1968, p. 112). While not detailed, this statement is revealing because it confirms – as many observers have suspected – that the clause at any rate when interpreted to include funds both from budgetary and non-budgetary sources encroaches on other spending clauses, and so is in part a misnomer. One might have been inclined to expect all scientific research to have been included within the science sub-clause of the major category social and cultural measures; this is not the case. As for state reserves, these or at any rate a major part of them must be relevant to defence; thus FNE probably encroaches on both the other two main expenditure clauses. The fact that coverage of FNE and of other main expenditure categories does not coincide exactly with their titles reduces the possibility of drawing meaningful deductions from changes in the size of these clauses, but it will be shown that interesting combinations can still be discerned.

A sizeable fraction of FNE must consist of subsidies, though the quantitative evidence is fragmentary and has been revealed only gradually. According to a table in Yevdokimov, FNE is divided up among thirteen numbered headings (nos 24–5, 27–34, 36, 42, 53). The amounts under these headings were indicated for the 9th Five-Year Plan. They were extremely uneven in size, a total of 83.14 bn roubles out of 100.544 bn being included under only two headings: no. 24, 'Centralised capital investments of *khozraschet* organisations and enterprises' (2.84 bn), and no. 32 'Other expenditures' (50.30 bn) (Yevdokimov, 1974, p. 141). Thus the minimally informative 'Other expenditures' comprised half the total. The difficulty of discovering what are the contents of a total, half of which is not itemised, needs no elaboration. The only other sizeable sub-item here mentioned is no. 31, 'Operational expenditures' (9.34 bn). These are described as being directed towards 'measures not connected with the basic activity of *khozraschet* state organisations and are not included in the estimate of production or in the calculation of the cost of production and services': this includes innovation and rationalisation, maintenance of waterways and icebreakers, geological prospecting and various other purposes. The next largest sub-item is capital repairs, only 2.05 bn. 'State subsidy' (no. 30) weighs in at only 0.80 bn (Yevdokimov, 1974, p. 141).

Thus Yevdokimov's classification did not at face value indicate that any large fraction of FNE consisted of subsidies at that time, yet such may well have been contained within 'Other expenditures'. Children's footwear, house rents, and 'various other' goods are subsidised from the budget, with subsidies for meat and dairy products amounting in 1975 to 'nearly 19 billion roubles' (Glushkov, 1977, p. 2); however, net subsidies within the budget for consumer goods, taking into account profits made in other branches, could have been smaller than this very large figure (cf. Nove, 1980, p. 199). On the other hand, items other than DEF – in particular FNE – may well contain subsidies to defence branches (see below, Chapter 9). By 1980, subsidies for 'basic goods', such as 'meat and meat products, milk, fish, children's items and others' were to amount to more than Rs 25 bn, while additionally about Rs 6 bn would go to subsidising house rents, and more than Rs 4 bn for covering the difference between the selling price to farms of agricultural machinery and its purchase price from industry (Glushkov, 1980, pp. 11–12). Total subsidies for these purposes in the 1980 budget would therefore amount to 35 billion roubles, equalling about 23 per cent of FNE as forecast for that year.

The proportion of FNE that is devoted to capital investment is according to Yevdokomov 34.0 (relating to the budget only and to investment in fixed capital), whereas according to Massarygin (1968, p. 112) it is 'more than 60 per cent' (relating to all sources and both fixed and working capital). While due to their different coverage these sources are not definitely in disagreement with each other, the two proportions are more widely different from each other than might have been expected. One must nevertheless draw the conclusion that capital investment, particularly in working capital, comprises a larger proportion of non-budgetary than of budgetary FNE, which is to say that budgetary FNE contains a larger proportion of non-investment.

Expenditure on defence consists of 'expenditures for maintenance of the army, aviation and navy' (Massarygin, 1968, p. 119). This could admit certain exceptions, such as the strategic rocket forces. Also, the Russian words translated here as 'for maintenance', *po soderzhaniyu*, could mean day-to-day upkeep rather than total costs including the supply of defence equipment. According to William T. Lee this last is excluded from the *oborona* clause (Lee, 1977, for example p. 54). Yet Massarygin goes on to include within expenditures via the estimate of the Ministry of Defence 'payment for military equipment and war supplies'. Piskotin mentions both 'the maintenance of the necessary Armed Forces and their provision with up-to-date equipment (1971, p. 161). A still more detailed definition is supplied by Aleksandrov: military schools, hospital networks, clubs and industrial enterprises are also included (Aleksandrov, 1965, pp. 382–3). These definitions apply to the estimate of the Ministry of Defence, not to the *oborona* vote. If one does not pay attention to that distinction, one may gain the impression that official sources are conveying that procurement of material, as well as much else, is included within the *oborona* vote. The distinction may well be a crucial one. These references are also not very recent, and it is possible that that situation may have changed in the direction of *no longer* including procurement of material; the evidence for this is examined in Chapter 9.

Defence has not always been reported as one item. The military health administration of the armed forces and transport protection within the country were once listed separately, but later were incorporated in the main *oborona* item. The paramilitary secret police (the OGPU, and subsequently NKVD and MVD troops) have always been listed separately, though under which clauses they are at present financed (in diminished numbers) is not clear. Military production until 1925/26 appeared within defence, but new investment in military industries at least since 1926/27 has been included within FNE (Davies,

1958, pp. 131–2). Since Davies wrote this it is not likely that this expenditure has been re-located with the imaginable exception that some elements might now be included under science, within SCM. So if more recently items included within defence have been reallocated, this would be no novelty. It *is* relatively recent that such reallocations can now only be inferred.

Ministry of Defence production and construction organisations work on a self-financing (*khozraschet*) basis, not on a basis of financial estimates (Massarygin, 1968, pp. 119–120; Aleksandrov's wording is quite consistent). If this means that such bodies are not financed by the budget, this amounts to further evidence that defence activity is funded from outside the *oborona* clause.

Defence industry (aviation, electronics, radio, and communications equipment) produces some consumer-durable goods, and the Soviet armed forces may on occasion be called on to help in some urgent work. The USSR is not unique in this latter respect. In Britain, the armed forces are liable to be called on for various activities not connected with their regular tasks, such as to supply firefighting teams to replace the regular firemen if the latter have gone on strike. In the USSR, that requirement is not present as strikes are not permitted. The Soviet Union prefers to maintain institutional arrangements to sustain a large effort in defence and defence-related production. As long as there is no emergency, fractions of that establishment may be spared temporarily for other work. On the other hand, reservists may be called up from civilian life to take part in military exercises, for instance in Belorussia in the summer of 1981.

Social and cultural measures (abbreviated in this book SCM) includes as major headings education and science; health protection and physical culture; social security; state social insurance; state stipends to mothers with many children and single mothers, and funds transferred to the centralised all-union fund for social security of collective farmers. These, particularly the first two, are also sub-divided.

SCM expenditures via republic budgets comprise: education, culture and science; health protection and physical culture; and social security. So far as the RSFSR budget is concerned, the first two of these have grown at about equal rates but the third four times faster, so that whereas in 1940 social security amounted to 13.1 per cent of total expenditures, by 1977 it had reached 38.5 per cent (Bobrovnikov, 1977, p. 42). Spending in the RSFSR on SCM from the republic budget comprised in 1975 63.4 per cent of total spending on SCM in that republic; the share had fallen slightly during the previous decade, owing to the growth of funds raised from enterprise profits and to union funds formed to benefit collective farmers (Bobrovnikov, p. 44).

Social-cultural items have basically a more stable character than FNE or DEF; the amount of pensions, for instance, depends chiefly on the number of pensioners. The absence of overtly recognised unemployment means that no dole is payable. But these expenditure clauses of very broad and partly undefined scope raise obvious questions. How, for instance, is the Communist Party financed? There is no mention of it anywhere. Very possibly, 'education' includes spending on Party propaganda, as suggested by Holzman (1955, p. 263).

Budget revenues and expenditures are classified according to the following scheme: divisions (*razdely*), paragraphs (*paragrafy*), and clauses (*stat'i*) (Yezhov, 1965, p. 248). These are divided among ministries, for example as described in 1953 the Ministry of Defence was apparently assigned divisions 108–120 inclusive (Gozulov, 1953, p. 394). The budgets of ASSRs and local budgets also include chapters (*glavy*), which group together expenditures of the same designation (Gozulov, 1953, p. 396). We find the following classification of expenditures: (1) general designation, (2) ministry or branch of the economy, (3) chief administration (*glavk*), association, plant etc. (more rarely, type of activity, and (4) subject designation of expenditure. In this series, (3) would correspond to paragraphs, and (4) to clauses.

UNION AND REPUBLIC BUDGETS

The budget is divided between 'union' (or 'all-union') and 'republic' sections, with the 'republic' section including the budgets of all the fifteen union republics. Unlike the union section of the budget, which always shows a surplus of revenues over expenditures, the republic section of the budget balances exactly.

The distinction between the union and the republic sections is highlighted by the following inequality. From 1960 onwards, the union budget forecast for year t + 1 has lain within the range of the forecast and the actual union budgets of year t in only 2 years out of 20 (up to and including 1979). By contrast, the forecast republic budget for year t + 1 has lain between the forecast and the actual republic budgets in year t in 16 out of 20 cases. (See Appendix I). This much larger difference than is ascribable to chance must signify that forecasts for the union and the republic sections are drawn up in a different way. It would seem that financial planners regularly fix the combined total of next year's republic budgets at just below the level they expect to be reached in the current year. Not exactly planning 'from the achieved level' (Birman, 1978, pp. 153–73), this has rather to be characterised as planning *down* from that level. The planners evidently envisage holding down next year's combined total of the republic budgets by setting a figure lower than could well be achieved; but this intention is then almost always frustrated, for the eventual republic total rides high above its forecast. The forecasting of the union section of the budget is apparently approached in quite another fashion. Every year since 1959 the target for the next year's union budget has been fixed well above the total reached in the current year, with the fairly obvious intention of encouraging its more rapid expansion; although invariably, save in 1966 and 1967, actual expenditure within the union budget has fallen short of the target. This behavioural contrast, together with the other differences, raises a question whether it is even proper to speak of 'the budget' – implying that it can be considered as a unity. Its two parts actually behave, and are treated, rather dissimilarly.[1]

The union budget comprises two groups of expenditures: (1) those undertaken only by the union budget (such as, according to all authorities, defence, and the upkeep of certain organs which fulfil a national function), and (2) expenditures which are borne both by union and by republic budgets. These latter are: financing of the economy (FNE), social and cultural measures (SCM), and upkeep of the government and judiciary. As regards the first group, the size of the union budget is determined chiefly by that of defence spending; as regards the second, by the size and number of all-union enterprises and the cost of upkeep of governmental bodies. As the magnitude of these elements, especially the number of all-union enterprises, has varied (due mainly to changes in their subordination), the union budget is one of the more variable proportions in Soviet budgetary history (see Chapter 6). Currently (1981) the union budget comprises about 55 per cent of the total budget, which is about mid-way between the highest and the lowest post-war proportions.

The comparative size of the two groups of expenditures within the union budget is not published. One may conjecture that it would shed unwanted light on some security-sensitive aspect.

No institution or measure may be financed from more than one budget, and therefore any which is budget-financed must be financed entirely from the union budget or entirely from the republic budget. The principles which govern that choice are subordination (*podchinennost*) and significance (*znacheniye*). Only the union budget finances defence and state reserves (Bescherevnykh, 1976, p. 145). Republic budgets are consequently to a greater extent absorbed by financing the economy and by social and cultural measures. Changes in the share of the republic division within FNE thus reflect in an enhanced degree changes in the proportionate share of the republic division in the total budget, and this is probably even more true of the share of the republic division in the financing of capital investment (Hutchings, 1971a, pp. 188–90). Yet only the minor part of investments is financed at the republic level. For instance, in the 10th Five-Year Plan capital investment in the RSFSR were planned at 375 bn roubles, of which only 144.4 bn were subordinated to the Council of Ministers of the RSFSR (Bobrovnikov, 1977, p. 152).

The implication that republic and lower levels are not at all concerned in the budgetary implementation of defence activity seems to be modified by an allusion which includes 'strengthening of the defence capability of the country' among functions to be executed basically via the plan and budget, by provincial governments at all levels (Piskotin, 1971, p. 216). Certain locally financed projects, such as aerodromes of local importance, for which 'substantial' sums are assigned (Bobrovnikov, 1977, p. 113) might have some defence relevance. Various other expenditures, for instance on physical culture, may be held to concern defence indirectly. However, any major devolution of expenditure may be presumed to violate another fundamental principle of Soviet behaviour, that of maximising secrecy.

Republic budgets

The budgets of individual republics closely resemble those of the whole USSR, apart of course from not including items which are reserved for the union budget. They use an identical terminology, and usually report the same sub-items in the same summary way.

In general, the budget laws of all the republics are the same. The RSFSR must in practice have a somewhat special status, its budget being so large relative to those of other republics. There are some unusual provisions in the budget laws of Georgia and Azerbaydzhan: the Supreme Soviets of their ASSRs when confirming their budgets are allowed to 'increase the total amount of revenues and change the total amount of expenditures' laid down by the republics (Piskotin, 1971, p. 104). This wording differs slightly from the wording of the law on the rights of union republics, which on confirmation may 'increase the total of revenues and the total sum of expenditures' (Piskotin, p. 103). Piskotin considers the former wording preferable, but it seems a distinction without any real difference.

Various principles tending towards territorial equalisation are supposed to operate: the equality of nationalities, the need to develop the economy and culture of all republics many-sidedly, ensuring their being factually on the same level, and so on (Piskotin, p. 91). There is an unwritten rule that services to the population should be about equal per head on the various republics (Bescherevnykh, 1976, pp. 143–4). In fact, outpayments of SCM to the various republics tend to make republic incomes per head of their populations less unequal (Wagener, 1969, pp. 127–8).

The proportion of turnover taxes gathered in its own territory which a republic is allowed to retain is listed in the annual budget law. As forecast for 1980, for example, this proportion varied from 42.4 per cent in Latvia to 100 per cent in Uzbekistan, Kazakhstan, Kirghizia and Turkmenia. It may vary quite abruptly from year to year even for the same republic: for instance, Armenia was to retain 61.8 per cent in 1979 but only 48.8 per cent in 1980. The republics fall into two fairly clear groups: the more favoured group retains 90–100 per cent of their turnover taxes, the less favoured one less than 65 per cent. The first group includes Uzbekistan, Kazakhstan, Lithuania, Kirghizia and Turkmenia; the second group nearly all the other republics.

The relatively few indices that are included in the budget law also include any subsidies allocated to republics. Subsidies are distinguished from percentage allocations of turnover tax (Bescherevnykh, 1976, pp. 140–1), and also from any hidden subsidy which may be supplied by the price structure, for instance for industry (Davies, 1958, p. 102). In principle, subsidies are allotted when a republic finances work of all-union importance. The strongest example of this principle in action is Kazakhstan, which throughout the period 1958 to 1975, except in 1973 and 1974, was receiving subsidies from the union budget, mainly in connection with non-ferrous metals and the virgin lands projects (Bescherevnykh, 1976, p. 144).

The TT proportions are apparently decided on the basis of considerations similar to those which govern whether a republic will be assigned subsidies from the union budget. If a republic is allotted such a subsidy, it will also be permitted to keep all its home-gathered turnover taxes. Retention of all these latter is the first recourse; only if that does not suffice is a subsidy added.

According to Piskotin, public opinion (*obshchestvennost'*) assesses the distribution of budget funds primarily by the scales of transfer of all-union taxes and revenues into the budget of each republic. These transfers actually only convey a roughly accurate picture, as republic revenues depend on how much industry is subordinated there to republic and local bodies; where this proportion is smaller, the republic needs larger subventions (Piskotin, 1971, p. 195).

The political importance of territorial redistribution of funds and the desirability of making explicit examinations of proposals of this sort found expression in the setting up of the Economic Commission of the Council of Nationalities of the Supreme Soviet, following the xxth Party Congress; however, the Commission has since been abolished. Perhaps its examinations became too explicit!

Little information has been published on the overall territorial distribution and impact of union financing; possibly such information has not been available even to some governmental bodies. But certainly this financing has been extremely uneven. Certain provinces in the RSFSR, Kazakhstan or other republics have benefited far more than others. Probably as an extreme case, between 1946 and 1965 the oil-rich Bashkirian ASSR received from union and RSFSR budgets 90.8 per cent of the funds spent on its economic development; while in 1966 this proportion was 74.8 per cent. Though the share of the union and RSFSR budgets in financing social and cultural measures in this ASSR was smaller, over the same twenty years it amounted to 25.9 per cent, in 1966 reaching 32.7 per cent (Piskotin, 1971, p. 90). If some areas or republics benefit to a greater than average degree, others must benefit less; or (what amounts to the same thing) some republics (and/or areas within republics) must be net donors. Outside the USSR, it has been demonstrated that the Ukraine has been one of these 'donor' republics (Melnyk, 1965).

In practice – despite the announced principles of equalisation – the budget apparently has not been used to counteract inequalities in the living standards of the various republics; at most, it has been so used to only a slight extent. Zwick even concludes that 'the ''worse off'' a union republic was socio-economically, the smaller its per capita socio-cultural budget, as compared with those of the other republics, was likely to have been over the subsequent ten year period' (Zwick, 1979, p. 394). The various republics are consequently left clustering in groups, characterised by socio-cultural indices, which are very similar to their groupings according to nationality and language; modifications of this similarity (Kazakhstan emerging as an 'adjunct' of the RSFSR, and Lithuania clustering with Belorussia rather than with the other Baltic republics of the USSR) being exceptional (Zwick, p. 392).

If the size of republic budgets is governed mainly by that region's prosperity, republic budgets should change only very slowly relative to each other. But it was already noted that the proportionate size of the all-union budget was relatively flexible, which implies that republic budgets are in aggregate equally flexible. How can flexibility of the aggregate be combined with stability of the components that make up this aggregate? When the total of all republic budgets changes, either in absolute terms or as a fraction of the total state budget, individual republics still maintain approximately the same relative positions within the larger or smaller total. This relationship can be pinpointed for the annual sequences 1957–8 and 1965–6: in the earlier pair of years the republic share increased, while in the latter pair it declined.

It seems therefore that despite its centralised form the national budget is either less able or less willing than could perhaps have been expected to redistribute funds among the constituent Soviet republics. Its controlling functions seems to enjoy a higher priority.

Given these controlling functions, the fact that each administrative unit is required by law to have its own budget also takes on a different aspect. Instead of appearing as a somewhat liberal feature of the system, it can be seen as an expression of mistrust that if an administration unit did not have such a budget, it would escape more readily from supervision. A parallel can be drawn with the legal requirement that every Soviet state undertaking must have an account with the Gosbank.

For a representative breakdown of republic budgets (actually as forecast for 1965) see Table 3.3.

TABLE 3.3   *Representative republic budget totals (bn roubles)*

RSFSR	31.55	Georgia	0.95	Kirghiziya	0.53
Ukraine	9.28	Azerbaydzhan	0.93	Tadzhikistan	0.49
Belorussia	1.66	Lithuania	0.77	Armenia	0.60
Uzbekistan	1.84	Moldavia	0.51	Turkmenia	0.46
Kazakhstan	3.98	Latvia	0.56	Estonia	0.41

SOURCE *Pravda*, 12 December 1964.

LOCAL BUDGETS

Local budget expenditures comprise administration, FNE and SCM. The lion's share (usually about 70 per cent) falls to SCM, while FNE takes about 20–5 per cent. Between 1940 and 1958 FNE enlarged its share, mainly at the expense of administration. There are no very

very marked differences in these shares as between republics, but the Baltic republics (Estonia, Latvia, Lithuania) spend slightly more than others on FNE (in 1958, 30–1 per cent against a national average of 26.2 per cent (*Mestnyye byudzhety SSSR*, 1960, pp. 100–30), the difference being possibly due to these republics' relatively prosperous handicraft industries (Hutchings, 1976, pp. 156–7), as well as to their relatively high living standards. Only just behind, the RSFSR in 1958 contributed to FNE 29.0 per cent, appreciably more than the Ukraine (20.3 per cent) or Belorussia (22.8). In Central Asia the share of FNE has been substantially lower. While this lower proportion is in part conditioned by more acute social needs in those areas, it cannot have helped to solve their problems of economic backwardness.

In all republics the share of FNE rose substantially after 1951–2 (which in most republics marked the lowest point). In most republics the sharpest rise in that share occurred in 1957, doubtless owing to the *sovnarkhoz* reform in that year.

The most noteworthy difference concerns the directions of expenditure at various levels. Taking the year 1958 as representative, we find the picture shown in Table 3.4 (percentage shares).

Expenditures on FNE are concentrated within higher-level and urban budgets, with rural budgets financing SCM overwhelmingly. For practical purposes, rural budgets make no direct contributions to development of the local economy. One may conjecture that this has been a not unimportant reason for the lagging behind of Soviet agriculture; it underlines also the extent to which rural localities are seen as recipients of relief payments, rather than as hotbeds of business enterprise.

Further breakdowns of local budgets become extremely complicated owing to the multiplicity of units involved, and as they also have limited importance in the present general survey the interested reader is

TABLE 3.4 *Percentage distribution of expenditures among local budget categories*

	FNE	SCM
Expenditures of republics (ASSR) and of territory, oblast and circuit (*okrug*) budgets	33.4	60.0
Expenditures of city budgets of republics	38.4	58.7
Expenditures of rayon budgets of republics	9.5	84.1
Expenditures of workers' settlements of republics	13.7	81.7
Expenditures of rural budgets of republics	2.5	82.0

SOURCE *Mestnyye byudzhety SSSR* (1960) pp. 131, 142, 158, 174, 190.

referred to official statistics, and to the noteworthy monograph *The Local Budget System of the USSR* (Stec, 1955).

We must now confront the question of how, when and where these myriads of empty boxes are filled up each year with revenue and expenditure totals.

NOTE

1. According to Birman, the 'entire riddle' of budget revenues belongs to the union budget. He further argues that 'use of the same mechanism [a transfer of revenues from emission to the budget not directly but via bank credit, which he believes is taking place] in the republic budgets would reveal the carefully-kept secret of the deficit nature of the Soviet budget to a considerably larger number of people' (Birman, 1981, pp. 24–5 and 204). If such a transfer is indeed occurring, it certainly would make sense to confine it – for the reason cited – to the union budget.

4 Composition, Presentation and Implementation

THE PERENNIAL CYCLE

Like other national budgets, the Soviet budget comes round every year; but unlike many economies, the Soviet economy is also regulated by economic plans, including plans of longer than one year's duration. If an annual budgetary cycle is not necessary for guiding the economy or for any indirect manipulative effects, why does this annual periodicity persist? Could not a budget be presented at shorter or longer intervals, or perhaps irregularly, when one was needed? There are probably five reasons why the budget is annual: conformity with the timetable of the economic plans; inertia; organisational complexity; the seasonal dimension; and international legitimacy. As listed here these five reasons may also be in the approximate order of their importance.

Conformity with the periodicity of the annual economic plans is probably the most influential reason. The annual plans being the operational ones, the budgets which are primarily (though not solely) their financial counterpart must be annual too. The argument is persuasive, though the absence of five-year budgetary plans to match the five-year economic plans seems then anomalous. (An objection that five-year economic plans are *not* operational is debatable, and in any case would leave open why similarly non-operational five-year *budgetary* plans are not promulgated.) Inertia is probably quite important too. Although in the 1921 period annual budgets were merely 'orientative' (Bescherevnykh, 1976, p. 71) budgets have always been presented annually, and there would have to be good grounds for diverging from such an obvious periodicity. Closely linked with inertia is the organisational complexity of budgetary composition. To get everything finished on time, a considerable number of bodies, both hierarchically and geographically dispersed, have to work in step with each other. This cannot be at all easy, and amending the timetable would make it still more difficult. The seasonal dimension is important because seasonal variations in the economy would make budgets compiled for unlike periods of the year non-comparable with each other. (Budget composition must naturally rely largely on forecasts of fulfilment, which in turn must be based mainly on past results.) Finally, an annual timetable makes the budget more comparable with the budgets of other countries, which confers both practical convenience and a sort of legitimacy – which may have both political and ideological importance.

Although these reasons, or something approximating to them, tip the balance in favour of annual budgets, the outcome has not always been so clear-cut as to preclude flirting with alternatives. The very irregular timing within the year of budget in the final Stalinist and early post-Stalin periods (see Table 4.1 below) apparently did not harm the contemporary performance of the economy (or if it did, we have no evidence of the fact). In 1964 the experiment was tried of presenting a budget which in outline would cover the two years 1964–5. It would seem that the experiment was not a success, since it has not been repeated. It proved evidently too difficult to look ahead reliably for even one extra year. This comes as no great surprise, deviations from the forecasts being sometimes quite substantial. These deviations are, however, of a different order of magnitude from those which are liable to occur in a pluralistic society, where the minister of finance has to anticipate the impact both of his own measures and of decisions taken by persons and institutions over which he has even less direct control.

The more emphasis is laid on financial aspects of planning, the more regular the financial cycle is likely to become – as in fact it has.

The Soviet budget is harder to compose even than the budgets of other socialist economies because of the size of the USSR, its federal structure, and unitary budget system. Because of its all-embracing character it is particularly important that the budget should be confirmed before the start of the year to which it applies, yet in principle the better advantage can be taken of available opportunities, the shorter is the interval between the start of the process of composition and the year to which the budget applies. Hence an expeditious process of compilation is preferable (Piskotin, 1971, p. 220). Deadlines for the various stages of composition and of submission to the Council of Ministers are therefore set well in advance (Piskotin, 1971, p. 221).

Because of the time taken up in composition, it is necessary to rely on forecasts as regards at least the final 5–6 months of the current financial year (Piskotin, p. 227), whereas next year's budget should ideally have as its starting point the actual results of the current year. As these cannot be to hand before the year's end, *forecasts* are compiled by the financial organs, and are among the most important measures needed for compiling the draft budget. The accuracy of the forecasts, or the degree to which they are taken into account, apparently vary a good deal as between sectors of the budget and types of expenditure (see Chapter 6).

PRESENTATION, COMPOSITION AND CONFIRMATION

The budget is invariably presented by the Minister of Finance immediately after the chairman of Gosplan presents its annual plan. This sequence matches the fact that on the whole, along its successive stages, the plan is confirmed earlier than the budget. For instance, when planning the compilation of its plan and budget for 1968 the Georgian government set the following deadlines: plan 26 June 1967, budget 3 July 1967 (Piskotin, 1971, p. 212). However, control figures which are the basis of the plan are worked out in financial terms and are drawn up with the participation of financial representatives, while the physical plans may then be made more precise on the basis of financial data (Piskotin, pp. 212–13).

The Supreme Soviet of the USSR is convened – and is informed of – debates and approves the plan and budget for the following year. Then ensues the republic stage of the proceedings. Supreme Soviets of the various republics usually meet 3–4 weeks later than the dates of the budget law for the budget of the USSR to be informed of, debate, and approve the annual plans and budgets for their respective republics. For example, the Soviet budget for 1977 was confirmed by the Supreme Soviet of the USSR on 29 October 1976, while the Supreme Soviet of the RSFSR was convened on 18 November 1976 (20 days later); analogous meetings of the Supreme Soviets of the Ukraine, Belorussia, Kazakhstan, Georgia, Lithuania, Latvia and Armenia were reported in *Pravda* of 21 November 1976.

At each national or regional level of authority, the convening of the legislative body is followed by the adoption of a budget law, which at any rate in theory means that it is obligatory to achieve the quantities set down in that document. Then follows the process of implementation of the budget, concerning which a summary statement (which at any rate so far as the Supreme Soviet of the USSR is concerned is very brief indeed) is made at a subsequent session of the same body that adopted the original law.

The whole budgetary process (composition, adoption, fulfilment, reporting back) takes up more than two years. Thus, the budget for 1974 began to be compiled in the first half of 1973, while the report of its fulfilment was confirmed by the Supreme Soviet in December 1975 (Bescherevnykh, 1976, p. 149).

As regards the budget for the whole USSR, both plan and budget are presented to joint sessions of the Council of the Union and the Council of Nationalities – the two divisions of the Supreme Soviet. Then, after a break separate sessions are resumed and deputies listen to the 'co-speeches' (*sodoklady*) of the chairmen of the planning-budget and branch commissions, following which a debate in which more deputies take part, but which still appears to be carefully structured, takes place. Vital aspects of the national finances remain almost or entirely unilluminated. There is no discussion at any point of alternative policies in general, merely of minor adjustments affecting a particular region or branch of the economy. Defence spending is not discussed at all. If it occurs to any deputy to wonder how the USSR can be militarily equal or superior to the United States while ostensibly spending on defence only one-seventh as much, in public he keeps such thoughts to himself. However, deputies find time to praise the performance of the economy in general and of their own sector in particular, while some-times adding useful specific suggestions. As a rule following only one full day of debating the finance minister sums up, and the final version of the budget is normally printed in the issue of the daily press which reports this summing up. This final version is set out only in outline, being adopted as a 'law', fulfilment of which is obligatory. The budget law summarises the main provisions of the budget in a standard manner. This procedure is in accordance with the law of 30 October 1959, clause 20 of which prescribed what the Supreme Soviet should 'confirm' and what it should 'establish' (Bescherevnykh, p. 158).

These proceedings certainly appear perfunctory, and their timetable over-hasty. Supreme Soviet deputies have no opportunity to express detailed views about the composition of the budget. Unless they have made individual analyses, or belong to one of the budgetary commis-sions of the Supreme Soviet (see pp. 53–4 below) they can have little idea of what is going on. For all the deputies, assent to the budget is a foregone conclusion: for the vast majority, raising a hand at the appropriate moments will be their sole contribution to the proceedings. Yet it must be recognised that if the budget of the whole USSR is to be confirmed before the budgets of the republics, and these in turn before the budgets of republic constituent units, then any prolonged debate at the Supreme Soviet stage is a luxury that cannot be afforded. If the centralised procedure is not to end in a shambles, it can tolerate no delay and few of the procedures or trappings of a political democracy.

While the conclusion seems inescapable, one may note as if in mitigation the geographic dispersion of the presentation and of the debates themselves: besides the Supreme Soviet, all the fifteen republics present and debate their individual budgets, which are reported in the press of that republic. At these intermediate levels the degree of public, or even popular, participation may be greater than in the Supreme Soviet of the USSR – though details are not available for perusal. One may ask too how matters are arranged in years when the annual budget is adopted long after the beginning of the year to which it applies. The problem is analogous to explaining how the system functions when no economic plans have yet been devolved. The solution is probably a built-in inertia at lower levels. However – as will be shown – delays in adoption of the budget law seem to be not altogether without repercussions.

It is often alleged that the Supreme Soviet merely rubber-stamps projects, such as the budget, which are placed before it. The invariably unanimous adoption of the budget supports that view. Deputies never draw attention in public either to discrepancies or to disagreements of principle. Are none perceived? Given the immense scope for error, or for divergence of view and interest, this seems very unlikely, but if important discrepancies are present, there is no evidence that either the Supreme Soviet or republic soviets are able instrumentalities for discovering them. However, deputies press for higher allocations for projects of special interest to their neighbourhoods, and the finance minister in his 'closing word' goes some way to meeting these requests (Hutchings, 1971a, p. 200). The eventual vote in the Supreme Soviet usually makes the largest proportionate further addition to SCM (White, 1982, p. 86). There having been scant time for consultation, the finance minister's alacrity of response seems suspicious. But it should be observed that some deputies serve on the budget commissions, and all are supplied with a little more information than is available to the general public. This is of two kinds.

(1) The 'co-speeches' by the two chairmen of the budgetary commissions respectively of the Council of the Union and of the Council of

Nationalities are the longest and most authoritative statements about the budgets of individual years with the exception of statements made by the Minister of Finance and data contained in the budget law. The chairmen of these commissions never make reference to their individual members or to any differences of view among them. The commissions, which are now referred to as planning-budgetary commissions, examine various estimates and materials which are not available to the public. Their members 'analyse the production and financial activity of ministries and departments, seek out possibilities of obtaining additional revenues, oversee the expenditure of state funds etc.' (Zlobin, 1971, p. 353). For example, in 1957 the Budgetary Commission of the Council of Nationalities was able to examine the 'supporting argument and estimates of measures projected by ministries and departments' (Safronov, 1957). This takes place usually a month before the Supreme Soviet session (Zverev, 1973, p. 174).

(2) Before the Supreme Soviet of the USSR meets to discuss the budget, deputies are supplied with a 'small brochure' about it (Bescherevnykh, 1976, p. 155). It is not stated *when* this is handed to them; presumably, not long before, considering that the budget would have been reviewed by the Central Committee perhaps only the previous day (see p. 55). The contrast with Western practice, which strictly forbids any disclosure in advance of the statement by the chancellor of the exchequer, seems striking, but since nothing is known about the contents of the 'brochure', further comment is difficult. Perhaps it merely explains in simple terms something about the budget's general make-up. The Minister of Finance in his published speech reveals nothing about taxation, mortgage rates, or much else that would normally be mentioned by a Western finance minister, and in the Soviet system of economy, which outlaws most types of enterprise and all 'speculation', there would be scant opportunity to profit from advance knowledge. Moreover, the date of presentation of the budget to the Supreme Soviet is only approximately synchronised when the budget comes into effect, and in some years (such as 1953) there has not been even an approximate synchronisation.

In countries such as the United Kingdom where new taxes come into force on announcement, and this announcement is made in the budget speech, the government may have an incentive to bring forward Budget Day so that extra taxes can be raised from that earlier date (or conceivably, though this is hardly encountered in practice, vice versa). In the USSR such considerations are inoperative, as both links are partially decoupled: higher rates of tax are not necessarily announced, and in any case no such announcement is made in the budget speech. However, the date when the budget is passed into law apparently does exert an influence on the degree of fulfilment of the forecast expenditure, as explained below.

The processes and stages of composition of any specific budget are not reported in the press, but since they are in essence inter-departmental it must be supposed that the Party leadership is kept informed to some extent. The lack of advance notification outside the Treasury which is the United Kingdom practice – the chancellor of the exchequer meets his Cabinet colleagues on the morning of Budget Day to inform them of the contents of the budget he will present to the House of Commons that same afternoon – would seem unlikely in Soviet circumstances. However, the practice in the USSR whereby the day before the meeting of the Supreme Soviet the plan and budget are presented to a special plenary meeting of the Central Committee of the CPSU, which following debate approves them in principle, clearly has some affinity to the British procedure. For example, the plan and budget for 1971 were heard, discussed and approved by a plenary meeting of the Central Committee of the CPSU on 7 December 1970, and were presented to the Supreme Soviet on the following day, 8 December 1970 (*Pravda*, 8 and 9 December 1970). Presumably if the plan and budget were not approved the Supreme Soviet would not meet, but as cancellation of the session, which many deputies must have travelled long distances to reach, would be very awkward, indeed barely possible, almost certainly the leadership has agreed already at any rate to the main directions of policy; it must be confident too that the Central Committee will not determine differently. Given the pliancy of the Supreme Soviet, many of whose deputies would probably not notice any change, an alternative recourse might, however, be simply to make alterations later, without convening or informing the Supreme Soviet. Such alterations are certainly made, without any formal precedure for approving or ratifying them.

As far as can be judged from the finance minister's manner, from what is presented, or from the reactions to his presentation, the budget never contains any element of dramatic surprise. Nobody seems to wait on news of the forthcoming budget with bated breath. The manner of passage proceeds with the smoothness that one associates in Britain with a royal procession, but arouses rather less public interest. The only visible disagreements are expressed in advocacy of marginal increases in budget spending for non-defence purposes. This can be seen as one of the culminations of attempts to enlarge spending, which are common to all levels in the Soviet business hierarchy (Hutchings, 1971a, pp. 198–204). In this case, several stages in the pressuring can be distinguished.

(1) During the process of examination of draft budgets, proposed expenditures are usually found to be inflated, whereas revenues are sometimes found to be understated (Piskotin, 1971, p. 234). Thus on the whole expenditures will exceed revenues. This means that financial organs cannot merely assemble the draft budgets reaching them. Actually, they make corrections; strictly speaking they have no right to do so, but if they did not the issue would go for decision to a higher non-specialised level which still would have to seek the advice of the financial body, and it is less time-wasting to anticipate that outcome.

Actual examples of draft budgets, and of the extent to which they exceed the budgets finally adopted, are rarely given. The budget of Kostroma oblast in 1968 was presented as a draft to the RSFSR Ministry of Finance at 124.1 m. roubles, but was accepted by that ministry at only 100.2 m. (Piskotin, 1971, p. 241). It can be regarded as certain that draft budgets are often substantially higher than confirmed ones. This is despite the fact that opposition to claims and pruning back of draft budgets must already have made inroads into the original demands of subordinate bodies. In fact, the process of submitting and advocating claims (*khodataystva*) has the inevitable result that some claims are thrown out while others are sharply cut; otherwise – Piskotin points out – draft budgets, financial plans and estimates would grow to 'fantastic proportions' (Piskotin, p. 234).

(2) Supreme Soviets of republics normally 'confirm' larger totals than are 'established' for them by the Supreme Soviet of the USSR. For instance, in 1968 all but one republic (Kirghiziya) confirmed their budgets at higher levels than had been laid down by the Supreme Soviet of the USSR. The RSFSR in the same year enlarged its total forecast revenues and expenditures by 1.1 bn roubles (equivalent to 3.2 per cent) (Piskotin, 1971, p. 103). Beschervykh (1976) examines in this connection the republic budgets of five republics (the RSFSR, the Ukraine, Belorussia, Kazakhstan, and Lithuania) for 1961–73 inclusive and for 1975: except only in Belorussia in 1964 (when the confirmed budget equalled the established one) the 'confirmed' budget was higher than what had been 'established'. In most cases the difference was less than 1 per cent, but this has varied considerably in different years and to some extent as between republics: in the budget of Kazakhstan the excess was below 1 per cent in 11 years out of 14, but in that of Lithuania in only 5 years out of 14. (Kazakhstan, which is

chronically in deficit and so dependent on union subventions, should be less able than most republics to contemplate further additions to 'established' levels.) On the whole there is no secular trend, but in the RSFSR budget – by far the largest – this trend has been definitely and quite sharply upwards, most recently reported additions being in the range of 2.5–3 per cent (Bescherevnykh, 1976, p. 161). Given the size of the RSFSR, these have been additions of not insignificant magnitude.

Given the obvious wish to exercise detailed control over spending, it may appear curious that confirmation applies only to *total* revenues and expenditures. (This applies at any rate to the majority of budgets, including the most important ones.) Even in cases where a wider circle of indices are confirmed, these are usually very few; most often they comprise large consolidated sub-divisions such as FNE or SCM. Thus the main part of budget expenditures is entrusted to the executive rather than the legislative branch of government (Piskotin, 1971, pp. 262–3). Evidently control is not exercised via the *legislative* apparatus.

The Supreme Soviet of the USSR belongs to the category of levels which confirm a little more than the revenue and expenditure totals. In this case the budget law confirms *three* indices: the total size of the budget, the total republic budget, and the amounts of transfers from the revenues used for such regulating purposes to the budgets of specific republics. Total revenues from the socialist sector, and expenditures in the main spending clauses, are not 'confirmed', merely 'established' (Bescherevnykh, 1976, pp. 158–9). The confirmation of only three indices may be seen either as a concession in practice to decentralised requests or – perhaps more realistically – as merely underlining the inability of the Supreme Soviet to insist on effective adherence to the specific provisions of the laws which it has adopted.

If the sums 'established' to be spent by republics, for example on FNE, can in practice be exceeded, one wonders whether there may not be some analogous procedure which would also enable DEF to be exceeded? Available Soviet literature contains no reference to such a possibility, but then of course none would be permitted. Without it, the system would have a pro-republic bias; however, there is also other evidence in favour of such a bias, since the union budget is usually underspent but the republic budget overspent, as will be explored further in Chapter 6.

The liberty to raise, but not lower, the budget as previously established clearly has strong affinities with 'counter-planning' – the accepted and recommended practice within the Soviet economy that business organisations should respond with more ambitious plans than the drafts devolved to them. The budget's bias is the financial counterpart of the bias in relation to physical quantities. The budgetary procedure was presumably drawn up so as to correspond to the other. Similarly, if more ambitious financial plans entail the requirement that a local authority must draw more heavily on revenues released from above, this in principle may match the enlarged need for physical inputs which is normally the concomitant of overfilled physical output plans.

Lower budgets on balance like to be assigned additional tasks, even when additional revenues are not assigned to them — as larger expenditures increase the role of the budget, and consequently of its managers. If the additional expense has to be met from the lower level's own resources, this increases the strain on its resources which by itself would be a counteracting factor. However, with the existing budgetary system that situation is virtually excluded, as in practice new financial tasks are accompanied by extra revenues which leave unaffected the net fiscal balance of lower levels and administrative–territorial units. Despite the additional responsibility imposed by the obligation to make further expenditures, lower budget bigwigs savour their extra consequential importance (Piskotin, 1971, pp. 199–200).

The normal rule is that the Supreme Soviets of republics have the right to increase the levels of revenue and expenditure in the budgets established for that republic by the Supreme Soviet of the USSR, but not to decrease them. This creates interestedness among governmental bodies in the republic and in its Supreme Soviets and their permanent commissions in seeking out additional sources of revenue, but deprives them of the possibility of reducing the total revenues and expenditures foreshadowed by the higher level. Similarly, legislation in all republics forbids any reduction of their budgets by autonomous republics. These prohibitions are connected with tasks of plan fulfilment; they are, however, necessitated also by the provision that additional revenues received in conjunction with implementing the budget remain at the disposal of republic councils of ministers and are spent as they please (with analogous provisions in respect of autonomous republics). Thus, if reduction of the revenue plan were permitted, republics or lower bodies could theoretically appropriate for themselves a larger proportion of total revenues — which cannot be permitted (Piskotin, 1971, pp. 105–6). This bias of the legislation naturally contributes to the readiness of republics and lower bodies to enlarge, but not reduce, expenditures.

Dates of presentation

The budget is usually passed in November or December of the previous year. Table 4.1 (shown graphically in Figure 4.1) which shows the number of days between 31 December of the year prior to the year to which the budget applies, and the date of the budget law (+ when the date is earlier than 31 December, − when it is later) reveals a very marked change from about 1956 or 1958 onwards: prior to that date, the budget was usually compiled tardily (that is after 31 December of the previous year) whereas since then it has been compiled before the end of December. This is the chief feature of this series. There is also a slight tendency since the 9th FYP (1971–5) for the date of the budget law to become even earlier: 23 October 1980, the date of the budget law for 1981, being the earliest date for 13 years.

What is the significance, if any, of these dates? Quite evidently, since about 1956 to 1958 much more serious attention has been paid to timeliness in the passage of the law. By itself, this would not tell us whether the change had a realistic or merely a cosmetic purpose. However, further analysis supplies a strong argument in favour of the view that the change did produce a certain result, although one which was

TABLE 4.1 *Dates of budget laws: numbers of days before (+) or after (−) 31 December of previous year, and durations of debates (days)*

Year	Date	Nos of days		Year	Date	Nos of days	
1950	17 June 1950	− 168	4	1966	9 Dec. 1965	+ 22	2
1951	10 Mar. 1951	− 69	3	1967	19 Dec. 1966	+ 12	4
1952	8 Mar. 1952	− 68	2	1968	12 Oct. 1967	+ 80	2
1953	8 Aug. 1953	− 220	3	1969	13 Dec. 1968	+ 18	3
1954	26 Apr. 1954	− 116	5	1970	18 Dec. 1969	+ 13	2
1955	8 Feb. 1955	− 39	5	1971	10 Dec. 1970	+ 21	2
1956	28 Dec. 1955	+ 3	2	1972	26 Nov. 1971	+ 35	4
1957	9 Feb. 1957	− 40	4	1973	19 Dec. 1972	+ 12	1
1958	20 Dec. 1957	+ 11	1	1974	14 Dec. 1973	+ 17	2
1959	23 Dec. 1958	+ 8	1	1975	20 Dec. 1974	+ 11	2
1960	30 Oct. 1959	+ 62	3	1976	4 Dec. 1975	+ 27	2
1961	22 Dec. 1960	+ 9	2	1977	29 Oct. 1976	+ 63	4
1962	8 Dec. 1961	+ 23	2	1978	16 Dec. 1977	+ 15	2
1963	12 Dec. 1962	+ 19	2	1979	30 Nov. 1978	+ 31	1
1964	19 Dec. 1963	+ 12	3	1980	30 Nov. 1979	+ 31	2
1965	11 Dec. 1964	+ 20	2	1981	23 Oct. 1980	+ 69	1

SOURCES *Pravda* of the corresponding dates (normally the day after the date mentioned).

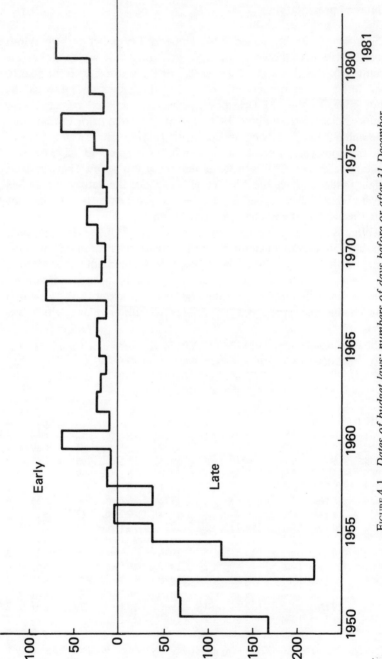

FIGURE 4.1   *Dates of budget laws: numbers of days before or after 31 December*

apparently in a strict sense unintended – although probably welcome. This evidence is as follows.

The later the budget begins to be compiled, the more closely the results it assumes for the year in progress should approximate to that year's actual results; so that, other things being equal, it should more accurately forecast the budget for the year to which it applies. On the other hand, delayed adoption would result in delay in transmitting the targets to the institutions which must implement them, which would produce the contrary result. It would seem that on the whole these effects approximately cancel out each other, since a rank correlation of numbers of days from the end of the previous year compared with deviations of actual from forecast expenditures yields (over the period 1950–79) an almost random result (R = 0.080). However, if the dates are compared not with deviations irrespective of whether they are positive or negative but with the degree of fulfilment of forecast spending from zero per cent upwards, the result is sharply different: now a comparison of numbers of days from the previous 31 December with the degree of fulfilment of forecast spending yields a significantly positive R = 0.600. That is to say, the earlier the budget law is passed, the larger actual spending is likely to be relative to forecast spending; and vice versa. As will be shown in Chapter 6, up to about 1962 actual spending usually fell short of its forecast, whereas since then it has usually exceeded it. The rank correlation just mentioned suggests the strong probability that this change is to be ascribed in large part to the adoption of the budget at earlier dates.

Soviet sources do not illuminate the origins or nature of the effort which must have gone into earlier preparation and presentation of the budget. The chronology of this change suggests that it might have been connected with the devolution of certain budgetary rights to the republics in the 1956–58 period. (See below, p. 74.)[1]

Whatever the precise circumstances of the change, it can be supposed that if the budget is presented extremely early or extremely late this indicates special circumstances in its composition or enactment. As in practice, from the governmental angle, enactment is not a problem – it is inconceivable that the Supreme Soviet should fail to adopt the budget placed before it – this can be narrowed down to unusual circumstances in its composition, that is to say either special difficulties or lack of them in the compilation of an agreed document.

It is important here to recall that the discussion of the budget is synchronised with discussion of the annual plan, and that on the whole (although not in any simple way) the budget is subordinate to the plan.

It can therefore be supposed that the timing of the budget discussion has in the first place to fit in with the timing of the plan discussion. This probably does not mean that the budget discussion is brought forward in order to be synchronised with the plan discussion; rather, that the timing proceeds at the pace of the slowest, with the plan having a slightly dominant status.

Extreme lateness in the presentation of the budget might be due to the rejection at some earlier stage of the original draft of either the annual plan or the budget, so that another had to be made ready from scratch. The budget for 1953, which was presented on 5 August 1953 — when the year was more than half over — can probably serve as an illustration. Stalin's death on 5 March of that year and the accession to power of new leaders intending to promote somewhat different policies must have thoroughly shaken up the annual routine. On the other hand, small differences in timing are perhaps due simply to the engagement calendar of members of the government or Party. One peculiarity of the recorded series of dates is the fact that presentation of the budget occasionally is very early, rather than occasionally very late; while it is not hard to imagine occasional circumstances when agreeing the budget would be unusually difficult, it is harder to think of occasional circumstances when agreeing it would be unusually easy. A near-regularity in the quantities comes to our aid. As Table 4.1 shows, the budget law in several instances has been adopted unusually early in the *second* year of a long-term plan. This applies to 1960 (the second year in the Seven-Year Plan), 1972 (not very markedly) and 1977. Perhaps, agreeing the budget for the second year tends to be easier than usual as the financial programme is still running directly along lines laid down in the five-year (or seven-year) plan? It is, admittedly, necessary in this case to switch to the periodicity of the Seven-Year Plan instead of the standardised five-yearly division which is employed normally in analysis in the present book (see in particular Chapter 10). Moreover, the earliest date (10 October 1967) referred to the budget for 1968, which was the *third* year of the 8th Five-Year Plan. This possibly can be explained by the fact that 1967 was the fiftieth anniversary of the Revolution: the earlier date would get the Supreme Soviet proceedings out of the way in good time, in preparation for festivities around the time of the Revolution anniversary on 7 November. Another exception is 1957, which was the last year when the budget was presented after the beginning of the year to which it referred; in this case the responsibility can perhaps be pinned on the economic difficulties which later that year led to the abandonment of the 6th Five-Year Plan.

The general uniformity of procedure does not mean that *no* differences can be detected in the activity of the Supreme Soviet at different years. One may in this connection measure the duration of the budget debates: the longer the debates, the larger the scope that one may assume to be permitted to the deputies. This duration may be measured approximately by the interval (in days) between the date of presentation of the budget by the finance minister and the date of the budget law. While this interval is taken up by joint discussion of both plan and budget, it will be assumed here that a stable share of the time is devoted to the budget.

In recent decades, the heyday of the budget debates as measured by this index was the mid-1950s, more exactly 1954 and 1955 – when Malenkov was in power. In April 1954 and February 1955 the interval between presentation and law was as long as five days. Never since then has it been so long. The average interval (in days) in successive five-year periods has been: 1951–5, 3.6; 1956–60, 2.2; 1961–5, 2.2; 1966–70, 2.6; 1971–5, 2.2; 1976–80, 2.2. These intervals, placed within a five-year framework, are shown in Table 4.2. There are clear traces of a cyclical sequence: the 6th, 9th and 10th FYPs, less closely also the 8th FYP, resemble each other. While the 7th (notional) FYP emerges as divergent, if the seven-year plan is reinstated and a series made to start in 1959 a sequence appears which quite closely resembles an elongated version of the others. Thus it would seen that the duration of the budget debates, and therefore (according to our hypothesis) the degree of freedom allowed to deputies, varies according to the position of the year within the five-year plan, with the longest debates often taking place at the time of the presentation of the budget for the *second*

TABLE 4.2   *Intervals between budget presentation and budget law (days)*

Five-Year Plan	Serial no. of year				
	1	*2*	*3*	*4*	*5*
4th					4
5th	3	2	3	5	5
6th	2	4	1	1	3
7th	2	2	2	3	2
8th	2	4	2	3	2
9th	2	4	1	2	2
10th	2	4	2	1	2
11th	1				

SOURCE Table 4.1.

year. This also matches the fact – already noticed – that the budget for the second year tends to be presented unusually early. Is it the case that, there being more time available in this year, more time can be allotted to debates? Or is it, rather, that a conscious attempt is made to allow deputies more scope for discussing the second year's budget, and therefore the proceedings are timed to start unusually early? The facts do not show which interpretation is correct, although the former seems the more likely. The unusually lengthy debates in 1954 and 1955 did not take place in the second year of a five-year plan, but those years did stand in approximately that relationship to the new order of economic policy which followed Stalin's death. So one might hypothesise that whenever a new phase of economic development begins, the budget debates for its second year are unusually prolonged. Would that be because the debates in that year are unusually important, so it is desired to benefit from the maximum discussion by deputies, or on the contrary, because (as already suggested) the financial programme at this time is already settled, and so the composition of the budget has been swifter than usual, permitting its earlier presentation to the Supreme Soviet? The latter seems the more probable.

The current procedure is for the results of the previous budget year to be confirmed by the Supreme Soviet at the same time as the project for the budget of the *following* year. This confirmation of the results of the budget of year t together with consideration of the project of the budget of year t + 2 serves no evident useful purpose, apart of course from simplifying the arrangements for calling together the Supreme Soviet. According to Piskotin, the previous year's results are consequently confirmed after some delay, and do not receive sufficiently careful attention. Some experiments in confirming the previous year's results somewhat earlier (around the middle of the year, rather than near its close) have been carried out since 1965 by the Supreme Soviets of the Ukraine, Belorussia, and certain other republics and autonomous republics, with what are described as 'very successful and fruitful' results (Piskotin, 1971, pp. 308–9; cf. Bescherevnykh, 1976, p. 175).

Comparing this cycle with the budgetary cycle in the US and the UK, one notices significant if fairly predictable differences. The budgetary cycle in the United States includes a congressional phase, during which the executive branch of the government has to supply relatively large amounts of information. (Some hearings are open to the public, but most are not.) The entire budgetary cycle lasts as long as thirty months. At first sight this seems similar to the Soviet duration of more than two years, but really there is no comparability as these thirty months in the US do not include the period which elapses before confirmation of the budget of the *previous* year, whereas for the USSR this is included. The US Congress obviously intervenes in defence budgeting, though perhaps not as much as it could (Aspin, 1975, pp. 155–74). As for the United Kingdom, British defence budgeting comprises two 'rolling' processes (that is, always looking ahead for a fixed span of years) one governmental and the other departmental. Both Western countries adopt rolling defence budgeting (Burt, 1975, p. 23); as these procedures are not known to operate in the USSR it is possible, though unlikely, that their defence spending is projected ahead for a longer period than Soviet defence spending, except when this latter is looking ahead from the first year of a long-term plan.

BUDGET IMPLEMENTATION

It was mentioned already that operational decisions relating to the budget are the province of the Ministry of Finance, which includes a budgetary directorate (*byudzhetnoye upravleniye*). The budget is implemented on a quarterly basis, and discussions of the quarterly budgets are the occasions for especially strong pressures from business organisations upon the Ministry of Finance (Zverev, 1973, p. 170). The quarterly subdivision matches the division into quarters of the annual economic plan, and it reflects, though not very closely, the seasonal rhythm. There are fairly marked and somewhat variable deviations from a perfectly smooth path; for example, total output in the final quarter is in normal circumstances always appreciably higher than in the preceding quarters, quite apart from any secular rising trend (Hutchings, 1971b, especially pp. 100 and 255). The quarterly distribution of revenues and expenditures of the union budget is confirmed by the USSR Council of Ministers (Bescherevnykh, 1976, p. 167), but is not made public. The budget has to be balanced within each quarter (Bescherevnykh, 1976, p. 166), yet the existence of discrepancies between annual financial plans and the sum of quarterly financial plans has been reported in the past, and led to delays in payments into the budget (Shvedskiy, 1946, p. 27). Subsidies are paid quarterly by the Gosbank, up to 70 per cent of the allotted sum being payable on the first day of the first month of the quarter, while the remainder is payable only after the accounts for the quarter have been received (Yevdokimov, 1974, p. 157).

While the budget has to take into account seasonal variations, the burden of adjustment to these of financial arrangements is chiefly borne by credit investments. For example, credits in heavy industry are planned by a 'selection' process, mainly according to whether stocks could be considered seasonal (Barkovskiy and Kartashova, 1966, p. 9). When it was discovered that the budget for the fourth quarter of 1937 would show a deficit equal to 5 per cent of the entire annual budget, a solution was found in a decision not to release credits which had been unutilised during the previous nine months (Zverev, 1973, pp. 145–6).

Credits are apparently emphasised as adjustment mechanisms because of the comparative inflexibility of budgetary arrangements relative to seasonal effects. Also, very possibly, the pervasiveness and variability of those effects tend to be underestimated. The official view of seasonal variations is that certain branches (the light and food industries, timber, agriculture, etc.) are seasonal whereas others (such as machine-building) are not (Barkovskiy and Kartashova, 1966, pp. 8–9; Hutchings, 1971b, especially pp. 9–10). While it is true that the very highly seasonal branches are a comparatively small group, they are not so much exceptions to the general rule as extreme expressions of it.

Admittedly, it seems to be not uncommon for the budget to be revised, this usually being done about the middle of the year (that is, following a review of the results for the first half-year), but as a rule this happens without any public announcement and the change has to be inferred from a comparison of initially promulgated figures with those apparently employed for comparing actual with forecast totals. Comparisons have not been undertaken for the wh ɔle post-war period, which would be very time-consuming. Table 4.3 shows the results of a comparison relating to the years 1958–62 of forecasts for total budget revenues and expenditures. In four out of these five years the initial forecasts appear to have been revised, although taking into account what appears to have been a shift in 1960 to calculation by a new series, the initial forecast in that year was either unaltered or altered inappreciably. The revision might be either downwards (1961) or upwards (1962) for both revenues and expenditures, or in the same year upwards for revenues but downwards for expenditures (1959). It is not certain whether these results can be extrapolated for subsequent years.

While the budget of the current year, revised or not, is being implemented, another is being concocted and in normal circumstances its bare bones emerge into public view in the final quarter of the calendar year prior to the year to which the budget applies.

TABLE 4.3 *Comparison of initial and revised forecasts and results*

Years	Total revenues (bn roubles)		Preliminary fulfilment	Final fulfilment
	Initial forecast	*Revised forecast*		
1958	64.30	—	66.12	67.24
1959	72.34	(72.35)	73.58	74.01
1960	77.30	(75.16*)	77.41	77.1
			75.24*	
1961	78.99*	(78.22*)	78.30*	78.0*
1962	81.92*	(84.5*)	84.7*	84.3*
	Total expenditures (bn roubles)			
1958	62.77	—	63.81	64.27
1959	70.76	(70.26)	69.88	70.40
1960	74.58	(72.84*)	74.31	72.60
			72.60*	
1961	77.59*	(76.62*)	76.7*	76.3*
1962	80.37*	(82.9*)	82.7*	82.2*

* Apparently represent figures of a new series.

SOURCE Budget laws, statistical handbooks and inference from percentages of fulfilment. Figures in brackets have been inferred: have not been published.

NOTE

1. Figure 6.6 shows that budget fulfilment improved at first (1952 to 1957) within the republic section of the budget, later (between 1957 and 1966) within its union section. A comparison with Figure 4.1 then permits the deduction that the most direct and immediate impact of the trend towards earlier adoption of the budget law was upon the degree of fulfilment of the republic section.

5 Legislative Provisions and General Trends

Soviet budgetary history exhibits swings both of centralisation and of decentralisation although the latter term is rarely found in Soviet literature as it clashes with the slogan of 'democratic centralism'. In any case, these are imprecise terms by comparison with a more concrete record. With that qualification: over a long period centralisation was in the ascendant. Successive stages of the process included the withdrawal from lower organs of the power to levy taxes (1920 onwards) and the inclusion of local budgets in the budget. The 'budget was gradually to include the gross income and expenditure of the whole economy' (Davies, 1958, p. 35), but by then a monetary economy was ceasing to operate (Davies, pp. 34–5). The New Economic Policy (1921–8) reversed or partially reversed these trends: for instance, in August 1921 it was acknowledged that local revenues could be collected for local use (Davies, p. 56). Various items were hived off. Introduction of a full system of republic budgets followed the adoption of the constitution of the USSR in 1922 (Davies, p. 80). By October 1924 'the main outlines of both the republican and the local budgetary systems were established' (Davies, p. 81). However, statutes in 1926 and especially of 27 May 1927 introduced modifications; in particular, that of 1927 attached to republics the revenues from three main taxes, as well as various non-tax revenues. A new expenditure classification was confirmed on 12 July 1927. In parallel with the shifting of the business year, the start of the budget year was shifted from 1 October to 1 January (commencing in 1931) (Bescherevnykh, 1976, pp. 76, 90–4, 105).

During the NEP financial arrangements, like other aspects of the economy, were more mobile and more openly reported than they became later, and between 1925 and 1930 financial planning lost ground relative to planning in physical terms. The financial authorities were split, the RSFSR People's Commissariat of Finance taking sides with the Gosplan against the USSR People's Commissariat of Finance (Bescherevnykh, pp. 84–5). Both the financial and the credit systems were reformed in a more permanent mould in 1930–1, with (by decree of 2 September 1930) turnover tax and deductions from profits becoming the two principal revenue sources. The turnover tax embraced 53 pre-existing taxes, deductions from profits, 6. Turnover tax going almost entirely to the all-union budget, part of it began to be transferred to republics as absolute sums, any other form of transfer being technically impossible. A decree of 31 December 1931 – the last major legislative act affecting budgetary rights, until 1959 – widened the income sources of republic and local budgets (Bescherevnykh, pp. 107–8 and 115).

Adoption of the turnover tax achieved five things: the tax system was immensely simplified: centralised revenue devolution was facilitated; monies could be diverted to varied and untraceable purposes and destinations; rates of taxation were concealed; and finally, it provided grounds for a plausible although specious claim that taxes on the population were being reduced. The concept of shifting tax incidence, familiar to every economics undergraduate in Britain, was not alluded to in the USSR (Hutchings, 1971a, p. 170). Soviet industralisation might have been achieved without the turnover tax; certainly this would then have encountered much bigger difficulties.

During the 1st and 2nd Five-Year Plans revenues were drawn overwhelmingly and increasingly from the socialised sector – which contributed 74.9 per cent of all funds in 1st Five-Year Plan, 82.5 per cent in the 2nd. 'Mobilisation of the funds of the population' supplied 17.9 and 12.5 per cent respectively. The financial plan for 1935 even forecast that revenues from the socialised sector would rise to 86.5 per cent while 'mobilisation of the funds of the population' would fall to 10.5 per cent (Bogolepov, 1935, p. 97). The dominating and still rising share of revenues from the socialised sector reflected the correspondingly dominating and rising share of the socialised sector within the whole economy.

Subsidies filtered down through hierarchical levels have a long history in the Soviet economy. Their heyday was the early and mid-1930s, until the decree of 1 April 1936 abolished subsidisation as a normal principle – though subsidies continued to be paid in a whole range of special instances. Budget subsidies required centralised accounting between industry and the budget. With the fixing of most prices at the (average) level of costs, the situation changed radically (Turetskiy, 1936, p. 25). The wholesale price system was framed basically in 1936–41 (Kondrashev, 1952, p. 35; cf. Hutchings, 1961, pp. 14–19).

The Constitution of 1936 incorporated a reference to the budget (see above Chapter 3). Since 1938 the budget has included the state social insurance budget – an inclusion said to have been requested by the trade unions (Voluyskiy, 1970, p. 104). These, of course, comprise one of the Party's transmitting belts. The inclusion brought about an enlargement of SCM which, however, was swamped by a contemporary sharp expansion in spending on defence. Also from 1938 onwards republics could confirm their budgets only *after* the national budget had been confirmed, which reversed what was set down in the statute of 27 May 1927 (Bescherevnykh, 1976, p. 49). Clearly this was a large step in the direction of greater centralisation. Piskotin makes the interesting comment that the Polish budgetary system until 1956 was similar to the Soviet post-1938 one (Piskotin, 1971, pp. 134–5).

A number of factors contributed to a high rate of pre-war inflation. Economic policy emphasised non-consumption. Shortfall in consumer goods production, and overfulfilment of producer goods production, would both intensify inflation; these two phenomena were both present and persistent. But even overfulfilment of consumer goods production would intensify inflation if it were accompanied by a more than proportionate rise in earnings, and this could well occur through a mixture of piecework and bonus payments. Labour productivity was held down by dilution and a high rate of labour turnover, while from 1937 onwards defence expenditures were rising steeply. A budget surplus should be disinflationary, but in the pre-war period there was marked inflation despite budget surpluses almost every year (Holzman, 1955, pp. 52–9 and 229).

Holzman attributes inflation during this period primarily to banking rather than to budget operations (Holzman, p. 28). Given that the budget was usually in surplus it is hard to find a superior alternative explanation of what permitted inflation to continue; its scale seems, all the same, incommensurate with the scale of banking operations. In my view the rapid expansion of the budget and the shift towards defence spending, at the expense especially of FNE, must also be numbered among the causes of inflation at this time. From the start of long-term planning (formally 1 October 1928) budget revenues and expenditures rose rapidly; expenditures, from 0.88 bn (post-1961) roubles in 1928/29 to 17.44 bn in 1940. Unfortunately, this growth is exaggerated by

TABLE 5.1   *Pre-War budget expenditures (percentages)*

Year	FNE	SCM	DEF	Total of the 3 columns on the left
1928/29	42.0	29.9	10.0	81.9
1932	65.2	20.0	3.4	88.6
1937	40.9	29.1	16.5	86.5
1940	33.4	23.5	32.6	89.5

SOURCE Plotnikov (1954) pp. 132–3, 193, 206, 209, 255, 260, 263.

the contemporary price increases for which one can make no reliable adjustment. The percentage shares of the main elements of expenditure altered as in Table 5.1. Reckoning in percentage terms, FNE at first rose and then fell, while DEF did just the opposite. Both changes were large in proportionate terms. SCM varied much less and on the whole was trending downwards. The table already illustrates a main characteristic of variations in the budget's internal proportions, that changes in FNE and DEF tend to be opposite in sign and fairly large in magnitude, whereas SCM is much less variable and is not correlated uniformly with the other main components. Over time, SCM had to yield ground to FNE between 1928/29 and 1932 and to DEF between 1937 and 1940, which implied giving priority to speeding economic development in 1928/29–32 and to strengthening defence in 1937–40. The rise in the proportionate share of DEF in the later 1930s is the budgetary reflection of Soviet rearmament, which gained momentum as the Nazi threat loomed larger.

Wartime finances had, of course, peculiar features. At once a 'fund for the defence of the country' was launched. The attempt was made to 'mobilise' hoards of gold and other precious metals. The campaign yielded 130.7 kg of gold and 9519.1 kg of silver, as well as platinum and other previous metals. On the whole, this harvest does not seem hugely impressive. By decision of the Council of Ministers on 19 May 1942, savings banks and cashiers' offices of communal banks were brought into the system of tax collection (Vaynshteyn, 1957, p. 50). Above all, through measures such as revision of the agricultural and personal income tax and the addition of a war surtax (July 1941), wartime saw a large rise in the absolute and relative importance of the private sector as a contributor to budget revenues (Millar, 1980, p. 114).[1] The war witnessed an intensified centralisation of budget outlays, although this trend had started even before the war (Millar, 1980, p. 113; see also above). This centralising was necessary for the sake of economising in resources in order to achieve the maximum concentration on military purposes.

The budget forecasts for 1942 and 1943 have not been published. Naturally, wartime public finance concentrated on defence spending, which left less to spare for other expenditure clauses. However, spending on SCM could be reduced also owing to the diminished population in the unoccupied areas (Hutchings, 1971a, p. 185). Possessing few external assets, the USSR drew on gold reserves in payment to her allies for war supplies; one shipment (largely recovered in 1981) being sunk in HMS *Edinburgh*. Considerable aid in war and other supplies was received via Lend-Lease.

Having got used to rising prices and wages during the 1st and 2nd Five-Year Plans the government not surprisingly had some recourse to deficit financing in 1942–43. According to Voznesenskiy, expenditures exceeded receipts in 1942 by 1.89 bn roubles (11.5 per cent) and in 1943 by 0.73 bn roubles (3.6 per cent). The excess was covered by currency emission and by 'commodity reserves and stocks of previous years' (Voznesenskiy, 1946, p. 79; cf. Turetskiy, 1948, p. 124). Another financial recourse was 'mobilisation of internal resources' (primarily surplus stocks of materials and equipment, and recovery of debts) (Tul'chinskiy, 1945, p. 20). During wartime, deductions from profits gained in importance relative to turnover tax (because retail trade shrank), although both declined as proportions of total revenues (Millar, 1980, p. 114). Eliminated in 1944, the budget deficit has never recurred if official statistics are truthful, but actually question marks can be raised here (see below, Chapter 6).

Having been disrupted early in the war, inspection by the People's Commissariat of Finance resumed its former role. The number of its inspections climbed from 17,000 in 1942 to 66,000 in 1943 and 95,000 in 1944, many deficiencies being discovered (Zverev, 1946, p. 157).

The budget participated in military arrangements, and not only through its financing of military production and servicemen's pay: a network of field units of the Gosbank accepted loan subscriptions, dealt with remainders of budgetary and extra-budgetary funds, and so on. The primary function of these units included cash implementation of the budget, the financial transactions of postal units and military trading centres, and operations connected with savings by servicemen (Vaynshteyn, 1957, p. 52).

On the whole, the war is considered to have shown the viability and indeed the special virtues of the Soviet financial system (for example Zverev, 1946, p. 129). This might be assessed simply as propaganda:

Soviet economists could say nothing else. The Soviet system *as a whole* held together – although during the first two years with much difficulty. The degree to which inflation was kept under control is, nevertheless, noteworthy. This was achieved partly through diverting excess purchasing power into the private sector, where collective farm market prices soared. However, the resulting accumulation of funds in peasant hands in turn tempted the authorities to enforce the currency reform of December 1947, which wiped out a large fraction of private monetary holdings. This set the tune for continuation of the policy of holding down inflation, which fundamentally is made possible in Soviet circumstances by restriction of the freedom of economic agents. As regards external relations, the Soviet Union in compensation for its immense war damage secured reparations from Finland, Bulgaria, Romania, Hungary, and Italy. Large quantities of equipment were removed from Germany and re-installed in the USSR (Rudolph, 1953, pp. 19–21).

As regards revenues, post-war history has seen several major developments. One notable event was the cessation from 1963 onwards of the practice of including savings bank funds within budget revenues (Bescherevnykh, 1976, p. 137). This move substituted the Gosbank for the Ministry of Finance as the recipient of household savings. It had no direct effect on the bank's credit policy, although at the beginning of 1967, 'savings deposits equalled almost one-third of all the credit extended by the Gosbank' (Garvy, 1977, p. 202). The move may have been made in anticipation of the switch towards financing capital investment by loan rather than by grant which was announced in October 1965, or it may have been envisaged that savings deposits could redouble their effect if they boosted bank credits rather than budget revenues (see also Chapter 11). A 'tax on non-commodity operations' was abolished as from 1 January 1958 (Tsypkin, 1973, p. 74 and Piskotin, 1971, p. 147). From 1960 onwards all state organisations were relieved from paying construction tax (*nalog so stroyeniy*) and land rent, this last according to Piskotin an over-hasty decision in view of the forthcoming switch to payment for capital and circulating funds, it being no less necessary to pay for the use of land (Piskotin, p. 189). Environmentalist considerations would also soon reinforce doubts about the wisdom of this course. Personal taxes (such as income tax) were to be discontinued by 1965, but this decision was later rescinded, which was one of the accusations laid against Khrushchev at the time of his dismissal. Regular subscriptions by the public to bond sales had been in practice (and since 1936, even in form) compulsory, but in 1958 compulsory subscriptions ceased (voluntary purchases being still possible), and regular drawings were soon made to repay them, with provision in the annual budget (Nove, 1980, p. 239; Hutchings 1971a, p. 171). (The Soviet premium bonds helped to inspire the introduction of a similar scheme in the United Kingdom.) On the whole, though the post-war period has seen further attempts to simplify revenue-gathering, these have not been comparable in scale with the introduction of turnover tax and more complicated considerations have increasingly gained the upper hand.

As regards cash circulation, the most important legal provision is the decree of the Council of Ministers of 8 December 1948; this demanded centralisation of all budget management in the Gosbank, with a centre of operational servicing concentrating within itself all main disposers of credit from the union and RSFSR republic budgets. (Cash implementation of republic budgets had been concentrated in republic offices even earlier (Vaynshteyn, 1957, pp. 55–6).) It was decided to set up a central administration (*Upravlenive*) for cash implementation of the budget of the USSR, communal and city banks being freed from these duties, or – in the case of the Moscow budget section of the Gosbank – abolished. Yet some lack of structural integration of budgetary sections continued to be felt, and in 1954 centralisation was carried a step further (Vaynshteyn, 1957, pp. 55–7). These moves can probably be interpreted as intending closer control over cash implementation, in part with the aim of curbing any inflationary tendencies.

As regards the division of expenditures between the state budget and the Gosbank, from 1 January 1953 projecting organisations, previously supported by the budget, were transferred to the Gosbank. Their work is said to have improved as a result (Dyskin, 1954, p. 54).

The *sovnarkhoz* reform of 1957 was accompanied by financial decentralisation; in particular, republic budgets expanded at the expense of the union budget (see Chapter 6 below, and cf. Hutchings, 1971a, p. 190). Decentralisation was effected also by the transfer to republic budgets as from 1 January 1958 of certain regulating sources of income, which until then had been relatively numerous (Bescherevnykh, 1976, pp. 156–7). Moreover, as from 1956 republics themselves determined which portion of their budget would be carried out by the republic budget and which by local budgets (formerly, this had been determined by the USSR budget law), while also additional revenues could remain at republics' disposal for financing the economy or social and cultural measures (Bescherevnykh, p. 51).

The law of 30 October 1959 besides regulating the publication of the budget (as noted already in Chapter 4) in conjunction with laws adopted in 1960–1 in all the republics codified all non-obsolete laws both before and after the 1936 Constitution, also generalising from experience and regulating individual points (Bescherevnykh, p. 126).

The economic reform of 1957 was virtually reversed by that of October 1965 – by decree of 4 October 1965 of the Central Committee of the Communist Party and the Council of Ministers of the USSR, in development of which various special decisions were adopted by the Council of Ministers and other bodies. No separate laws were passed concerning the financial provisions of the decree, which according to Bescherevnykh amounted to an irregularity relative to the law of 30 October 1959 (Bescherevnykh, pp. 130–1).

Four main changes occurred in the budget after the economic reform of 1965: the role of financial levers and indices in business organisation and activity was greatly increased, the gross production index being replaced by one of sold production, and the costs index being replaced by that of profits; the role of the share of profits remaining at plants' disposal was increased, the share going to the budget being reduced; the tax named deductions from profits ceased to exist, its place being taken by this trio: payments for productive funds, rent, and levies of free profit margins (some rates of turnover tax being reduced, to assure a sufficient margin of profitability); fourth, capital grants to plants were curtailed in volume and the free supplementing of their working capital stopped, while in this connection the application of bank credit was widened (Piskotin, 1971, pp. 26–7). Thus, on the whole the budget was to participate less in business activity. Financial indices in a few cases took the place of natural ones, that is in these cases the financial plans became the operative ones (Piskotin, p. 25).

As regards the control exercised over republic budgets by the union budget, extreme centralisation involving the imposition of differentiated limits upon funding authorisations (*limitirovaniye*), which was practised until 1965, was abolished. (The text actually has '1955', but in view of the immediately following reference to the 1965 decree this is presumed to be a misprint.) As described in 1971, the union budget was still fixing five limits for republic budgets: in regard to FNE, SCM, organs of state administration of the republic, wages, and budget subsidies. Seen from the republic, limits thus applied to four items of expenditure and one of revenue (the final one in this list). This simplified form of central control dated from a Council of Ministers decree of 4 May 1965.

To the extent that these changes augmented the sums effectively left at the disposal of plants, they must have been welcome; whereas they must have been unwelcome to plants to the extent that they replaced free budget grants by repayable loans. In practice, one observes little shrinkage of the budget's role in financing economic development.

On the whole, events since 1930–1 have confirmed the basic stability of the financial arrangements settled at that time. 'Stability' would be very far from describing the trend over time of the amounts of revenues and expenditures – the subject of Part II.

NOTE

1. As an extreme example of this trend, a private individual, Ferapont Golovatyy, bought a fighter plane! (Zverev, 1973, p. 202). One is reminded irresistibly of voluntary subscriptions in Britain in the Second World War for buying Spitfires. (The price is remembered to have been £5,000.)

PART II
Growth, Fluctuation and Variation in Visibility

6 Main Quantitative Trends

GROWTH OF THE TOTAL BUDGET

In Part II, elements of the budget are examined and their behaviour over time depicted. The following general scheme may be borne in mind: general trends, any cycles that are synchronised with the economic plans (especially those of five years' duration), and irregular movements.

The growth of the budget between 1940 and 1979 (actual total expenditures), according to official statistics, is set out in Figure 6.1. This growth has been very rapid: from 17.43 bn roubles in 1940 to 276.37 bn in 1979, that is by 15.9 times. Total revenues rose over the same period from 18.02 bn to 281.53 bn roubles, that is by 15.6 times. If these increases represent real values – a caveat will be entered here – they are by any standards very imposing.

Main revenue trends

Appendix II exhibits total (actual) revenues annually since 1945, the amounts contributed by turnover tax or deductions from profits (after 1965, the latter becomes payments out of profits), and the relative shares of each of these two principal sources in total revenues. During the 1930s an overwhelming reliance was placed on the turnover tax. (Hutchings, 1971a, p. 179). After 1946, deductions from profits gradually became relatively more important, and following two periods (1947–55 and 1958–61) when total turnover tax revenues remained almost constant (Ames, 1965, p. 161), deductions from profits by 1967 had become the largest revenue item. One of the reasons for the relative decline in revenues from turnover tax was the decision of the March 1965 Party Plenum to give tax encouragements to agriculture (Gumpel, 1967, p. 114). The share of payments out of profits has since fallen slightly, and the two sources, now about equal

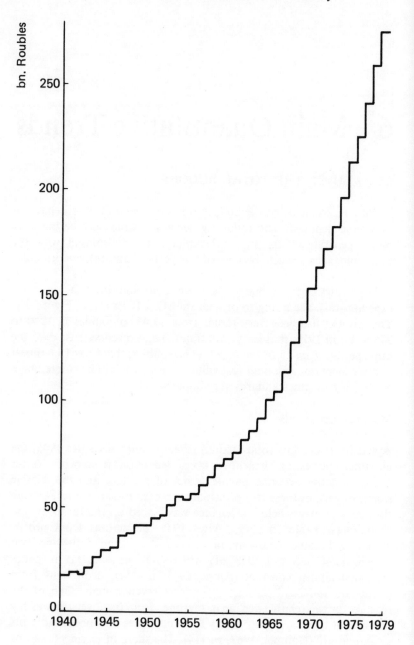

FIGURE 6.1   *Growth of budget expenditures 1940–79*

in size, are each currently contributing slightly less than one-third of total revenues.

From the exchequer's point of view it is not absolutely fundamental whether to raise revenues through turnover tax or through deductions from profits, as both are paid by the 'socialist sector'. In fact, changes from year to year in their respective shares in total revenues have usually been in opposite directions, as if payment via the one were substituted for payment via the other. Since 1970 this relationship has been less marked, as the relative shares of both items have been marking time. This stabilisation has perhaps resulted from an acceptance by the authorities of arguments by budgetary specialists that too large a displacement of turnover tax by payments out of profits would bring negative consequences (for example Piskotin, 1971, pp. 190–1).

Slightly more than one-third is therefore contributed by other sources, whose proportionate share declined from 1953 to 1966 but subsequently has inched up again.

Principal expenditure trends

To focus now on the expenditure side of the budget, and first on total expenditures. Although very occasionally total spending declined from one year to the next, on the whole growth has been continuous as well as rapid. But one can observe one fairly marked discontinuity. Up to about 1961 its growth can be described as linear, as was noted at the time (Hutchings, 1962a, Tables I and II). Growth then accelerated, but without becoming exponential. Rather, growth continued to be approximately linear, but now with larger annual additions. The latest period available for study again exhibits an approximation to linear growth, as shown in Table 6.1.

As the strong upward trend makes it hard to discern variations in the rate of annual growth, these rates are set out in Figure 6.2. Between

TABLE 6.1   *Annual additions to actual total budget expenditures (bn roubles)*

1973–4	13.4
1974–5	17.1
1975–6	12.2
1976–7	16.1
1977–8	17.4
1978–9	16.2
Average of above	15.4

SOURCE Appendix I of this volume.

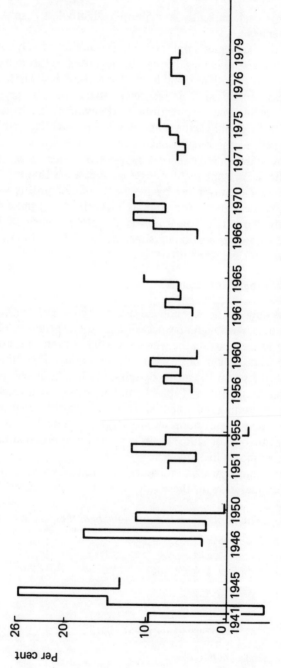

FIGURE 6.2 *Variations in rates of annual growth of budget expenditures (relative to previous year)*

1940 and 1955 growth rates were much more variable than they have been since; this of course is partly due to the War, but post-1955 also exhibits in this respect some internal differences. Until 1966–70 the growth rate was tending to become more variable, whereas it has since been less variable. There has not been any phase of persistently below-average growth.

In Figure 6.2 annual growth rates of budget spending are set out in a five-year grouping based on the sequence of five-year plans (1961–5 being entered as a notional seventh FYP). Judging by this diagram the turning-point in annual growth rates appears to have been 1965, whereas a comparison of actual with forecast spending suggests a turning-point as early as 1962, when actual total spending began to exceed the plan whereas in 1959 to 1961 it had fallen short. Up to 1961, total budget spending normally fell short of the forecast: from 1946 to 1961, this was so in 14 years out of 16. But from 1962 onwards total forecast expenditure has been almost always exceeded, the only exception being 1972. The extent of overspending has risen also, both absolutely and proportionately. *Forecast* expenditures at least were still adhering approximately to a linear projection.

The comparison of average growth rates during successive five-year periods since 1940 shows 1965–70 to be anomalous, the average annual growth rate of budget spending during this period having been 8.8 per cent as compared with 6.8 per cent in each of the flanking periods of the same length. Within this span, the individual years which exhibited the fastest rates of growth were 1967 to 1968 and 1969 to 1970 (11.6 per cent in each case).

Reversal of quinquennial rhythm

Until 1965 (neglecting the war years, and 1945–6 which was dominated by the changeover from war conditions) budget growth always accelerated in the first year of a new five-year plan, and decelerated in its final year. But starting in 1965, budget growth has always *decelerated* in the first year of a new five-year plan and *accelerated* in its final year. Furthermore, until 1962–3 budget growth usually decelerated in the middle year of a five-year plan (1952–3 was exceptional, but can be explained by Stalin's death and by the new government's adoption of modified economic policies), whereas since 1962–3 budget growth has always accelerated in the plan's middle year. This means that from 1963 onwards the quinquennial rhythm has been reversed (see also Chapter 10).

Total budget spending from the period of the early or middle 1960s is thus marked by several changes: a faster rate of growth on the whole, overspending of the forecast instead of underspending, and a reversed quinquennial rhythm.

Main expenditure items

Budget spending on the economy (FNE) is the most characteristically Soviet feature of Soviet budget spending; for national budgets generally (though in different proportions) allot money always to defence, and normally also to some kind of social expenditures. By contrast, it is characteristic of a socialist system that the budget finances either all or the larger part of investment in the economy. This is also one of the main components of Soviet budgetary FNE. It is not the whole of it: FNE also includes subsidies, and other items, some of which are not readily identifiable.

FNE is not only the most characteristic feature of the Soviet budget but, increasingly, the dominating one. In 1946, actual FNE comprised 31.1 per cent of total actual expenditure; the corresponding proportion in 1979 was 54.9 per cent. The intermittent but, on the whole, relentless rise in this proportion is shown in Figure 6.3. In absolute figures, 9.57 bn roubles were spent in 1946, 151.4 bn in 1979 − an increase of 15.8 times. While these totals are reckoned in current prices, the rise reckoned in stable values would also be very large.

It would be desirable also to present total spending on FNE from all sources (including enterprises' own funds and bank credit), but here the available data are much more scanty; indeed, that total is not usually published. We can report only that between 1957 and 1966 forecast allocations to FNE from all sources rose from 37.6 bn to 81.8 bn, an increase of 2.2 times − which was somewhat larger than the increase in forecast allocations to FNE from the budget over the same period (1.7 times). Almost certainly this 2.2 : 1.7 ratio did not hold good throughout the whole post-war period: 1957 to 1966 would have witnessed an unusually large relative rise in allocations to FNE from all sources, which is probably why this larger total is published only for this specific period. But if allocations from all sources on the whole may not have risen much faster than allocations from the budget alone, they probably did not rise more slowly. Thus, an index of increase of allocations from all sources would not be less impressive than one relating to budgetary allocations alone.

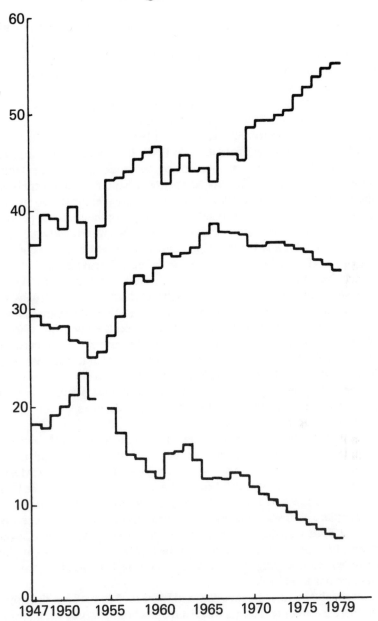

FIGURE 6.3 *Percentage shares of FNE, SCM and DEF in total budget expenditures*

The only other item of expenditure that can compare in size with FNE during most of the post-war period is spending on social and cultural measures (SCM). Generally, SCM has amounted to a figure in the region of three-quarters of FNE; illustrative percentages are: 1940 70.0; 1945, 84.4; 1950, 74.0; 1955, 63.1; 1960, 73.0; 1965, 85.1; 1970, 74.9; 1975, 69.6. This ratio has therefore undulated, but the proportions in 1940 and 1975 were almost the same. As a proportion of total spending SCM rose from 23.5 per cent in 1940 to 35.9 per cent in 1975. SCM is much more predictable than FNE; its estimate is more often overspent than underspent, but not by any wide margin. It exhibits little or no five-year periodicity (see below, Chapter 10) and there is no sustained take-off after 1961. FNE has consequently stayed as the largest item of budgetary expenditure throughout the post-war period. Though the two items started almost level, FNE was quickly drawing ahead of SCM. Only between 1961 and 1966 was SCM again coming close to FNE, and since then FNE has taken a decisive lead.

Relative to total expenditure, FNE exhibits ups and downs but on the whole the post-war period can be divided into three spans of approximately equal length. Between 1946 and 1960, the share of FNE in total spending rose from 31.1 to 46.6 per cent, while from 1969 to 1979, this share rose from 45.0 per cent to 54.9 per cent. Thus, between 1960 and 1969 the share of FNE *declined* from 46.6 to 45.0 per cent. Whereas between 1946 and 1960 the share rose by an annual average of 1.1 per cent, and between 1969 and 1979 by an annual average of 1.0 per cent, between 1960 and 1969 this share declined by an annual average of 0.2 per cent.

As may be seen by reference to Figure 6.3, the unusual behaviour of FNE in the middle sub-period was the result of unusual trends in the behaviour of both the other two main expenditure clauses: SCM and DEF. SCM was rising almost throughout this sub-period, while DEF contrary to the previous trend rose sharply from 1961 onwards to a higher plateau of spending. The coincident decline in the rate of expansion of FNE was slightly moderated by a fairly regular decline in the proportionate size of the budget residue (see below, pp. 88–90, in this chapter). Considering the post-war period as a whole, the share of defence has been declining.

In absolute terms, defence declined from 1945 to 1948 but since then has risen in three great surges which have reached their peaks or plateaux at intervals of 9–11 years, that is to say in 1952–5, 1961 and 1970–3 (see Figure 6.4). This three-stage movement shows affinities with the division of the post-war period into three spans of approximately equal length

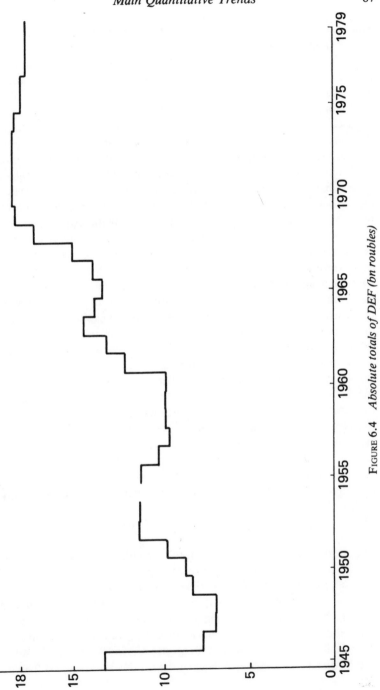

FIGURE 6.4   *Absolute totals of DEF (bn roubles)*

which characterises FNE relative to total expenditure, as described in the previous paragraph but one.

As Figure 6.3 shows, since about 1954 FNE and DEF have usually tended to move in opposite directions, whereas a similar alternation of DEF and SCM is only found within the approximate span 1947 to 1961.

Reasons for variations in the proportionate size of budget expenditures can according to Piskotin be divided into two groups, though these are interconnected. The first group comprises reactions to events, such as the size of the annual harvest and the international situation, or some natural disaster (such as an earthquake); the second, changes in state policy, such as the decision following the XXth Party Congress to increase substantially allocations to housing and communal economy, or to agriculture following various plenums of the Party (Piskotin, 1971, pp. 166–7). As expenditure cuts in some directions would have very unfavourable effects, such cuts are effected chiefly in areas such as housing repairs, city improvements, or the purchase of institutional equipment. (Piskotin, p. 166). Agreeing that these connections do exist, one must point out that Piskotin's illustrations are far from being exhaustive. He (of course) does not make explicit the effect of decisions to increase spending on weapons, as well as many other connections. On the whole, the Soviet budget, like the whole economy, has to compensate for unforeseen expenses by unforeseen savings. In this respect it is no different from any other budget or economy, unless in the Soviet Union the requirement is more strict, its budget already comprising an unusually large proportion of the national income while the economy in terms of fullness of employment, although not of efficiency, is also near to its maximum level.

It is of course also conceivable that spending clauses change in apparent size owing to changes in their coverage. Usually, variations in coverage can only be inferred. (See in this connection Bahry, 1980.)

BUDGET RESIDUE AND BUDGET SURPLUS

The residue is calculated here as total expenditures minus DEF, FNE and SCM – thus (for this purpose) ignoring administration, which is probably understated in official statistics (see Schroeder, 1976, pp. 23–44). Its trend since 1945 is shown in Figure 6.5. The dominant feature has been its very marked decline relative to total actual expenditure: from 19.1 per cent in 1946 to only 2.7 per cent in 1963. This decline was interrupted by an abrupt rise in 1953 which, however, can be disregarded in the analysis of the residue as it resulted from the

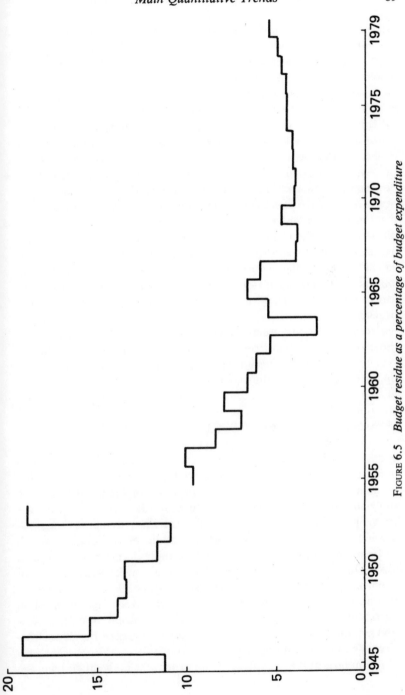

FIGURE 6.5 *Budget residue as a percentage of budget expenditure*

extraordinary and fictitious procedure in that year and in the following year of registering price reductions (see Chapter 1). Since 1962 the trend of the residue has been generally upwards, though the gradient is much more gradual than the previous fall had been. The contraction of the residue if the post-war period is considered as a whole substantially enhances the validity of analysis based mainly in changes in the size of the three largest named items of budget expenditure.

The surplus of total revenue over total expenditure has also tended to shrink, not only in relative terms but even absolutely: for example, the surplus was 3.96 bn Rs in 1948, only 1.89 bn in 1972. The fall has been especially marked in the forecast surplus, which in the same years were 4.11 bn and 0.20 bn respectively, despite the considerable enlargement of the total budget during the same period. The steepest drop (by nine-tenths) in the forecast surplus occurred between 1963 and 1966. The actual surplus now exceeds the forecast one by a wide margin: in 1971 and 1972, being more than nine *times* larger. It is not that actual expenditures have fallen short of forecast: both revenues and expenditures actually have exceeded their forecasts, but revenues in the bigger proportion.

Except in 1940–1 the actual residue has invariably been smaller than the forecast one, almost certainly owing to the allocation during the year to specific expenditure clauses of funds originally held in reserve by the Council of Ministers of the USSR.

UNION AND REPUBLIC SECTIONS OF THE BUDGET

It has been pointed out already that the budget has to be divided into union and republic sections, and that these exhibit significantly different characteristics. What have been their respective trends? The share of the union budget declined between 1953 and 1961, then rose (more gradually) until 1970, since when there has been little change. A significant crossover point was 1967, when the union budget regained the leading place (51.5 per cent of the total budget) for the first time since 1957. This occurred in the aftermath of the economic reform of 1965, and can be regarded as one of its results. In 1979, the share of the union budget was 52.1 per cent. This relatively high proportion currently is firmly buttressing 'democratic centralism', or more exactly and meaningfully, Moscow is again in direct control of the larger fraction of budget expenditure.

All budgets of the individual republics are constantly on the increase, but not at equal rates. While their relative positions are usually unchanged from one year to another over decades there have been some displacements. Between 1960 and 1980 Lithuania, Moldavia, Tadzhikistan and Estonia improved their positions in a league table, whereas Georgia, Azerbaydzhan, Latvia, Kirghizia, Armenia and Turkmenia fell back. Belorussia, which between 1960 and 1965 was overtaken by Uzbekistan, by 1975 had regained fourth place; the two republics are now running neck-and-neck. Over 20 years one observes a falling-back of the RSFSR (from 59.8 to 54.9 per cent of the total for all republics), and marginally of the Ukraine (from 18.0 to 17.0 per cent); while the Transcaucasus raised its proportion slightly (from 4.0 to 4.3 per cent), the chief gains were registered in the east (Uzbekistan, Kazakhstan, Kirghizia, Tadzhikistan and Turkmenia – their sum total rose from 11.5 per cent to 14.1 per cent), and even more strikingly in the west (Belorussia, Lithuania, Latvia, Estonia, and Moldavia – from 6.6 per cent to 9.6 per cent). To the extent that it is reflected in the comparative size of republic budgets, the eastwards shift in the centre of gravity of the Soviet economy has come to a halt.

If the observed pattern cannot be characterised as an eastwards shift, does the analysis suggest any other simple formula? Both in the east and in the west are found small republics, but these have not fared especially well, on an average. If anything, over the past thirty years the larger budgets to start with have also grown the faster, though the correlation falls well short of being statistically significant.

On the whole, it seems most likely that comparative shifts have to be ascribed not to any general principle but to factors which are specific to the particular republics. The 'republic bias' of the budget (see above, Chapter 3) is therefore not translated into privileges for specific republics. In the first case we are dealing with a horizontal category of the budget, in the second with a regional distribution. Besides being conceptually distinct, the two series obey different rules. The differential rates of budget growth have doubtless been affected importantly by the much more rapid growth of population in Central Asia.

OVERSPENDING AND UNDERSPENDING

On the whole since the war budget forecasts have been overspent, and this weakness – as the financial organs presumably see it – has become chronic. But we need to distinguish here between various sub-periods. Up to 1952 forecasts were approximately accurate, whereas performance has since become much less predictable. Yet this applies only to the republic section of the budget. While the union section of the budget is currently underspent, on an average, to about the same degree (around 4 per cent) as before 1952, the republic section which formerly was just about on target is nowadays overspent by 10 per cent or more; in 1978, even by 16 per cent. Figure 6.6 illustrates the sequence of over- and underspending of annual union and republic budgets, by comparison with forecasts of them, since 1944. In almost every year the union budget has been underspent but the republic budget overspent. However, three sub-periods and two transitional years can be distinguished: 1946–52, union budget slightly underspent, republic budget on target; 1953–65, union budget markedly underspent, republic budget even more markedly overspent; 1966, union budget overspent, republic budget underspent; 1967, union budget slightly overspent, republic budget overspent; 1968 at least until the present day, union budget underspent, republic budget overspent.

Considering the whole period since 1944, reduced underspending of the union budget is not correlated with either increased or decreased overspending of the republic budget. Until 1952 and again from 1965 onwards both degrees of fulfilment moved in the same direction, whereas in the middle phase they were moving in opposite directions. Also during the middle phase the ratio of the union budget to the republic budget was changing, whereas in the earlier and later phases this ratio was more static. While from 1953 to 1967 inclusive degrees of fulfilment of the two sections of the budget are roughly mirror images of each other, this is not true of the earliest and latest phases.

Figure 6.5 shows an increasing degree of overspending of the republic budget from 1953 onwards, which reached its culmination in 1957. Overspending in that year was the direct result of Khrushchev's *sovnarkhoz* reform, which has always been regarded as rather precipitate: criticisms were being levelled at ministries during 1956, preparations for the reform were initiated with proposals to that effect published on 30 March 1957, the reform was promulgated on 10 May and it was to be carried into effect by 1 July 1957. The rising degree of overspending of republic budgets suggests, however, that events actually were moving in the direction of the reform appreciably earlier, even from as early as 1953. Similarly, the substantial overspending of the republic budget in 1959–60 and simultaneous underspending of the union budget suggests a continued process of financial decentralisation even after the reform was formally effected. Or, putting matters the

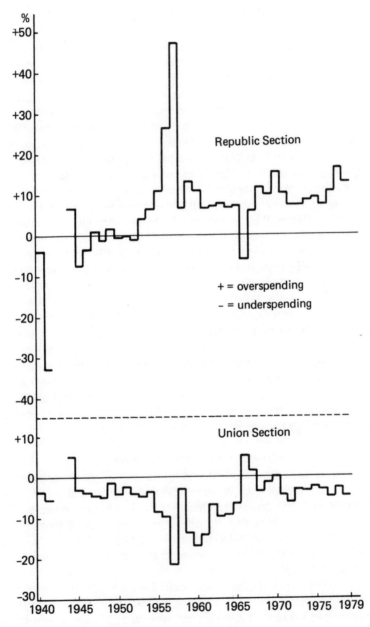

FIGURE 6.6 *Overspending and underspending of union and republic sections of budget*

other way round, the greater the degree of decentralisation, the greater apparently is the likelihood of overspending; that is, the more spending is decentralised, the more the government loses control of it.

While the suggestion cannot be found in Soviet sources, it is perhaps arguable that these results were grasped and accepted by the authorities as part of the price to be paid for pursuing a wider variety of objectives via decentralisation, or a narrower one via centralisation. In 1957 a wider variety of aims began to be pursued: to overtake the United States in production of meat, milk and butter per head of the population, and then to launch the world's first sputnik, with all that that implied in scientific and technical advance. But by the end of the Seven-Year Plan Khrushchev's targets for agricultural production were being clearly seen as unrealistic, while the headlong promotion of science and technology was perceived to be becoming altogether too expensive (Hutchings, 1976, pp. 75–83). This sequence of objectives and of their accompanying perceived constraints chronologically matches the decentralisation of budget spending in 1957 and its recentralisation in 1965.

PROBLEMS AND INCONSISTENCIES

Various shorter-term fluctuations in the amounts recorded under these clauses will be examined subsequently. But first: how nearly do the uncovered trends of total spending and of the main components of expenditure conform to what might reasonably have been expected? There are several unexpected or even peculiar features.

(1) From about 1962–5 budget expenditures accelerated: although growth continued to be basically linear so far as concerned total revenue or expenditure, the annual additions became larger. Looking at Figure 6.4, one prominent change around that time was an enlargement in defence spending. In Soviet circumstances of basically full employment it is not clear why that should have been accompanied by (or should have resulted in, or from) a faster expansion of total budget expenditure.

(2) From about 1962 onwards, actual total expenditure exceeds its forecast rather than falls short of it. Apparently, financial planning has become less taut. It is not evident why such a change should accompany higher defence spending; if anything, one might expect the contrary result. Furthermore the extent of overspending has risen,

though as planning techniques improve, any deviation of actual from forecast spending should be expected to become smaller rather than larger.

(3) Throughout, the Soviet Union has ostensibly been striving towards 'communism'. In budgetary terms, that striving would presumably entrain an expansion in the share of spending that was devoted to 'social and cultural measures'. The share of SCM has actually risen, but by no means steadily. As already noted, since 1965 SCM relative to FNE has fallen – contrary to the expectation of Gumpel and his collaborators (Gumpel, 1967, pp. 118–19).

(4) The growth of defence spending in waves which reach a peak or plateau at intervals of 9–11 years is not correlated in any obvious way with post-war trends in international relations. For example, 1966–8 which is regarded as a period of détente saw a sharp rise in Soviet defence spending, which since the early 1970s even has been falling. The generally declining share of defence relative to total spending also by no means matches the fact that armaments have been growing much more expensive.

(5) Throughout the post-war period, although at a slackening rate, the Soviet economy has been undergoing expansion. It might have been expected that in consequence, spending on the economy as a proportion of total spending would level off or even decline. Such a trend is in fact found only in the middle third of the post-war period. The rather marked, and continuing, enlargement in the share of FNE at other times does not fit such an expectation.

(6) As regards quinquennial rhythms, the Soviet system of economy does not profess either to generate them or *a fortiori* to instigate reversal of them; indeed, it professes to eliminate them.

Thus in both actual and relative terms, the post-war movement of the main expenditure clauses presents a number of unexpected and surprising features. Forces other than those mentioned so far must have played a substantial part in shaping the size of expenditures and their trend. In subsequent chapters, further explanations of these, and other, problems are sought in more detailed analyses of the budget's components. In the present chapter, attention is drawn to the various possible forms of budget growth.

(1) The budget while remaining a stable share of the gross national product might increase as the GNP increases.

(2) The budget might become a larger share of the GNP.

(3) Both the above alternatives presuppose that the budget and the GNP are expressed in quantities (value totals) which can be related to each other. However, since the budget has two sides — revenue and expenditure — if these are in balance the budget total might grow due to multiplication of the sums appearing on both sides of the account, if sums are merely flowing in a circle from enterprises to the budget and back again. Within a given period, this would correspond to a faster velocity of circulation of budget funds. If the budget exploits *this* channel for growth, it expands into a dimension which is not employed on the computation of the GNP (or of its variants, such as the net material product).

If an expansion of type (3) took place, how could it be detected? First, the budget would expand more rapidly than the GNP (or the net material product), and more rapidly also than net budgetary financing. Second, elements in the budget which participated in the circular flow of funds would expand relative to elements which did not. Third, the presence of the phenomenon might be corroborated by collateral information (from economists, bookkeepers etc.). There might be more or less explicit statements of intention to achieve a particularly high rate of budget growth. Fourth, revenues and expenditures would be in balance or at least near to so being, and over time any surplus or deficit would be likely to shrink relative to total revenue or expenditure.

All these signs (or very similar ones) can in fact be observed. First, as shown below (Chapter 9, pp. 133–4) in recent years the ratio of the budget to the net material product has risen. As the gross national product, as reckoned by the Soviet *valovoy obshchestvennyy produkt*, has risen about as fast as the *proizvedennyy natsional'nyy dokhod* (between 1965 and 1977 the former rose 2.11 times, the latter 2.10 times — *Nar. khoz. SSSR v 1977 g.*, 1978, p. 30) the same is extremely likely to apply to the ratio of the budget to the *valovoy obshchestvennyy produkt*. Also, as noted in Chapter 2, between 1971–5 and 1976–80 the budget's share in the state's total financial resources increased slightly. The measurement of net budgetary financing is difficult, but the more rapid increase of the budget than of net budgetary financing is clearly affirmed by Liberman (1970, pp. 269–70) who (second) also corroborates the relatively more rapid expansion of elements in the budget which took part in the circular flow. Liberman's statement may be included also in evidence of the third type. Fourth, reference to the statistical tables (Appendix I) will reveal an approximate balance of revenues and expenditures, and over time a diminution of the budget surplus. (Liberman's allusion is examined further in Hutchings, 1981.)

Thus it can be determined that the expected signs are in fact present, which leads to the conclusion that the budget has grown at any rate partly owing to the especially rapid growth of an internal circular flow.

Another partial explanation of the inflationary aspect of budget growth may be found in an upward drift of prices due to the replacement of lower-priced items by higher-priced items. Of course, the primary source of budget growth is to be found in the expansion of the whole economy, which has on the whole been matched by that of the total budget.

7 Spending on the Economy

INTRODUCTION

Preceding chapters looked at FNE as a whole relative to other major items and trends. The analysis is now carried into the interior of FNE, so far as the available data permit. Unfortunately, for no single year is there anything even remotely resembling a complete breakdown of this vitally important segment of budgetary spending. In principle, the clause might be split up in two ways: horizontally between investment and non-investment, and vertically among industry, agriculture, or other *branches* of the economy. But not a single year exhibits *both* breakdowns. Despite this lacuna in the sub-division of FNE, a great deal can still be accomplished, and will shed light on the behaviour of the budget and of the economy generally.

VERTICAL SUB-DIVISIONS

Budget FNE

The economy is financed both from within the budget and from outside it. Considering first budgetary allocations, their distribution among branches of the economy is shown in Table 7.1 in the form of percentages of the forecast totals. A less detailed but more consistent breakdown of the actual sums spent (over a shorter period) is shown in Appendix III. Looking at the *forecasts*: as a rule, rather less than half has gone to industry and the rest to other branches (agriculture in particular). Industry's share over time has declined slightly, but there is no clear trend and this share has always been between 37.7 (1970) and 63.0 per cent (1948). Agriculture's share has varied within somewhat wider

TABLE 7.1 *Finance of national economy from budget: percentages of forecast totals*

	(i)	(ii)	(iii)	(iv)	(v)	(vi)	(vii)	(viii)	(ix)	(x)
1941	53.8				18.5		9.1			18.6
1944	55.3		2.7		16.1		14.1	3.8		8.0
1945	55.6		2.6		14.2		15.2	4.5		7.9
1946	62.4		3.1		12.3		10.6	3.8		7.8
1947	60.6		2.9		12.3		10.0			14.2
1948	63.0		2.8		13.4		9.3			11.5
1950	51.9				22.3		9.1			16.7
1951			6.3		21.8					71.9
1952					19.2					80.8
1953	42.9			20.7						36.4
1954	36.8	6.6			28.9		9.9			17.8
1955	45.5	4.8	0.4		24.8		10.3			14.2
1956	42.5				20.5		9.2			27.8
1957	48.4				21.6					30.0
1958	50.2				20.8					29.0
1959	47.0				9.8		8.1			35.1
1960	46.2				9.8					44.0
1961	47.5				12.4			10.6		29.5
1962	45.6						7.7			46.7
1963				16.2			6.9			83.8
1964										100.0
1965	48.6			16.5			6.8			34.9
1966	51.1			14.8			6.2	9.6		34.1
1967	46.7		6.8		13.4		5.8			33.7
1968	47.6			17.9						34.5
1969	38.1		11.1	15.8				8.4		37.7
1970	37.7		9.6							62.3
1971	38.4		7.8	14.2			3.9			35.7
1972	38.7			14.6			3.9	6.8		36.0
1973	39.2		4.0	17.3			3.7			39.8
1974	38.6			15.9			4.0	6.5		35.0
1975	41.2			17.2			4.4			37.2
1976	41.9			16.0			4.3	7.2		30.6
1977										100.0
1978	42.7		2.3	16.1			5.0			33.9
1979	42.5		0.7		15.9		4.8	6.5		29.6
1980	45.7		2.1		16.1		5.2	6.2		24.7

(i) Heavy industry; (ii) Light industry; (iii) Internal trade; (iv) Procurements; (v) Agriculture; (vi) Forestry; (vii) Transport and communications; (viii) Communal economy; (ix) Housing; (x) Remainder.

SOURCE Budget speeches and annual articles in *Finansy SSSR*.

limits (9.8 per cent in 1959 and 1960, to 28.9 per cent in 1954), although more recently this share has been almost stable, at about 16 per cent. Transport and communications has obtained between 3.7 per cent (1973) and 15.2 per cent (1945). Trade, procurements, forestry, communal economy and housing, are indicated less frequently.

Expenditure on agriculture has, of course, risen very greatly in absolute terms, yet as a proportion of total FNE it was no higher in 1969 than in 1941. The trend here as disclosed by the budget figures differs a good deal from what is often supposed. The proportion doubled between 1948 and 1954, but in 1959 (the first year of the Seven-Year Plan) it fell to the lowest level since the Second World War and subsequent increases have only partially recovered the lost ground.

Also forecast in most years is expenditure on transport and communications. Not surprisingly this rose in proportionate terms in 1945 (war damage to the rail network had been very severe) and then remained for several years at above the 1941 proportion. There was another rise in 1955, probably in connection with improving communications, in particular with the construction of narrow-gauge railways, to serve the virgin lands being opened up about that time. The share of transport and communications declined slowly until 1975, but has since risen slightly. Trade and procurements, or simply trade (state and co-operative) has varied erratically, owing perhaps to changes in coverage (National Foreign Assessment Center, 1977, p. 10). In years when its proportion is high, the main component of the Trade allocation must be subsidies aimed at keeping down retail prices, although total subsidies in some years at least, are much larger than could be contained within the stated trade allocation (see above, Chapter 3). Part of the trade subsidy would compensate foreign trade organisations for differences between the rouble cost of imports and the sums received by them from retail sales. The only other item that is reported more than a few times is communal economy (at times linked with housing), which lately has been rather stable at just over 6 per cent.

FNE from all sources

Turning to forecast expenditures on the economy from all sources (Table 7.2), one finds somewhat more abundant and regular data from 1963 onwards; perhaps the Garbuzov new broom. Other differences are also seen. Industry was to receive relatively more from all sources than from the budget alone, the proportion from all sources being

TABLE 7.2 *Finance of national economy from all sources: percentages of forecast totals*

	(i)	(ii)	(iii)	(iv)	(v)	(vi)	(vii)	(viii)	(ix)	(x)
1960	53.4	2.8**			9.7		11.0			23.1
1961					11.0					89.0
1962	54.0				13.5		11.2			21.3
1963	53.3	4.0	15.3				10.9	6.2		10.3
1964										100.0
1965	52.9	3.8	16.4				11.9	5.7		9.3
1966	52.3	4.5	16.1				10.3	5.6		11.2
1967	52.8	4.9		15.6			10.2			16.5
1968								both (viii) and (ix)		100.0
1969	51.3	6.8	14.8				9.5	4.8		12.8
1970	50.0	5.7	15.0				9.5			19.8
1971	50.9	5.0	15.4				8.6			20.1
1972	51.2	1.5*	16.3				8.5	3.9		18.6
1973	51.8	1.9**	17.2				8.8			20.3
1974	51.7	1.5*	16.5				8.8	3.8		17.7
1975	52.5	2.0**	17.6				8.9			19.0
1976	53.0	1.6*	16.4				8.6	4.3		16.1
1977										100.0
1978	52.7	2.3		16.7			9.3			19.0
1979	52.4	1.4		16.7			8.9	4.1		16.5
1980	54.0	2.3**		16.9			8.9	3.9		14.0

(i) Heavy Industry; (ii) Light industry; (iii) Internal trade; (iv) Procurements; (v) Agriculture; (vi) Forestry; (vii) Transport and communications; (viii) Communal economy; (ix) Housing (x) Remainder.

* state trade   ** state and co-operative trade.
Intermediate placing means that a total applies jointly to the columns on either side.

SOURCE Based mainly on annual articles in *Finansy SSSR*.

much the more stable: from 1960 to 1980 this varied only between 50.0 per cent and 54.0 per cent. Agriculture receives on average about the same share from all sources as from the budget alone, although again, over time its share from all sources is the more stable. Transport and communications also receives a larger share from all sources than from the budget alone. Obviously, some sector or sectors must receive *less* from all sources, and this turns out to be communal economy and housing economy. However, these relatively small items cannot account for the whole difference in degrees of coverage. A comparison of Tables 7.1 and 7.2, shows at once that there are more blanks in the budgetary division than in the all sources division. Take for example

TABLE 7.3   *Summation of named items (percentage of total)*

	Budget	All sources
1969	62.3	87.2
1974	65.0	82.3
1979	70.4	83.5

SOURCE   Tables 7.1 and 7.2.

the years 1969, 1974 and 1979 — separated by five-year intervals: summation of the named items leads to the results in Table 7.3.

The sectoral division therefore brings to light a larger relative volume of unitemised allocations from the budget alone than from all sources together — a very interesting finding. The additional gap is in the region of almost 20 per cent of total budget allocations to FNE. This certainly strengthens the case for the existence within budgetary FNE of large subsidies, and perhaps of other special features.

The restricted range of variations stands out as the most fundamental feature of the distribution shown in Table 7.2. The distribution of allocations from all sources is much more stable than that of budgetary allocations. A comparison has admittedly to be based on partly different time-spans. It appears, however, that variations in budget financing are largely smoothed out by compensating variations in funding from other sources; or at any rate, that this is the intention. The large variations in budget financing suggest that this is the more directly under central control. So far as total allocations are concerned, the lack of marked variation in the proportions over a fairly long period, when different priorities might have been expected to assert themselves, evokes some doubts about the ability of the authorities to manoeuvre as they may well have wished.

Budget and non-budget allocations to industry generally

Forecast allocations from the budget to industry between 1953 and 1980 rose by over eight times, as shown in Table 7.4. Forecast allocations to industry from all sources over the marginally more recent period 1955–81 rose by 8.5 times. *Actual* spending from all sources over seventeen years (1962–79) rose by 4.8 times. These increases are reckoned in current prices, and as usual no price-deflating index is available.

Comparing allocations to industry from the budget and from all sources, which is done in column (c) of Table 7.4, shows that the

TABLE 7.4   *Budget and non-budget allocations to industry generally (bn roubles)*

Year	(a) Industry budget only forecast	(b) Industry all sources forecast	(c) (a)/(b)%	(d) Industry all sources actual	(e) (d)/(b)%	(f) Total all sources forecast	(g) (b)/(f)%
1953	8.26						
1954	9.23						
1955	11.18	18.96	59.0				
1956	11.19	18.47	60.6				
1957	11.84	20.14	58.8			37.6	53.6
1958	12.90						
1959	14.53	25.24	57.6			48.43	52.1
1960	15.18	27.91	54.4			52.24	53.4
1961	16.10					56.4	
1962	14.80	30.5	48.5	30.53	100.1	56.50	54.0
1963		33.7				63.2	53.3
1964				35.64		68.5	
1965	20.6	40.1	51.4	40.07	99.9	75.8	52.9
1966	22.4	42.8	52.3	42.59	99.5	81.8	52.3
1967	21.9	45.7	47.9			86.5	52.5
1968	23.9	51.8	46.1	52.36	101.1		
1969	22.2	59.8	37.1	61.49	102.8	116.5	51.5
1970	23.9	64.5	37.1	68.34	106.0	129.0	50.0
1971	29.6	78.8	37.6	79.38	100.7	154.9	50.9
1972	32.0	87	36.8	87.03	100.0	169.8	51.2
1973	33.9	93.3	36.3			180.0	51.8
1974	36.7	102.5	35.8			198.4	51.7
1975	42.3	110.7	38.2	114.20	103.2	210.8	52.8
1976	48.0	120.6	39.8			227.6	53.0
1977		128.9		130.20	101.0		
1978	53.6	134.5	39.9	134.80	100.2	255.1	52.7
1979	61.4	146.8	41.8	146.60	99.9	280.3	52.4
1980	68.3	157.6	43.3			291.9	54.0
1981		162					

SOURCE Annual budget laws, statistical handbooks and articles in *Finansy SSSR*.

budget's share in total spending fluctuated between 35.8 per cent (in 1974) and 60.6 per cent (in 1956). A low point in 1962 was followed by a rise to 1966 and then by a further fall which, however, was followed by a partial recovery. In absolute terms, between 1966 and 1968 budget allocations to industry rose by 6.7 per cent, non-budget allocations over the same period by 36.8 per cent. Between 1955 and 1980 non-budget forecast allocations to industry rose 11-fold.

While the decline from 60.6 per cent in 1956 to 48.5 per cent in 1962 expresses a degree of financial decentralisation which accompanied the *sovnarkhoz* reform, it is interesting to see that this proportion was rising even before October 1965, when that reform was reversed.

The fall in non-budget allocations to industry in 1956 can be reckoned to have been among the reasons for the disappointing growth of industrial output in 1956 which in 1957 led to the abandonment of the Sixth Five-Year Plan.

Comparing Table 7.4 and Appendix III, we find that the forecast budget allocations to industry (heavy plus light) have usually been exceeded by actual budget spending on industry and construction; this was in fact the case in all years from 1955 to 1970 except in only 1955, 1961 and 1966. The excess varied from 1.0 per cent in 1968 to a staggering 27.7 per cent in 1970.[1] The actual sums spent on industry from all sources in most years when comparison is possible were very close to the forecasts, with appreciable deviations only in 1969, 1970 and 1975. Two out of these three years, and also the same two when the proportionate deviations were largest, were 1970 and 1975 – both of which were final years of five-year plans. This is to be expected, as special efforts would be being made at that stage to fulfil and overfulfil output plans. We shall see later that something more can be said about the category of industry to which that particularly applied.

The available data for allocations from the budget only and from all sources mainly do not overlap. Where they do, forecast allocations from all sources seem to increase more smoothly than allocations from the budget alone. Actual allocations from all sources may show a similar difference by comparison with forecast allocations from all sources. There is a noticeable lack of information as regards 1964 (in which connection see Chapter 1).

As regards percentage changes from year to year in the amounts (in absolute terms) of budget or non-budget allocations to Industry, we first note that for certain years only forecast allocations are published. The relevant data are set out in Table 7.5, and are analyzed further in chapter 10 (in particular, Tables 10.7 and 10.8). At this point one may merely draw attention to the quite marked variations in the year-to-year rates of change especially of forecast budgetary allocations.

Budget and non-budget spending on heavy industry and light industry

Expenditure on industry can sometimes be divided among the following groupings: Total; heavy industry; light industry. For available years, when this sub-division is possible (that is to say, omitting years when a figure is available only for allocations to all industry) forecast or actual expenditures have been as in Table 7.6.

TABLE 7.5   *Percentage rates of change of allocations to industry relative to previous year (plus except where minus sign indicated)*

| Year | Forecast allocations | | Actual allocations |
	From budget (a)	From all sources (b)	From all sources (c)
1954	11.7		
1955	21.1		
1956	0.1		
1957	5.8	9.0	
1958	9.0		
1959	12.6		
1960	4.5		
1961	6.0		
1962	−8.1		
1963		10.5	
1964			
1965			12.4
1966	8.7	6.7	6.3
1967	−2.2	6.8	
1968	9.1	13.3	
1969	−7.1	15.4	17.4
1970	7.7	6.2	11.1
1971	23.8	24.1	16.2
1972	8.1	10.4	9.6
1973	5.9	7.2	
1974	8.3	9.8	
1975	15.3	8.1	
1976	13.5	8.9	
1977		6.9	
1978		4.3	3.5
1979	14.6	9.1	8.8
1980	11.2	7.4	
1981		2.8	

Note Earlier post-war data not available. Blanks signify absence of data.

As Table 7.6 shows, the amount of recent information about spending on different major categories of industry from the budget alone is amazingly restricted, being indeed confined to the forecast figures for 1955, in which year the division of budget and non-budget spending was to have been as in in Table 7.7. So in that year the division of budget and non-budget allocations to industry would have been: budget to heavy industry 90.5 per cent, to light industry 9.5 per cent; non-budget to heavy industry 40.8 per cent, to light industry 59.2 per cent. Thus budget spending would have been overwhelmingly on heavy industry, non-budget spending largely on light industry. It would not

TABLE 7.6   *Budget and non-budget expenditure on heavy and light industry*

		Total	Heavy (bn roubles)	Light	Light as % of total
From Budget Only					
1955	Forecast	11.18	10.12	1.06	9.5
	Actual	–	–	–	–
From All Sources					
1955	Forecast	18.96	16.36	2.60	13.7
1956	Forecast	18.47	15.87	2.6	14.1
1964	Actual	35.64	30.16	5.48	15.4
1965	Forecast	40.1	34.2	5.9	14.7
	Actual	40.07			
1966	Forecast	42.8			
	Actual	42.59	38.22	4.37	10.3
1967	Forecast	45.7	40.5	5.2	11.4
	Actual			7.21	
1968	Forecast	51.8	43.7	8.1	15.6
	Actual	52.36			
1969	Forecast	59.8	52.3	7.5	12.5
	Actual	61.49	52.8	8.69	14.1
1970	Forecast	64.5	55.1	8.4	13.0
	Actual	68.34			
1971	Forecast	78.8	65.7	13.1	16.6
	Actual	79.38			
1972	Forecast	87	71.5	15.5	17.8
	Actual	87.03			
1973	Forecast	93.3			
	Actual	92.35	77.6	14.75	
1974	Forecast	102.4	86.4	16	15.6
1975	Forecast	110.7	98.0	12.7	11.5
	Actual	114.20	97.6	16.59	14.5
1976	Forecast	120.6	103.1	17.5	14.5
1977	Forecast	128.9	108	20.9	16.2
	Actual	130.20			
1978	Forecast	134.5	112.1	22.4	16.7
	Actual	134.80			
1979	Forecast	146.8	120.2	26.6	18.1
	Actual	146.60			
1980	Forecast	157.6	129.4	28.2	17.9
1981	Forecast	162.	133.5	28.5	17.6

SOURCE   Primarily annual articles in *Finansy SSSR*.

TABLE 7.7   *Budget spending on heavy and light industry in 1955 (bn roubles)*

	Heavy industry	Light industry
Budget	10.12	1.06
Non-budget	6.24	1.52
Totals	16.36	2.60

be surprising if the picture had been similar in other years, but this can only be conjectured.

We are a good deal better informed about the division of total allocations (both from budgetary *and* non-budgetary sources) as between heavy and light industry. This is shown in Table 7.6. Available figures relate mainly to the 8th, 9th and 10th FYPs. Over time, the proportion going to light industry has risen, but only slightly – to an average of 16.7 per cent in the 10th FYP (see also Table 10.11).

HORIZONTAL SUB-DIVISIONS

Table 7.8 indicates the sums stated to be allocated for capital investments as mentioned in the budget speeches of the finance minister in successive years. The precise coverage of the statistics is never stated, nor is it made clear how the various categories relate to one another. The table is set out according to my interpretation of what has been said. Four categories are used, which in order of size are: (a) budget allocations to centralised capital investments from the budget, enterprises' own funds and bank credit; (b) capital investments from the budget, enterprises' own funds and bank credit – thus (a) is included within (b); (c) state capital investments; and (d) total volume (*obshchii ob'yom*) of capital investments.

The sums allocated to capital investments from the budget approximately quintupled between 1952 and 1979, while total allocations to investments rose probably in a somewhat greater proportion.

In Table 7.8, column (a) matches the column 'Budget Capital Expenditures' in Table 10 of *Soviet Economic Development* (Hutchings, 1971a, p. 182), apart from certain corrections.

Over time, column (a) has fallen relative to column (b): thus in 1952 (a) was 68.6 per cent of (b), in 1962, 63.5 per cent; in 1972, 47.0 per cent. However, relative to column (c), column (a) in 1972 was 39.6 per cent; in 1979, 41.7 per cent.

TABLE 7.8 *Capital investments from and not from the budget (bn roubles)*

	(a)	(b)	(c)	(d)
1952	9.81	14.31		
1953				
1954	12.11	18.49		
1955				
1956	11.84	16.08		
1957	12.94	17.86		
1958	14.27	20.38		
1959	16.21	23.12		
1960	18.03	26.19		
1961	19.5	29.5		
1962	19.7	31		
1963	20.4	33.8		
1964		36.5		
1965	23.5	38.7		
1966	22.8	40.6		
1967	22.2	41.3		
1968	23.1	43.6		
1969	25.5	52.5		
1970	25.8	54.4		
1971	29.5	62.2		86.3
1972	31.5	67	79.5	
1973		70.5	82.4	
1974			90.4	
1975	40+	85.4	98.6	113
1976		88.3	102.5	
1977			106.7	
1978			110.6	125.5
1979	48.6		116.5	
1980			119.1	
1981			124.1	

The budget therefore finances only the smaller part of capital investments, but in all probability this includes a disproportionately large share of the investments in heavy industry and in other sectors of large-scale development. The actual division of capital investments among sectors is rarely given. In 1956, the planned shares of capital investments (bn roubles) were to have been: heavy industry, 9.66; agriculture, 2.13; transport, 2.15; light and food industries, 0.78. In the budget of the same year, sums were allocated as follows to the various branches: heavy industry, 42.5 per cent; agriculture, 20.5 per cent; transport, 9.2 per cent (the light and food industries not being mentioned). This yields the comparative division as shown in Table 7.9

TABLE 7.9   *Capital investments in budget sectoral financing*

	Heavy industry	Agriculture	Transport
Capital investments	1.0	0.22	0.22
All financing	1.0	0.48	0.22

In this table, Heavy industry = 1.00

which relative to heavy industry shows transport in the same proportions for capital investments and total financing, but agriculture sharply higher in total financing than in capital investments. In the RSFSR (11 union-republic ministries and departments) the budget funded 71.3 per cent of total investments in 1967, 64.3 per cent in 1975, 55.4 per cent in 1977 (Bobrovnikov, 1977, p. 95). As for non-industrial branches of the economy, the extent of their self-financing is very diverse. In 1977 in the RSFSR the budget was to provide the following percentages of funds for the branches named: state trade, 23.0; automobile transport, 17.8; river fleet, 45.0; road construction, 32.4; household services, 29.1; dwelling-communal economy (housebuilding and repairs), 78.1; measures to link together executive committees of local soviets, 100 (Bobrovnikov, p. 108). The relatively high percentage share of forecast budgetary financing in housebuilding and its relatively low share in transport are especially noticeable.

It is never claimed that capital investments are entirely included within the FNE clause, and the inference must be that some fraction of total capital investments may be found outside FNE, though much the larger part must surely be contained within it. It is known that a portion of SCM consists of capital investments; this is itemised intermittently in the statistical annuals, but is reported for every year from 1970 onwards. For available years, capital investments which are included within SCM are shown in Table 7.10.

TABLE 7.10   *Capital investments within SCM (bn roubles)*

1940	0.07	1974	1.63
1960	0.78	1975	1.78
1965	1.01	1976	1.87
1970	1.29	1977	1.91
1971	1.43	1978	1.92
1972	1.48	1979	1.95
1973	1.37		

SOURCE Annual statistical handbooks.

TABLE 7.11   *Capital investments and FNE from the budget (bn roubles)*

	(a)	(b)	(a)/(b) (%)		(a)	(b)	(a)/(b) (%)
1952	9.81	18.04	54.4	1965	23.5	42.36	55.5
1954	12.11	21.63	56.0	1966	22.8	43.85	52.0
1956	11.84	23.72	49.9	1967	22.2	46.92	47.3
1957	12.94	24.47	52.9	1968	23.1	50.19	46.0
1958	14.27	25.72	55.5	1969	25.5	58.32	43.7
1959	16.21	30.89	52.5	1970	25.8	63.48	40.6
1960	18.03	32.85	54.9	1971	29.5	77.03	38.3
1961	19.5	33.91	57.5	1972	31.5	82.63	38.1
1962	19.7	32.47	60.7	1975	40	102.63	39.0
1963	20.4	34.54	59.1				

(a) capital investments; (b) FNE.

SOURCE Annual statistical handbooks.

While it is conceivable that DEF too should contain capital invest-ments, in fact this is extremely unlikely as this clause is too small (see Chapter 10). The estimate of the Ministry of Defence is stated to con-tain 'military construction' (Massarygin, 1968, p. 119), but such ex-penditure would not assist economic development. Certain invest-ments, especially for housing and administrative building, must be contained within the budget residue. Unfortunately, these are not itemised.

The amount of capital investments therefore cannot be validly com-pared with any single one of the main budget vertical divisions, or more exactly, any such comparison must include the reservation that part of capital investments are not contained within the clause with which the investment total is being compared. This does not mean that such a comparison might not uncover *something* of interest. The least invalid comparison would be of capital investments with FNE. Such a com-parison produces the series presented in Table 7.11 (forecasts in all cases, and omitting years when comparison is not possible).

The ratio of capital investments to FNE has varied in an interesting manner. Short-term movements are examined in Chapter 9. As regards the longer-term trend, whereas between 1952 and 1966 this ratio lay between 49.9 and 60.7 per cent, subsequently it has fallen to about 38 per cent. Thus, the proportion of budgetary FNE consisting of capital investments is now well under half, even if no account is taken of the certainly not negligible fraction of investments which is *not* contained within the FNE clause; allowing for that fraction would reduce the proportion of FNE which consists of capital investments still further.

34.0 per cent, which is the ratio of capital investments (both centralised and non-centralised) to total FNE quoted by Yevdokimov in respect of the Ninth Five-Year Plan (Yevdokimov, 1974, p. 141) would perhaps be near to the correct proportion. In any case, the trend of the third column in Table 7.11 is complicating even more the difficult question of how to account fully for that portion of FNE that does not consist of investment. Suspicion as to what is being concealed here is further enhanced by the tailing-off of our information from 1972 onwards.

The rise in non-investment financing is, however, compatible with a reported rise between 1958 and 1966 in the number of bodies in receipt of subsidies. During this period, subsidies from the centre to local budgets increased (*Ekon. gaz.*, no. 23 of 1966, p. 10). In 1969, within 10 out of 15 republics a whole range of budgets of ASSRs and other directly subordinate units were receiving subsidies. This was *not* the case only in the Ukraine, Belorussia, Kazakhstan, Lithuania and Moldavia. In the first four of these exceptional republics, territorial–administrative units of republic subordination managed to balance their budgets without having recourse to subsidies: this is connected with the fact that the Ukraine, Belorussia and Kazakhstan are divided into oblasts, which have more substantial sources of revenue than rayons (Piskotin, 1971, p. 184). Whereas in the 1930s subsidies were directed via the hierarchical network, by the late 1960s they had become to a greater extent territorial. This trend may not have continued over the most recent decade, judging by the fact that whereas in 1968 40 per cent of rural and rural settlement (*poselkovykh*) soviets in the RSFSR were receiving subsidies from higher-level budgets, by 1977 the proportion had fallen to 0.9 per cent (Bobrovnikov, 1977, p. 39).

According to Massarygin, writing in 1968, the budget was financing 300 000 plants and constructions, including more than 50 000 administrative–territorial units (Massarygin, 1968, p. 85). Vaynshteyn implied that there were at that time about 666 000 accounts (Vaynshteyn, 1957; p. 95). If half the budget accounts involved financing from the budget (a guess), the number of units receiving funds would have declined slightly between 1957 and 1968; this decline, if it occurred, may have been more marked, given a 'considerable' growth prior to 1970 of administrative–territorial units in receipt of subsidies from higher-level budgets (Piskotin, 1971, p. 184). The argument here is that more was going to administrative–territorial units, leaving less for plants and constructions. Though a decline in this latter figure is probable, given the shift (decreed in 1965, but carried out only partially) from financing by grant to financing by loan, the average volume of funding per unit almost certainly increased − a conclusion which is supported by a simultaneous enlargement in the average size of enterprises.

SUMMING-UP

This chapter has focused on visible trends in spending on various components of FNE, both budgetary and non-budgetary, rather than on attempting to discover their causes. A considerable amount of information is available, but there are also important gaps, which prevent the presentation of any complete analysis. As a general rule, vertical sub-division is more detailed than horizontal, while scarcely any knitting together is possible of the results of both vertical and horizontal sub-divisions. The analysis can advance a stage further when account is taken of the sequence *within* five-year plans, as is done in Chapter 10.

NOTE

1. The inclusion here of 'construction' in actual budget spending should not falsify the comparison, as it is believed that construction would be included also in the combined forecast totals of heavy industry and light industry.

8 Spending on Social and Cultural Measures

The growth of the SCM clause was mentioned in Chapter 6, where it was pointed out that its irregular and spasmodic expansion was evidently influenced by a variety of forces. In this chapter we look more deeply into this clause, partly with the aim of identifying those forces.

The most important divisions of SCM are: education (sometimes defined as education and science), health and physical culture, social security, state social insurance, and 'aid to mothers with many children and to single mothers'. (I shall say for short 'aid to mothers'.) The amounts in billions of roubles allotted to each of these purposes, and also (from 1965 onwards) to funds, transferred into the Centralized All-Union Fund of Social Security of Collective Farmers (for short, 'Collective farmers') are indicated in Table 8.1. These items as percentages of total SCM are mentioned in Table 8.2. In certain years, SCM is indicated minus capital investments (the ordinary total, which is also given in the handbooks, *includes* capital investments).

From Table 8.1 it can be seen that all sub-items have grown almost continuously except aid to mothers, which reached a peak in 1958 and since then has been gradually falling.

Clearly, the biggest component of SCM is education. This always occupies just under half the total, the percentage varying only between 40.1 (1958) and 48.5 (1950). In recent years this proportion has settled down at 41–2 per cent. Next in magnitude (except in 1953–6) is social security, which for most of the post-war period has taken up about one-quarter of SCM. In third place in most years has been health and physical culture, which only since 1975 has been overtaken by state social insurance. The fourth place, therefore (except since 1975) has been occupied by state social insurance. Fifth, until 1967, but far behind the others, has been aid to mothers. Collective farmers started in 1965 and by now this item is firmly holding fifth place. The four largest items — education, social security, health and physical culture and state social insurance — together normally make up almost 97 per cent of SCM (e.g. in 1950, 1970 and 1979 — 96.8 per cent).

TABLE 8.1   *Components of social and cultural measures (bn roubles)*

Year	Education* (1)	(1)**	Health and physical culture (2)	Social security (3)	State social insurance (4)	Aid to mothers (5)	Collective farmers (6)
1940	2.25	2.18	0.90	0.31	0.50	0.12	
1950	5.67		2.16	2.21	1.27	0.37	
1951							
1952	5.85		2.23	2.25	1.52	0.42	
1953	6.11		2.42	2.28	1.62	0.45	
1954							
1955	6.89		3.12	2.56	1.66	0.49	
1956	7.36		3.57	3.15	1.86	0.50	
1957	8.07		3.83	5.28	2.35	0.52	
1958	8.58		4.11	5.73	2.44	0.53	
1959	9.41		4.46	6.07	2.67	0.50	
1960	10.31	9.53	4.82	6.48	2.81	0.50	
1961	11.35		4.99	7.15	3.21	0.49	
1962	12.43		4.94	7.67	3.44	0.48	
1963	13.71		5.26	8.13	3.41	0.47	
1964	15.10		5.66	8.58	3.50	0.47	
1965	17.51	16.50	6.67	9.05	4.04	0.46	0.44
1966	18.73		7.10	9.74	4.33	0.46	0.40
1967	20.09		7.45	10.37	4.72	0.45	0.40
1968	21.84		8.14	11.26	5.47	0.45	1.14
1969	23.30		8.55	12.02	6.29	0.44	1.26
1970	24.77	23.48	9.28	12.74	7.33	0.43	1.38
1971	26.29	24.86	9.62	13.62	7.77	0.43	1.69
1972	27.95	26.47	10.03	14.45	8.30	0.42	2.34
1973	29.81	28.44	10.49	15.11	9.12	0.41	2.40
1974	31.57	29.94	10.97	16.08	9.89	0.39	2.39
1975	32.79	31.01	11.47	18.17	11.85	0.39	2.38
1976	33.79	31.92	11.85	19.21	12.75	0.37	2.77
1977	35.12	33.21	12.46	20.18	13.33	0.35	2.83
1978	36.93	35.01	13.49	21.41	14.00	0.34	2.88
1979	38.34	36.39	14.13	22.64	14.75	0.32	2.63

* Education is sometimes called education and science.
** Education minus capital investments.
SOURCE Annual statistical handbooks.

Certain of these can be sub-divided, in particular education, which is shown in Table 8.3. The main component of education is general education and upbringing of children and youths and general educational work among adults (here called 'general education'): this usually comprises just under half the education item. Science comprises

TABLE 8.2   *Main components of SCM as percentages of total*

Year	(1)	(2)	(3)	(4)	Year	(1)	(2)	(3)	(4)	Year	(1)	(2)	(3)	(4)
1940	55.0	22.0	7.6	12.2	1960	41.3	19.3	26.0	11.3	1970	44.3	16.6	22.8	13.1
1950	48.5	18.5	18.9	10.9	1961	41.7	18.4	26.3	11.8	1971	44.2	16.2	22.9	13.1
1951	n.a.	n.a.	n.a.	n.a.	1962	42.9	17.1	26.5	11.9	1972	44.0	15.8	22.8	13.1
1952	47.6	18.2	18.3	12.4	1963	44.3	17.0	26.3	11.0	1973	44.3	15.6	22.4	13.5
1953	47.4	18.8	17.7	12.6	1964	45.3	17.0	25.8	10.5	1974	44.3	15.4	22.6	13.9
1954	n.a.	n.a.	n.a.	n.a.	1965	45.9	17.5	23.7	10.6	1975	42.6	14.9	23.6	15.4
1955	46.8	21.2	17.4	11.3	1966	46.0	17.4	23.9	10.6	1976	41.9	14.7	23.8	15.8
1956	44.8	21.7	19.2	11.3	1967	46.2	17.1	23.9	10.9	1977	41.7	14.8	23.9	15.8
1957	40.7	19.3	26.6	11.9	1968	45.2	16.8	23.3	11.3	1978	41.5	15.1	24.0	15.7
1958	40.1	19.2	26.8	11.4	1969	44.9	16.5	23.2	12.1	1979	41.3	15.2	24.4	15.9
1959	40.7	19.3	26.3	11.6										

(1) Education; (2) Health and physical culture; (3) Social Security; (4) State social insurance.

SOURCE Appendix I and Table 8.1.

TABLE 8.3   *Components of expenditures on education from budgetary SCM (bn roubles)*

Year	(1A)	(1B)	(1C)	(1D)	(1E)	(1F)	Year	(1A)	(1B)	(1C)	(1D)	(1E)	(1F)
1940	1.19	0.08	0.77	0.11	0.06	0.03	1966	8.75	0.47	3.56	4.61	0.36	0.10
1950	3.04	0.17	1.83	0.54	0.06	0.05	1967	9.12	0.52	3.95	5.05	0.43	0.12
1952	3.16	0.19	1.82	0.56	0.06	0.05	1968	9.89	0.58	4.29	5.52	0.50	0.12
1953	3.22	0.21	1.93	0.63	0.07	0.05	1969	10.36	0.65	4.60	5.88	0.57	0.12
1955	3.35	0.25	2.33	0.83	0.07	0.06	1970	10.75	0.70	4.85	6.42	0.63	0.12
1956	3.45	0.26	2.42	1.03	0.09	0.07	1971	11.22	0.75	5.15	6.92	0.71	0.12
1957	3.76	0.31	2.42	1.36	0.10	0.07	1972	11.88	0.80	5.57	7.30	0.80	0.11
1958	3.98	0.31	2.35	1.70	0.13	0.09	1973	12.91	0.87	6.18	7.50	0.86	0.12
1959	4.43	0.33	2.39	2.00	0.12	0.09	1974	13.37	0.93	6.63	7.90	0.97	0.14
1960	5.00	0.33	2.42	2.34	0.10	0.07	1975	13.85	0.98	7.02	7.89	1.12	0.14
1961	5.60	0.34	2.53	2.68	0.09	0.07	1976	14.28	1.03	7.39	7.90	1.18	0.15
1962	6.21	0.33	2.72	3.01	0.09	0.07	1977	14.72	1.14	7.73	8.19	1.28	0.14
1963	6.73	0.30	2.89	3.46	0.24	0.06	1978	15.33	1.25	8.11	8.78	1.40	0.15
1964	7.37	0.32	3.08	3.97	0.28	0.06	1979	15.73	1.32	8.39	9.28	1.50	0.16
1965	8.31	0.42	3.25	4.13	0.30	0.08							

Note From 1950 to 1964 figures include capital investments. From 1965 onwards figures do not include capital investments. Data are lacking for 1951 and 1954.

(1A) General education and upbringing of children and youths and general educational work among adults; (1B) Cultural-enlightenment work; (1C) Training of cadres; (1D) Science; (1E) Art and radio; (1F) Press.

SOURCE Annual statistical handbooks.

about one-quarter of education, while other components share the remaining quarter. These other components include cultural enlighten-ment work — which in substantial part may be a euphemism for political propaganda — and training of cadres, which last includes both higher education and specialised technical education.

Over time, the relative shares of education, health and social security within total SCM have not changed very sharply or markedly, taking the post-war period as a whole. The main, although gradual, change has been a shift in favour of social security and state social insurance and away from health and physical culture: the first two relative to the third changed as follows in decennial years: 1950, 1.61:1; 1960, 1.93:1; 1970, 2.16:1; 1979 2.65:1. This substantial and persistent shift takes its origin from 1957, when health and physical culture fell back from 21.7 per cent to 19.3 while social security rose from 19.2 to 26.6 per cent — in absolute terms, from 3.15 bn roubles to 5.28 bn. This was due primarily to a rise in pension rates decreed in 1956, which has had mounting consequences owing to the more rapid growth in the number of pensioners due to the rising average age of the population. The shift away from expenditure on health appears to have brought unfavour-able repercussions. (While certainly various factors are responsible, since 1964 the Soviet crude death-rate has been rising.)

The statistical reporting of social security and state social insurance (included above under social security) is confusing: although these two categories are listed separately in handbooks as regards their total amounts, a part of social security is funded from the state social insurance budget and a breakdown is then provided of this larger total. For instance, in 1965 this combined total was 10.54 bn, consisting of 4.04 bn from state social insurance and 6.50 bn from social security on account of state social insurance funds (*Nar. khoz.* 1965, 1966, pp. 785–6). Relative to this larger total, pensions rose from 43.6 per cent in 1960 to a dominating 70.3 per cent in 1965, while other items often seen as more characteristic of the USSR declined, such as funds to enable working people to attend sanatoria and resorts from 9.9 per cent to 3.5. By 1979, pensions were comprising 70.1 per cent of social security and state social insurance. This category has gained also relative to education, but less markedly: between 1950 and 1979 the ratio of social security and state social insurance to education altered as follows: 1950, 0.61:1; 1960, 0.90:1; 1970, 0.81:1; 1979, 0.98:1. Between 1960 and 1970 social security *lost* ground relative to education, though also during this period actual spending on welfare (although not recorded as social security or state social insurance) has to be augmented by the amounts of state subsidies to collective farmers' pensions.

Between 1960 and 1970 the sums allotted to education rather more than doubled − rising from 10.31 to 24.77 bn. Only two of its components − science, and art and radio − exhibited faster growth rates during the same span: science rising from 2.34 to 6.42 bn, art and radio from 0.10 to 0.63 bn. Over the full span 1950−79, spending on science has been by far the most dynamic element of spending on education − rising from 9.5 per cent in 1950 to a peak of 27.8 per cent in 1971 but since then falling slightly to about 25 per cent. The largest percentage increases in the share of science relative to education were in 1957 and 1958 − 2.9 per cent in each case. The chronological match with the launching of the first Sputnik in October 1957 is so good that one can be almost sure that this was the single most influential factor. The share of science within education in fact rose continuously from 1953 (probably − the share in 1954 being unknown) to 1964, since when it has been maintained at near to one-quarter of the education allocation. Here again, one principal reason seems fairly plain: in 1964 Khrushchev was ousted by Brezhnev, who imposed ceilings on the growth of appropriations for science (Vladimirov, 1971, pp. 20−1, 119, 139−40). Science rose from 22.7 per cent of the education vote in 1960 to 27.7 per cent in 1970 (from 2.34 bn to 6.42 bn). Without that addition, education in 1970 would have been 20.69 bn rather than 24.67 bn, which would have signified an increase as compared with 1960 of 101 per cent; that would not have been much above the increases in 1950−60 (82 per cent) or 1970−80 (about 93 per cent). Thus, a substantial fraction of the growth in the share of education within SCM over 1960−70 has to be ascribed to the unusual growth of spending on science, the remaining part to the specially fast growth of allocations to art and radio.

These increases in science (and art and radio) were naturally in part, at any rate, at the expense of other elements of education. The brunt was borne by spending on training of cadres, which actually declined between 1957 and 1958 and indeed did not grow at all between 1956 and 1960, whereas spending on science grew by 160 per cent over the same period. Within training of cadres, higher educational institutions (*VUZy*) experienced a marked deceleration in the growth of their appropriations, which rose only from 10.2 bn roubles in 1955 to 11.7 bn in 1960; yet those appropriations did continue to rise every year, though very slowly. By contrast, expenditure on specialised secondary education declined. It is thus clear that during this period spending on education shifted towards theoretical work and research. The foundation in 1957 of the Siberian Branch of the Academy of Sciences was another expression of this trend. The reform of the educational system, adopted in December 1958, seems to have had as one of its objectives to enable higher and secondary education to manage on a more restricted budget (Hutchings, 1976, p. 76). As for the other rapidly growing item, art and radio jumped from 0.09 bn in 1962 to 0.24 bn in 1963 (Hutchings, 1976, p. 169). No explanation is provided in official sources, which also do not define the contents of this clause.

Surveying the comparative magnitudes of these series over the whole period since 1950, one is struck by their smoothness and uneventfulness. The enlargement of pensions from 1957 onwards, the faster growth of spending on science also from about that time with concomitant variations in priorities within education, and the introduction of subsidised pensions for collective farmers after 1964, are the only large changes that can be definitely attributed to deliberate decisions. In other respects the series appear to have been governed by demographic trends, such as the decline in the birth-rate and the ageing of the population. The net result has been a steep rise in expenditure on pensions: in the whole USSR, over 20 times between 1950 and 1975 (equivalent to an annual growth of 13.1 per cent).

At the same time, the comparatively small expenditure on what might be described as welfare, apart from pensions, is noticeable. For example, aid to mothers, which one might have expected to be fairly prominent in this connection, has never amounted to more than 7 per cent of spending on education, and at present amounts to less than 1 per cent of that item. Within the combined state social insurance clause, spending on pensions was in 1950 4.6 times as large as payments in connection with pregnancies and births, but in 1975 the former was more than fourteen times as large as the latter. Almost half the expenditure on education is for higher education or research. Subsidies to collective farmers' pensions currently absorb only about 3 per cent of SCM. The impression of a concentration on education, and especially on its higher reaches, is confirmed by Soviet commentators. For instance, education and science are mentioned by Piskotin among categories of financing which, having come to be seen as 'normal', escape strict investigation. Even if theoretically spending on science should prove profitable for the economy, Soviet economists are by no means agreed on *how* profitable (Hutchings, 1976, p. 55). Substantial sums are in practice wasted, because lines of research are pursued which turn out to be dead-ends, or which are overtaken by research conducted elsewhere. The 'army' of foreign-language teachers, whose efforts – not only in the USSR! – fail to provide most pupils with a grasp of a foreign language, is another illustration cited by Piskotin (1971, p. 243). Public provision for old people can be limited by the still common practice whereby surviving grandparents lodge with their children; it seems all the same quite inadequate. For example, in 1975 old people's homes in the RSFSR had available 216 100 places (Bobrovnikov, 1977, p. 143): while this may seem an imposing figure, it would have represented only one place for every 623 of the republic's inhabitants of all ages.

TABLE 8.4   *SCM from budget and from all sources (bn roubles)*

Year	From budget	From all sources	
	(a)	*(b)*	*(b)/(a)*
1950	11.68	13.0	1.11
1955	14.72	16.5	1.12
1960	24.94	28.3	1.13
1965	38.16	45.3	1.19
1970	55.94	69.8	1.25
1975	77.04	97.6	1.27

SOURCE Annual statistical handbooks.

In reckoning the total volume of spending on SCM (see Table 8.4), we must also take into account expenditure from outside the budget. In years separated by five-year intervals these totals have altered as in Tables 8.5 and 8.6. Total spending on SCM has risen somewhat faster than spending from the budget alone, but the difference would hardly be great enough to alter the general picture, even if spending on SCM from outside the budget concentrated on filling the welfare gaps. Actually, adding in SCM from outside the budget intensifies the bias already mentioned, for it is concentrated in spending on science (less than half of which by 1975 was from the budget), to a lesser degree on education and on health and physical culture, and least of all on social security or social insurance. The conclusions reached in the previous paragraph are therefore confirmed, and indeed reinforced.

There is one pronounced exception to the impression of drift in the proportions allotted to the various categories of SCM expenditure: this relates to expenditure on science. As in the case of state social insurance, its statistical presentation is confusing, handbooks of different years giving different series. Using what seem to be comparable

TABLE 8.5   *Main components of SCM from budget and from all sources*

| | Education | | Science | | Health and physical culture | | Social security and state social insurance | |
	b	all	b	all	b	all	b	all
1950	5.69	6.47			2.14	2.57	3.57*	3.83
1955	6.89	8.06			3.12	3.69	4.47*	4.77
1960	7.98	9.3	2.34	3.3	4.82	5.9	9.29	9.8
1965	13.38	16.1	4.13	6.9	6.67	7.9	13.09	14.4
1970	18.34	23.5	6.42	11.7	9.28	11.8	22.51	22.8
1975	24.89	31.1	7.89	17.4	11.47	14.5	30.0	34.6

b = from budget only; *all* = from all sources.
* Includes funds from *byudzhet sotsial'nogo strakhovaniya*.
SOURCE Annual statistical handbooks.

TABLE 8.6   *Budget component as proportion of total*

	Education	Science	Health and physical culture	Social security and state social insurance
1950	0.879		0.833	0.932
1955	0.855		0.846	0.937
1960	0.858	0.709	0.817	0.948
1965	0.831	0.595	0.844	0.909
1970	0.780	0.549	0.786	0.987
1975	0.800	0.453	0.791	0.867

SOURCE Table 8.5.

figures, the budget's share in total spending on science rose from 1940 to (probably) 1967, but has since declined again: the relevant percentages are 35.0, 1940; 60.1, 1967; and 45.9, 1979. If since about 1964 spending on science has been held down to relatively stable proportions of SCM or of education, total spending on science has risen relatively to budgetary spending. While the rise in the budget's proportion during and after the war, further intensified between 1956 and 1959 almost certainly in connection with space research, reflects a centralisation of management to match the greater importance of science to the nation as a whole, it is difficult to believe that the trend of decentralisation since 1967 reflects the opposite.

Throughout this whole period, Soviet propaganda announcing a 'scientific-technical revolution' has been strident; moreover, the apparent decentralisation of scientific spending does not match the return after 1965 to a less decentralised pattern of industrial administration, or as regards budgetary structure, the enlarged share of the union section of the budget. By 1979, total spending on science had reached 20.2 bn roubles, rather more than spending on defence in the same year (17.2 bn). Yet in 1950, spending on defence had been eight or nine times larger than total spending on science! Of course the scientific element in defence spending has greatly increased, yet it is far from evident why there should have occurred such a very marked change. According to William T. Lee, it is 'totally implausible' that spending on science now exceeds spending on defence (Lee, 1975, p. 5); it is most difficult to disagree. This must raise a question whether some fraction of what is called science ought more properly to be included within some other clause, or perhaps should be sub-headed as contributing to national defence.

In any case the evidence shows that progress in science and technology (for multiple purposes), as well as raising the pensions of collective farmers — rather than health protection or any more far-reaching measures of social engineering — have been the chief consciously considered influences in recent decades upon the growth of spending on social and cultural measures. It must be emphasised that this growth also in a strong degree reflects demographic changes, and of course it has been made possible by the expansion of the whole economy.

9 Spending on Defence and Administration

SPENDING ON ADMINISTRATION

'Defence' and 'administration' are considered jointly in this chapter for four reasons: in published budgets neither is broken down into components; they are sometimes considered under the same heading by Soviet economists (Lavrov *et al.*, 1961, p. 21; Massarygin, 1968, p. 118); in official statistics the size of both is minimised (Schroeder, 1976, p. 23); and in the Stalinist period 'administration' covered part or all of the costs of paramilitary forces. As there is little to say about administration it can be dealt with first.

Spending on administration rose until 1952–3, then declined until 1962–4, since when it has been rising very gradually (Table 9.1). The only sudden change occurred between 1953 and 1955, when spending fell from Rs 1.43 bn to 1.25 bn; according to Schroeder, this is attributable to the 'dismantling of part of the Stalinist prison and ministerial *apparat* in 1953–54' (Schroeder, 1967, p. 34).

As a proportion of total budget expenditure it has declined almost continuously, despite the growth in scale and complexity of the economy and the society (Hutchings, 1971a, p. 187), which is difficult to understand. Moreover, the stated sums are very low in absolute terms and do not match the considerable volume of state administration of which every visitor to the Soviet Union is likely to become aware. The explanation seems to be that only a fraction of the administrative bureaucracy is covered by the budget heading (Schroeder, 1976, pp. 23–44).

THE CREDIBILITY OR OTHERWISE OF OFFICIAL DEFENCE EXPENDITURE

Soviet defence spending is discussed in this book to the extent that budgetary data shed light on it. Unfortunately it is clear that the budget

TABLE 9.1   *Expenditures on administration*

1945 Forecast	0.95	1958	1.20	1970	1.71
Actual	0.92		1.20		1.66
1946	1.17	1959	1.15	1971	1.72
	1.16		1.12		1.8
1947	1.28	1960	1.11	1972	1.77
	1.32		1.09		1.8
1948	1.35	1961	1.07	1973	1.82
	1.30		1.08		1.9
1949	1.37	1962	1.07	1974	1.86
	1.35		1.09		1.9
1950	1.39	1963	1.10	1975	1.94
	1.39		1.09		2.0
1951	1.43	1964	1.11	1976	2.01
	1.40		1.11		2.1
1952	1.43	1965	1.15	1977	2.03
	1.43		1.28		2.2
1953	1.43	1966	1.32	1978	2.11
	1.43		1.41		2.3
1954	*	1967	1.43	1979	2.29
	1.38		1.51		2.4
1955	**	1968	1.53	1980	2.42
	1.25		1.62		
1956	1.25	1969	1.64	1981	2.54
	1.21		1.72		
1957	1.19				
	1.20				

* No explicit figure given: stated to be economy by comparison with 1953 of 3 855 564 thousand roubles, i.e. of 0.39 bn post-1961 roubles.
** No explicit figure given: stated to be economy by comparison with 1954 of 6 057 000 thousand roubles, i.e. of 0.61 bn post-1961 roubles.

SOURCE   Statistical handbooks.

is intended to shed minimum light on the subject; hence, analysis here cannot reach any definite or detailed conclusions as to the magnitude of Soviet defence spending or its allocation to particular branches of the armed forces. For only an annual total, not sub-divided in any way, is made public. How much goes to the ground forces, to the air force, navy, rocket forces, training or administration, is not stated. Consequently, for discovering the extent of the Soviet defence effort it is necessary to have recourse to other methods, such as spy satellites, and estimates of the physical quantities of hardware and other equipment, multiplied by available price-lists or by reference to the price of analogous items within the inventories of the armed forces of other advanced countries, with regard of course to the peculiarities of the

Soviet economic system and to its defence needs and defence doctrines. Such surveys and estimates of a global nature being within the capability only of governments, the present book cannot emulate them.

Allusions to defence spending in the speech of the finance minister are invariably brief, and convey an impression that Soviet spending in this field is small relative to the expenditure of 'capitalist' powers; but this can be dismissed as propaganda. In more specialised literature a rather different impression is created. Budget expenditures are intended for strengthening the 'economic and defence might of the state', including for 'strengthening its defence capability' (Garbuzov, 1979, p. 3), while expenditures on defence comprise 'no small burden' for the budget (Massarygin, 1968, pp. 119–20). According to Piskotin a 'very important part' of budget funds is assigned to defence. (Piskotin, 1971, p. 11). These expressions suggest a larger volume of defence spending than is indicated by the announced totals.

Methods of verification have been devised (Holzman, 1975), but would demand a large improvement in the international political climate, which in turn would make them less necessary.

It is obvious that a number of influences, both internal and external, affect Soviet defence spending. For instance, among the external influences would be the level of defence spending by NATO countries, especially the United States, which has been explored by Paul R. Gregory (Gregory, 1974, pp. 72–80; also subsequent contributors to the ensuing debate in *Soviet Studies*). Of course the very much higher admitted total of United States defence expenditure if translated into roubles at the official exchange rate lends further support to the view that Soviet spending must surely be larger than they admit.

Yet this by no means signifies that budgetary analysis cannot contribute to the study of the subject. The DEF item is embedded within the structure of the budget, and therefore affects the size and behaviour of other items, which can be subjected to analysis. It is entirely possible that the credibility of the official figures, like the extent of official secretiveness, has varied over time, and analysis may bring to light such variations. The observation and recalculation ('building-block') method is more effective in reckoning output than input, since it is not possible to observe and measure all component materials or other constituents of defence equipment as accurately as complete items, whereas if the defence *burden* is estimated the former rather than the latter has to be the object of attention. Further, the margin of superiority of the 'building-block' method, though still enormous, may lately have been reduced, for two reasons: the upward revision in 1976 of the CIA's estimate revealed substantial errors in its previous approach, while the alternation of FNE and DEF relative to total budget expenditure suggests that changes in DEF are a genuine phenomenon. Or might this be simply a statistical appearance, with little or no basis in reality? A fluctuation in arms exports (see Chapter 10) argues against this; indeed, it is difficult to see what would be the cause of a simulated alternation which did not exist in reality. There would be no reason to invent it! However, a comparison of DEF with the longer-term trend of arms exports shows the considerable unlikelihood of a sequence based directly on official DEF totals, for if they were true, Soviet exports of arms to the Third World would have increased enormously relative to total defence expenditure.

If DEF actually represents only a fraction of total defence spending it is clearly possible that a much broader overview of defence spending would not show a fluctuation of precisely those dimensions, but that argument is compatible with a larger fluctuation just as readily as with a smaller.

If one accepts official statistics at face value, one can immediately construct a trend of Soviet defence spending since the Second World War. One needs then only to refer to official figures of spending on defence (Russian: *oborona*), which show that spending under this head rose from 7.26 bn roubles in 1946 to 17.2 bn in 1979, that is to say increased by under $2\frac{1}{2}$ times (see Appendix II and Figure 6.4). In relation to total budget spending, defence spending declined from 23.6 per cent in 1946 to 6.2 per cent in 1979. Unfortunately to halt the analysis at that point would brand one almost as an imbecile among students of the subject, as nobody in that group believes completely in the official figures while many regard them as being intended simply for propaganda.

The present writer has not been among this last group. It would be quite a strong claim that any budget data lack *all* economic basis, and if one did believe that one would not find it worthwhile to attempt any careful analysis of the budget. But there are also more reasonable grounds for giving *some* credence to some official totals. The trend over time is not wholly absurd. It appears that spending on defence fell after the Second World War; rose about the time of the Korean War; it was stable from 1953 to 1955; declined until 1957 and then stayed about level until 1960; rose in 1961 (the year of the Berlin crisis) to a new peak in 1963; and then following a dip in 1965, rose to a new plateau in 1970–3, since when there has been a very gradual decline. The directions of movement at various moments are quite plausible.

But credence is fatally undermined when one looks at the finishing point. It suffices to compare announced, forecast, British and Soviet defence spending in 1981, which respectively are £12.2 bn and Rs 17.05 bn. At the official exchange rate, £0.75 = R.1, so that officially, Soviet defence spending is scarcely larger than British. For a country which has more than four times the population of the United Kingdom and which claims a higher gross national product per head, and whose military power is in every way comparable to that of the United States – which spends on defence almost seven times as much as the United Kingdom – this is absurd and out of the question. It is true that personnel pay is much smaller per capita in the Soviet than in the British armed forces, which is appropriate to mainly conscript forces as opposed to entirely voluntary ones. Against this, the Soviet officer corps is much better paid relative to other ranks and is un- usually numerous. It is no longer believed that Soviet armaments pro- duction is extremely efficient relative to other branches (Agursky and Adomeit, 1979, pp. 106–24). Other considerations cannot all be ex- plored here; the conclusion is that DEF cannot possibly comprise all actual defence spending. Evidently, by the time they come up to the present day the statistics have gone gravely awry. Even if their direc- tions of movement at various times are perhaps not incorrect, the relative magnitudes have become hopelessly distorted.

The impossibility of relying simply on the official totals springs also from their presentation and from their trend, when these are examined more closely. At times, the stability of the figures passes belief. Thus, it is claimed that 17.9 bn roubles were spent on defence in 1970 *and* in 1971, 1972 and 1973; 17.2 bn in 1977 *and* in 1978 and 1979. What kind of 'control by the rouble' could possibly achieve such immobility? Yet at other times, as in 1961, immobility has been interrupted by abrupt increases – as if the possibilities in a planned economy of achieving more gradual transitions planned in advance had been wholly fore- gone. If we accept the statistics at their face value, we must apparently conclude that Soviet economic planning so far as spending on defence is concerned is a myth. Again (as previously noted) the gradual and persistent decline since 1970–3, despite continual increases in the cost of weapon systems and lack of progress towards disarmament, is – to say the least – puzzling.

Thus evidently something can be said on both sides, but the argu- ments suggest a possible way to resolve the contradictions: it may be the case that the credibility of the official DEF figures over time has diminished – or perhaps has altered in some more complex sequence.

The *oborona* totals actually look a lot more believable for the first half, or first three-fifths, of the post-war period than for the most recent period. During the earlier period the trends are at least understandable; during the most recent period, they are not. At what point does the credibility gap become unbridgeable?

DECLINE IN VISIBILITY OF SOVIET DEFENCE SPENDING

Various arguments bear on this subject: they tend towards the conclusion that Soviet secretiveness in reporting defence spending has varied, and in the most recent period has increased.

(1) From 1967 onwards, Soviet statistics list the same figure for forecast and actual defence spending; more precisely, the figure is the same within the limit of precision of our number of decimal points, which is one fewer in what is stated to be the actual figure than in what is stated to be the forecast one. Even from 1963 to 1966 differences between the forecast and the actual totals were extremely small. This is an important change: before 1963 the two totals always differed, sometimes substantially.

The implied coincidence of actual and forecast totals is very unlikely. If it were true, it would imply (a) that nothing happened during any year that persuaded the authorities that any deviation whatever from the planned figure was required, and (b) the introduction suddenly in 1963 of a novel and miraculously perfect system of expenditure control. The former seems quite out of the question (one needs only to recall the invasion of Czechoslovakia in 1968), and there is no hint in the literature of the latter.

It may be concluded that the coincidence is not possible, and in fact has not occurred. The release of figures which suggest that it has occurred has to be assessed as a falsification. How should we interpret this? As Soviet sources do not even allude to the change, let alone propose any reasons for it, we have quite a free hand to propose reasons and to draw our own conclusions.

The information watershed may have been a result of the choice of V. F. Garbuzov as the new Finance Minister. Chapter 1 indeed suggested an interconnection between these events. Or it may have been a riposte to Western analysis, which had become increasingly active.

It is also conceivable that the decision stemmed from some developments of a domestic nature relating to the planning or financing of defence expenditure. The only known change in budget arrangements in 1963 was the exclusion henceforward from budget revenues of additions to savings bank deposits (see above, Chapter 5). As a result, such additions could finance loan investments from the Gosbank. This change would have contracted the revenues received by the budget, but also would have made them more predictable. From a slightly different perspective, the change would have blocked a channel through which additional funds could flow into budget revenues on a rather unpredictable basis, and therefore made it more necessary for budget expenditure to conform to its forecast. Thus if DEF were to start to do just this, it would not be an irrational consequence. However, the same should then apply to the other expenditure clauses, and actually neither FNE nor SCM showed any tendency to adhere more closely to forecast expenditures after 1963 than before (see Appendix II). In fact, the most pronounced overspending of FNE occurred in the 8th FYP – 1966–70 (see Table 10.10).

From 1965 onwards, budget spending on *science* was more closely confined; the post-Khrushchev government took occasion to scale down the growth of scientific expenditure, including expenditure on space exploration (Hutchings, 1976, pp. 81–2). However, this relates to a little later than the year we are considering, and a change of government happened first.

The year 1963 was the middle year in a notional 7th FYP, and was just after the mid-point of the operational Seven-Year Plan (1959–65). As will be shown, around the mid-point of a five-year plan it has been normal for spending on defence to be granted rather more latitude. Against this background, any special insistence then on not overspending the defence estimate would have been out of phase.

It is now reported that in 1963 the DEF forecast was (in a very small degree) underspent, which it had been according to official statistics in almost every earlier post-war year. In particular, while DEF as originally forecast for 1961 had been Rs 9.255 bn, on 8 July 1981 Khrushchev announced that the figure had been raised to Rs 12.399 bn, that is by 34 per cent (*Pravda*, 9 July 1961). Actual spending according to the statistical annual was, however, only 11.6 bn, implying a shortfall of 6.4 per cent. The leadership may well have reasoned that a comparison of these figures showed too clearly the limits upon the capacity of the economy to achieve a swift increase in defence spending.

Summing-up on this issue: contrasts in spending relative to forecasts, in particular recent ones (overspending in 1961, underspending in 1962) were probably seen as too revealing, and therefore it was decided to make impossible any comparison of forecast and actual spending. From 1963 to 1967 the coincidence was drawn closer and was fixed through inertia, or more probably was confirmed by the incoming finance minister who would have had no strong motive to oppose more intense secrecy if this was insisted on by the defence authorities. Thus we may reject the hypothesis that the move was dictated by any actual changes in budget arrangements, in favour of concluding that it was decided mainly or exclusively on security grounds. But this means that we are left uncertain as to what DEF actually was in 1967 and in every subsequent year, except of course that it might be conjectured that actual spending would not diverge enormously from forecast totals.

By this move, the Russians took the only step still open to them to reduce the amount of information they provided about their own defence spending, without reducing this information provided on an annual basis to zero. That is to say, as long as they intend to offer any annual total for defence they have left themselves with no margin for reducing the amount of information any further. It would still be possible for them to provide a less comprehensive figure; to provide such a figure at more infrequent intervals; or in culmination, to provide no information at all about defence spending. This last, however, is scarcely a practicable option, as it would deprive the Russians of the opportunity to claim on the basis of their own published figures that they are spending less than the Americans, or less than anyone else, and also would deprive their leadership of the possibility of backing with their own figures any announced change towards détente or away from it. For similar reasons, any move towards reporting defence spending at less frequent intervals is unlikely, although it is not entirely impossible. The nearer analysis of the Soviet budget gets to the mark, the less improbable such a development becomes.

While the reporting change in 1963 is the clearest and most direct indication of enhanced secretiveness in Soviet reporting of their defence expenditures, it is by no means the only such indication.

(2) Previously, for instance in the budget for 1951 and the reporting of actual spending in 1950, appropriations were stated to be destined for the 'Military and Navy Ministries' (*Voyennoye i Voyenno-morskoye ministerstva*); nowadays no ministries are mentioned.

(3) Previously, there were occasional references to rather precise totals of actual spending, as in *Gosudarstvennyy byudzhet SSSR i byudzhety soyuznykh respublik* (1962, p. 19) which gave actual defence spending in 1957 as 9 123.2 m. post-1961 roubles. From 1967 onwards *oborona* totals are rounded off to the nearest zero.

(4) From about 1970 onwards the dovetailing fluctuation of FNE

and DEF has virtually become invisible, although there have been no changes in budget arrangements which would make such a fluctuation less likely than before – or at least, the present writer is not aware of any.

In this connection, allusion can be made to more complicated relationships or sequences, which involve assumptions that some defence spending may be accommodated outside the DEF clause.

A provisional conclusion that Soviet secretiveness concerning their defence spending has become more intense does not point in any certain direction as regards the magnitudes of such spending. Relative to what is revealed, this might remain as before. However, that seems unlikely: why then would one trouble to amend the reporting? More probably, there has been some change in that relationship. But then the real total of spending might turn out to be either smaller or larger than what is reported. If it were smaller, there would be difficulty in accounting for the whole of the defence appropriation, which would appear too large for what one presumed it to contain. Actually, the situation is the contrary, which strongly suggests that enhanced secretiveness has concealed a larger total of defence expenditure. Also not irrelevant, and tending towards the same conclusion, is the fact that the peaceloving stance in which the USSR portrays itself would necessitate an ostensibly modest defence budget; stability of the totals at various periods would exert a calming effect on international opinion (as long as this was the only information available to it, which in fact has gradually ceased to be the case), while also presenting an uncomplicated background against which any increase that it *was* decided to make public would appear more conspicuous. The balance of the argument is clearly on the side of the conclusion that enhanced secretiveness conceals a larger rather than a smaller total of actual expenditure. This means that some spending must be included in clauses which are external to budgetary DEF.

(5) According to William T. Lee, procurement of defence material is entirely excluded from DEF. Among the evidential material he cites in this connection is a diagram of Yevdokimov (1974, p. 160), which Lee claims to show that the Ministry of Defence and some other ministries share a group of budget clauses (*stat'i*, or as he calls them 'articles'), which contain no entry for procurement (Lee, 1976, p. 124). In fact, this diagram appears not to have been reproduced correctly, which invalidates the argument. (This is explored in more detail in Hutchings, 1981b.) This particular argument therefore does not appear to strengthen the case for the view that procurement is not included with DEF. But there are others.

(6) Indirect evidence strongly suggests that some element was transferred from DEF to FNE in 1959, and from FNE to DEF in 1962 (Hutchings, 1962b, p. 42: this was deduced on the basis of a comparison of changes in FNE and in other expenditure clauses, including the residue). One is then left with the result that some procurement of defence material would have remained within DEF. Yet that too need not have been the end of the story. (See below, p. 135.)

(7) As has been shown earlier (Hutchings, 1977, pp. 257–82), the post-war period as regards visibility of Soviet defence spending in the Soviet budget may be divided into three periods of approximately equal length, and which roughly correspond to the Stalin, Khrushchev and post-Khrushchev periods. This conclusion was reached through a comparison of year-to-year changes in DEF with year-to-year changes in FNE and SCM: apparently, during the middle sub-period excess spending was not accommodated within FNE, whereas in the other two sub-periods (before 1954 and after 1964) it was (or is).

(8) From about 1970, the ratio

$$\frac{FNE_t}{FNE_{t-1}} \times \frac{DEF_t}{DEF_{t-1}}$$

changed over from a convex to a concave sequence (Hutchings, 1981b, Diagram 3); this again appears to reflect a shift to lesser visibility of DEF, as concavity shows the influence of FNE rather than of DEF in a five-yearly sequence. However, in this case the changeover point is later than 1964 (the year indicated in the previous formula). The choice of 1964 in that formula was partly influenced by the fact that this year tends to be unusually skimpily reported in Soviet economic statistics, but evidence is now to light that that may have been not so much deliberate as resulting accidentally from a routine of reporting performance in certain years in less detail than that of other years (Hutchings, 1982, pp. 36–7). Perhaps therefore enhanced secretiveness, as regards defence spending, dates from a later year than 1964, or secretiveness may have been enhanced more gradually than seemed previously to be the case.

A possible proxy for more gradual enhancement of secrecy might be the ratio of budget allocations to capital investment to budgetary allocations to FNE generally. This last series in fact smooths down what would otherwise be a sharp discontinuity. But Chapter 7 has now gone further in that analysis. As noted there, the vertical division of FNE is more detailed than the horizontal one, which suggests that the horizontal division, if elaborated in detail, would convey more than the present vertical division about concealed items of defence spending. Is it nevertheless possible to infer anything from the present horizontal division? Capital investments are made both in defence and in non-defence activities. However, it might be the case that investment comprised different proportions of total funding in the two cases, or that its timing was different relative to the five-year plans.

Given the relatively high value of the rouble in the purchase of military equipment,[1] which would entail paying substantial subsidies to plants producing such equipment, large sums would have to be allotted as subsidies in total budgetary spending, which would reduce the proportion available for capital investment. Again, some item of investment for military purposes could be represented as having also a civilian purpose, as indeed it might really have. That too would lower the investment proportion.

As regards timing, investment for military purposes would compete with investment for other purposes for certain supplies, but due to organizational separation the two sectors would not be so directly in competition with each other as one project of non-defence investment would be with another within the same category. While investment for non-defence purposes must ensure gaining a place in the sum of budgetary allocations right at the start of a five-year plan, that constraint should be less binding on defence investment.

Any very unexpected, and otherwise inexplicable, shift in the proportion of capital investment relative to total FNE also deserves attention, as possibly signifying a change in the comparative importance of capital investment for defence and non-defence purposes.

From these angles, the chronological patterns of budget-financed capital investment are possibly significant (see Table 10.9, right-hand side). The sequences (in Table 10.8) from 1–2 to 5–1 (the '1' referring to the next FYP) in the 6th and 7th FYPs of year-to-year percentage changes in budget allocations to capital investments are quite similar to each other (up-down-down-down-down in each case). Also in each case there is a bigger drop from the increase registered in the first year of the next plan to that registered in its second year (from 12.6 to 5.1, and from 4.9 to 1.7). However, the 3–4 and 5–1 (next) transitions in the 8th FYP are suddenly and sharply higher (3–4, 20.4; 5–1 (next) 14.3). These abrupt rises are curious. The replacement of the clearly marked rhythm of the 6th and 7th plans by something which is rather different and less determinate suggests the intervention of some external influence, but it is not clear whether this would have been defence-related. Very possibly, the whole explanation is to be found in higher prices adopted in 1967 (cf. Clarke, 1972, p. 13; National Foreign Assessment Center, 1979, p. 4).

If a large share of FNE is devoted to defence purposes (that is, mainly to weapons procurement, though partly to R and D connected with defence purposes), there would be ample room to finance the defence programme – perhaps even too much. But here it may be necessary to take into account an artificial inflation of the FNE clause, due to the inclusion within it of sums which are repaid by business organisations, and which therefore figure both in the expenditure and in the revenue sides of the budget. As stated by Liberman in 1970, the inflation would amount to not less than 20 per cent (Liberman, 1970, pp. 269–70); this referred apparently to total revenue and expenditure, and almost certainly, mainly to the FNE clause. If this is correct, the residue of FNE which might house sums spent on defence purposes would be substantially reduced.

The budgetary evidence nevertheless on the whole suggests that FNE now houses amounts by which defence spending is augmented, either directly in payment for defence material or in the form of subsidies enabling the prices of such material to be reduced.

(9) As has been shown already, both the budget residue and the budget surplus have declined, taking the post-war period as a whole; in recent years, however, both have been slowly drifting upwards, which possibly lends further credence to the view that secretiveness has lately been increasing.

Let us now examine other relationships which arouse difficulty in the analysis of budget spending categories, and which are at the very least compatible with a volume of defence spending that is larger than is officially admitted.

RATIO OF BUDGET TO NATIONAL INCOME

The ratio of the budget to the net material product (*natsional'nyy dokhod*, or *proizvedennyy natsional'nyy dokhod*) has risen, especially in recent years: in 1965 the ratio was 53 per cent, in 1970 54 per cent, but in 1978 the budget would 'accumulate' nearly 60 per cent of the national income (Garetovskiy, 1978, p. 50). To say 'accumulate' here is a little curious, but the percentage was apparently meant to be comparable with those cited for 1965 and 1970. It is possible that in 1978 the ratio was to be unusually high. The increasing ratio seems to confirm Melnyk's view (Melnyk, 1965, p. 96), yet seems puzzling in view of the October 1965 reform, which was intended to increase the relative share of non-budgetary financing of capital investments. In fact, due to this reform budget revenues did rise at a slightly lower rate than that of the state's financial resources (Garetovskiy, 1978, p. 11), which is also confirmed by Liberman who indicates that the ratio of budget revenue to the *natsional'nyy dokhod* in current prices declined from 54.3 per cent in 1959 to 51.9 per cent in 1967 (Liberman, 1970, p. 265).

Sitaryan seems to be trying to explain the paradox. Admitting that with the transition to intensive growth the role of redistribution declines, he claims that the role of the *budget* in the development of the economy nevertheless increases. He gives the following reasons: the economic reform ensures an organic link between productive and financial plans (because sold output and profits become the most important indices; indices confirmed to the plant include its mutual relations with the budget under the new arrangements, indices having been chosen with certain purposes in mind); the fact that plants' relations with the budget have been made dependent on their factors and circumstances of production; the dependence of material and financial stimulation on the results of plants' activities was linked with the mutual relations between plant and budget (Sitaryan, 1968, p. 17). Yet these reasons sound a little contrived, hence not wholly convincing.

The problem is evidently recognized also by Massarygin, who writes:

As is known, as a result of the business reform of 1966–68 there took place a substantial widening of the sphere of credit investments at the expense of a corresponding contraction in the sphere of budget financing. Despite this, the role of the state budget of the USSR in financing the economy has grown in strong degree in connection with the emergence of novel structural problems of development of the country's economy, and of problems of raising its general effectiveness, which cannot be solved successfully without large budgetary redistributions of funds aimed towards capital investments (Massarygin, 1968, p. 84).

In other words, budget financing of the economy has contracted, but also it has expanded! The interpretation here of these puzzling statements is that their authors were rather desperately trying to expound explanations in which they did not really believe.

While these explanations are by no means completely clear, their very lack of clarity, being surely not accidental, can perhaps shed some light. Although the natural inertia of the system in resisting replacement of budget grants by loans must have been considerable, were this the main reason why the budget has retained a much more important role than had been intended there would not be sufficient motive to employ such vague and circuitous language. It could be simply stated, with regret, that old habits of being accustomed to spending free grants were dying hard. There being no complaint to that effect, the main reason is likely to be different.

DEFENCE AND THE ACCUMULATION AND CONSUMPTION FUNDS

The relationship of budget clauses to the consumption fund (*fond potrebleniya*) and the accumulation fund (*fond nakopleniya*) is highly interesting. In 1950, the 'overwhelming part' of expenditures on state and state security belonged to the consumption fund (Allakhverdyan, 1951, p. 30). However, in 1955 defence was mentioned *not* in relation to either of these divisions (Ostrovityanov *et al.*, 1955, p. 551). In 1960 the 'material-technical supply' of the 'army' (which presumably here was meant to stand for all the armed forces) was stated to come from the accumulation fund, while its 'material and monetary satisfaction' came from the consumption fund (Allakhverdyan, 1961, pp. 176–7). By 1967, however, according to Massarygin, expenditures on defence were made from the consumption fund (Massarygin, 1968, p. 108). On the face of it, the difference in wording suggests that between 1960 and 1967 spending on defence was shifted from being partly within the accumulation fund to being wholly within the consumption fund. The apparent meaning is that between these dates spending on procurement of defence material was shifted out of defence spending. If this is correct, it can be assessed as a very important disclosure. The problem alluded to in (6) above, that after 1962 some element of procurement was left within DEF, is then solved: at a later date it was shifted out again (cf. also Becker, 1969, pp. 156–66).

OTHER INTERRELATIONSHIPS OF FNE AND DEF

Given the connection postulated between FNE and DEF, to reckon either (FNE + DEF) or (FNE − DEF) might yield interesting results.

Since their sequences are essentially dovetailing, with FNE concave and DEF convex,[2]

$$\frac{FNE + DEF}{Total\ exp.}$$

should within each plan period trace approximately a straight line and

$$\frac{FNE - DEF}{Total\ exp.}$$

a concave one. Between 1950 and 1961 changes in (FNE + DEF) were found to trace a stepwise sequence, each movement lasting two years. (Hutchings, 1973a, pp. 60–2). As for

$$\frac{FNE - DEF}{Total\ exp.}$$

this generates one perfectly concave sequence (the 9th FYP). Three FYPs (the 5th, notional 7th and 8th) exhibit concavity only in the second half of the plan period; the 4th FYP shows convexity (but this of course was abnormal, in the war's aftermath); while the 6th and (so far) 10th FYPs show approximately a straight line. Thus expectation is to some extent borne out. On the whole, (FNE − DEF) is angled upwards, and has opened out remarkably, starting with the 8th FYP, since thereafter FNE rises rapidly whereas DEF from 1969 onwards does little more than mark time. The steep rise in (FNE − DEF) in 1970 (+ 12.0 bn roubles as compared with + 2.7 bn the previous year) inaugurated the current phase of this series, which is quite sharply distinguished from its preceding phase.

The sequence admittedly adds nothing fundamentally new, but does sharpen perception of several trend-relationships. From 1969 onwards the entire sequence looks inflationary. If FNE and DEF are still dovetailing, the former has grown so large that it overwhelms the latter.

Thus summing up the arguments for or against the proposition that defence spending has grown more rapidly than DEF, we obtain a balance sheet as follows. First arguments are listed for the proposition.

(1) DEF appears too small for the sums that it should contain.
(2) DEF has been continuously shrinking as a proportion of total budget spending.

(3) The secrecy surrounding DEF has been intensified since 1963.
(4) Evidence, though neither certain nor unambiguous, suggesting that DEF no longer includes procurement of defence material.

No arguments are found against the proposition.

Next, for or against the proposition that some actual defence spending has come to be included within FNE; first of all for the propositions:

(1) FNE appears too large for the sums it should contain.
(2) FNE has been continuously rising as a proportion of total budget spending.
(3) The large unitemised fraction of FNE.
(4) The reduction in the amount of detail concerning FNE since about 1963.

Once again no arguments are found against the proposition.

DEFENCE SPENDING AND THE BUDGET SURPLUS

All expenditure items share the following relationship to the budget surplus: other things being equal, the larger the item, the smaller will be the surplus. But particular expenditure items might be related to the size of the surplus more closely than this, or than others are. This could be discovered if changes in that item and in the surplus bore a stable or fairly stable ratio to each other, and especially if they were approximately equal and opposite, that is the ratio of change in the one to change in the other was about −1. It can be shown that this is in fact the case for only one of the three main expenditure items.

This result can be demonstrated by comparing changes in the actual amounts of FNE, SCM or DEF with changes in the amounts of the surplus, over the period 1946 to 1976. Directions of change of the surplus and of the expenditure items are sometimes the same, sometimes different. Whenever there is a transition from same to different, or from different to same, the sub-period is terminated at that point and results over the sub-period are aggregated. The change in the expenditure item is then compared with the change in the budget surplus.

For example in 1946–9 FNE rose successively by 3.70 (billion roubles), 1.48 and 1.44, while the surplus rose successively by 0.68 and 1.49 but then declined by 1.49. Thus in the first two years the directions of change of the compared items were the same while in the third year they were different. Over the first two years, the ratio of change in FNE to that in the surplus was 2.387.

Performing these operations for the three main expenditure items we obtain the following ratios in successive sub-periods (naturally, the starting and finishing dates of the sub-periods may differ for the various items):[3]

FNE, successively 2.387, −0.966, 6.731, −2.690, −0.985, −6.519, 20.855, −3.690, 8.747, −4.679, 20.283, −20.172, 10.353

SCM, successively 3.838, −0.227, 0.232, −0.623, 0.259, −9.808, 2.490, −1.109, 4.226, −3.908, infinity, 5.033, −5.071, 6.800, −17.500, 4.794

DEF, successively 1.241, 0.408, −0.860, 8.810, −1.282, 0.333, 0, 0, −1.111, 0

Comparing the results from analysis of these series, we find that: (a) the number of sub-periods is fewer for DEF (10) than for FNE (13) or SCM (16); (b) the FNE and SCM ratios fluctuate within much wider limits than that for DEF; (c) the DEF ratios are the nearest to −1, and this is also the case over the longest period: if 0.0 to −2.0 is accepted as a standard range, the number of years during which each of the main expenditure clauses falls within this range is: FNE 2, SCM 6, DEF 11. Thus here too DEF scores easily. Among the two other ratios there is little to choose, but that of SCM may be slightly less uneven than that of FNE.

The results indicate rather clearly that sums are included either within DEF or within the budget surplus much more often than they are included either within FNE or SCM or within the surplus. That is to say, the surplus forms a hiding place for sums alternatively attributable to DEF much more often than it forms a hiding place for sums alternatively attributable to FNE or SCM. It is also possible to detect when increased defence spending is being kept secret, and when it is being deliberately revealed. In 1950−2 the ratio of the increment in DEF to that in the budget surplus was almost +1, whereas in 1960−1 it was almost −1, which surely means that in the earlier sequence of years higher defence spending was being kept secret, but in the later pair was disclosed deliberately.

SCM AND DEFENCE SPENDING

This chapter has so far paid little attention to the SCM clause. It appears in fact much less likely that extra spending for defence purposes is accommodated within SCM than within FNE or the budget surplus. On the other hand, spending on 'science' is largely (though not exclusively) within SCM. What proportion of this is devoted to defence purposes is a matter about which there is no consensus among Western Sovietologists. As pointed out in Chapter 10, series connected with *innovation* are concave, and therefore (as it appears that such sequences tend to be connected with economic development, whereas convex sequences are more likely to relate to defence activities) those series probably relate to economic rather than to defence affairs. However, this tells us nothing about other kinds of scientific spending.

FINAL REMARKS

The reader has been warned already that no definite or detailed conclusions would be reached concerning the magnitude or distribution of Soviet defence spending. What budgetary evidence does clearly show is that Soviet secretiveness relative to their defence expenditure has increased, probably after having *decreased* in or about 1961. The official totals have entirely ceased to be believable, not only because of external evidence but because of their internal trends and the manner of their presentation. It is concluded that a gap between actual and reported spending started to open, or opened wider, about 1963–4, and that it has gone on widening ever since, at a rate which from year to year is affected by a propensity of DEF to dovetail approximately with FNE within each five-year plan period except when abnormal international events supervene and in abnormal circumstances by Soviet reactions to those events, as long as those reactions do not extend to any announcement of a dramatic enlargement of defence expenditure.

NOTES

1. The comparison is normally made in terms of the relative value of the rouble and the US dollar; the value of the rouble in terms of the dollar is much higher for military expenditure than for investment or consumption. See for example JEC (1980, p. 150).
2. These terms are explained on p. 140.
3. It is assumed that actual DEF in 1954 was 10.55 bn, as deduced below (pp. 153–4).

10 Cyclical Sequences in Budget Quantities

INTRODUCTION

Previous chapters have already contained allusions to movements in budgetary quantities which are apparently synchronised with the periodicity of the five-year plans. The present chapter focuses directly on these fluctuations, mentioning also one important non-budgetary fluctuation which may be connected with them.

As the budget as a whole, and consequently most or all of its components, are growing almost continuously, to describe any one of them as growing in absolute terms would add little to the characterisation. Consequently, the analysis looks mainly at ratios of one element to another (the former being, as a rule, included within the latter) or at year-to-year changes in ratios or quantities. Naturally, ratios may be translated back into absolute figures if so desired. A fluctuation is described as 'convex' if the quantity is relatively highest near the midpoint of a plan, as 'concave' if it is relatively higher at its beginning or end.

The budget participates in cyclical movements which are approximately synchronised with the duration of the long-term plans, and which – there being no *other* cycles in the Soviet economy of the same periodicity – must surely be generated by those plans. These cycles are not necessarily visible in budget *totals*; one has to dig more deeply. There is, for instance, no quinquennial cycle in differences between 'established' and 'confirmed' sums (see Chapter 4), though even here it is possibly significant that the two largest proportionate differences (over 6 per cent, in Belorussia and Lithuania) both occurred in 1966 – the opening year of a five-year plan (the 8th). There may be a few traces of a two-year alternation (cf. Hutchings, 1973a, pp. 60–4). This writer formerly thought that defence spending exhibited cycles of about seven years (Hutchings, 1962b, p. 2), but no longer thinks so. The official *oborona* totals suggest a ten-year cycle (see Chapter 6). The normal periodicity of budget quantities, if they exhibit any regularity of fluctuation, appears to be five years.

The most readily visible of these cycles, and the one that affects the largest aggregates, is the cycle of spending FNE and DEF. While spending on SCM is not stable from year to year or over longer periods, either in absolute terms or relative to total expenditure, it does not exhibit any cycle that is synchronisable with the five-year plans; thus, when one focuses on that periodicity, SCM can be neglected. By contrast, FNE and DEF have at times shared an approximately dove-tailing cycle, FNE tending to be highest in the final year of the plan while DEF tends to be highest in its middle year.

This can be shown in various ways, but perhaps most suitably in the ratio of FNE to DEF (actual totals in both cases). This is done in Table 10.1. The comparison is, however, partly obscured by a long-term rise of FNE and decline of DEF. To offset this, Table 10.2 records the differences between ratios of FNE to DEF in successive years.

TABLE 10.1   *Ratio of FNE to DEF*

FYP	1	2	3	4	5
4th	1.32	2.00	2.22	2.04	1.90
5th	1.92	1.65	1.68	n.a.	2.17
6th	2.52	2.93	3.10	3.45	3.67
7th	2.81	2.87	2.80	3.06	3.51
8th	3.37	3.64	3.52	3.52	4.16
9th	4.49	4.74	5.10	5.63	6.36
10th	6.81	7.55	8.22	8.80	

SOURCE Appendix I.

TABLE 10.2   *Differences in year-to-year ratios of FNE to DEF*

FYP	1	2	3	4	5
4th		+0.68	+0.22	−0.18	−0.14
5th	+0.02	−0.27	+0.03	n.a.	n.a.
6th	+0.35	+0.41	+0.17	+0.35	+0.22
7th	−0.86	+0.06	−0.07	+0.26	+0.45
8th	−0.14	+0.27	−0.12	+0.00	+0.64
9th	+0.33	+0.25	+0.36	+0.53	+0.73
10th	+0.45	+0.74	+0.67	+0.58	

SOURCE Table 10.1.

However, any smooth sequence is then interrupted by abrupt changes in particular years, especially 1961. The 4th Five-Year Plan was affected by the transition from war to peace, and then from peace to Cold War, while the difference in the ratio cannot be calculated for 1953–4 or 1954–5. Since 1963 the picture is again confused by the refusal of the authorities to admit any deviation of actual from forecast defence expenditure. Despite all these difficulties, fairly clear tendencies emerge for DEF to be accented (relative to FNE) in the middle (third) year of the plan and sometimes also (although not in the latest period) in its first year, while FNE is accented (relative to DEF) especially in the final (fifth) year of the plan and to some extent also in its second year. While these regularities must not be exaggerated, they seem to be sufficiently marked to require an explanation.

The rationale of the alternation could very well be that FNE rises soon after the start of the FYP to get the plan off to a good start, but in particular in the final year of the five-year plan to bring it home to a storming finish, whereas DEF is able to expand especially at times when pressure to fulfil economic plans or to get them well under way is less acute. Certainly this seems the most probable general explanation.

This explanation requires an assumption that in normal circumstances, that is to say in the absence of a perceived *unusual* overriding military need, spending on the economy enjoys priority over spending on defence. The assumption is justified because the opposite would be untenable. Over any extended period, to award the priority to defence would contract the economic base which (except for incomes earned through arms exports) alone can support defence spending. Over short periods defence may indeed be assigned the priority, but if that priority is prolonged the impact on the economy is liable to be dire, as British experience incidentally also shows: on the only two occasions during the past half-century when the normal British policy of subordinating defence policy to overall economic policy was reversed, that is during the Second World War and during the Korean War, the economic consequences were extremely serious (Kennedy, 1977, p. 17). In the Soviet economy, where as a rule there is less surplus capacity than in a market economy, this is likely to apply even more strongly.

Collateral evidence (1) Lee's NSE series

Other students of the subject have not drawn attention to this regularity in the mutual displacement of FNE and DEF. Yet William T. Lee (1977) provides estimates of NSE (national security expenditures)

TABLE 10.3   *NSE as a percentage of GNP*

FYP	1	2	3	4	5
5th					11.5
6th	9.5	8.5	8.5	8.5	9.0
7th	9.5	10.5	10.5	10.0	10.0
8th	10.0	10.5	12.0	12.0	11.5

as a percentage of Soviet GNP in column (5) of his Table 6.2; expressed in our standard format these are as in Table 10.3. It will be seen that the percentage traces a convex shape in two out of the five-year periods (Lee, 1977, p. 98). The out-of-step 6th FYP was, of course, also irregular in being superseded after only two years. The *SOVMOD I* study found that for marginal changes 'defense and investment (not consumption) are rivals for resources, with changes in defense spending being reflected almost entirely in (opposite) changes in investment' (Ellman, 1978, p. 583). Here the only puzzling thing is that its authors were apparently surprised by this predictable finding. (This is quoted also in Hutchings, 1981b, p. 221).

Collateral evidence (2) The special case of arms exports

As noted above, only through arms exports might defence be self-financing (provided that the capacity to produce arms already exists, which demands previous spending in appropriate economic and scientific directions). This might be deemed merely an academic exception, of no practical importance, were there not evidence to the contrary. Over the period 1955–70, Soviet exports of major arms (aircraft, warships, armoured fighting vehicles and missiles) to the Third World, as recorded in statistics of the Stockholm International Peace Research Institute, exhibit an almost regular fluctuation with a periodicity equalling that of the five-year plans. The sequence is non-random by every obvious mathematical test, and as it is not reasonable to suppose that the causation could reside in some autonomous regularity of international events, the responsibility for this has to be pinned upon the Soviet Union herself, and almost certainly, upon the rhythm of five-year plans. The most common sequence, starting from the first year of a FYP, was up-down-down-up-up. Arms exports tended to reach a peak in the second year of the five-year plan (see Hutchings, 1978a, pp. 378–89, and 1978b, pp. 182–202, and Abouchar, 1981, pp. 147–8).

While the regularity seems to be established, it is less easy to find the reasons for it. It must however be presumed that administrative or financial pressures, or some mixture of the two, promote arms exports at certain times within the five-year timetable while inhibiting them at other times. If the origin is to be found in financial constraints, these apparently are most acute in the second or third years of a five-year plan, that is to say at a time when defence spending has apparently been *less* constrained than at other times by pressures to spend more on the economy. At first sight, this seems contradictory.

The contradiction may be avoided if the proceeds from arms exports, or some fraction of them, are diverted to the benefit of arms exporting organisations via some other clause than DEF. On that hypothesis, which specific gaps would those funds be intended to fill? The expenditure clause which would be most naturally complemented from a chronological angle is FNE, since its gross totals tend to dip during the phase of the five-year plan when arms exports rise, and these dips within the successive five-year periods corresponding to the 6th, 7th (notional) and 8th FYPs were of about the same amplitude, which is true also of the simultaneous convex motions of major arms exports. Moreover, FNE contains sums for compensating exporters for differences between internal and external prices. But why should the defence authorities promote a sequence of arms exports which compensates for unevenness in FNE? The presumption then must be that they are seeking to supplement the fraction of FNE which would be devoted to their own networks. Is it plausible that this fraction would need to be supplemented at exactly those times? In fact, this seems not unlikely, since FNE as a whole is being squeezed towards the mid-point of five-year plans and the defence authorities, which are benefiting at precisely this time via the DEF allocation, could well find themselves especially *disadvantaged* as regards the share then due to them from FNE. Since investment in defence factories is included within FNE, this would almost certainly be among the principal areas of expenditure where the defence authorities would look for extra support.

The argumentation in the previous paragraph must be very tentative, there being a complete absence of direct evidence. It is therefore necessary to remain alert for the possibility of alternative (or additional) explanations.

Collateral evidence (3) Soviet weapons production

In September 1981 the US Defense Intelligence Agency made public its estimates of Soviet weapons production in the period 1976 to 1980.

TABLE 10.4 *Soviet weapons production: directions of change from year to year*

	1976–7	1977–8	1978–9	1979–80
up	13	6	6	4
level	11	14	16	17
down	5	9	7	8
ups/downs	2.60	0.67	0.86	0.50

SOURCE US Defense Intelligence Agency (1981), Table 44.

An extensive summary of the analysis was published by the International Communication Agency dated 4 September 1981, and is the basis for the present note. As one type of weapon is not commensurate with another, the totals do not summate; however, each can be examined to see whether its production rises, remains stable or falls from each year to the next. Totalling up the numbers of cases when production went up (u), remained level (l) or went down (d), the results as shown in Table 10.4 are obtained. Although the total number of up and down movements is the same (29 in each case, as compared with 58 instances where production stayed level), the ups and downs are unevenly distributed: from 1976 to 1977 there were 2.6 times as many ups as downs, in 1977–8, and 1978–9 slightly more downs than ups, and in 1979–80 twice as many downs as ups. In other words, the series probably traces a convex sequence, which it was already concluded was the configuration of DEF relative to total budget spending.

Furthermore, according to Admiral Stansfield Turner, Director of the CIA, giving evidence in June 1979 before the Joint Economic Committee of the US Congress on Soviet defence programmes, 'another cyclical increase in defense spending is likely in the early to mid 1980's' (JEC, 1980, p. 14). It is possible but not certain that 'cyclical' here was referring to a plan-cycle.

CYCLES WITHIN FNE

Fluctuations are examined now *inside* the FNE clause, both from and not from the budget. Within a five-year matrix (Table 10.5), neither agriculture nor transport and communications exhibit any regularity; however, industry does. We find that for year 2 the industry proportion lies between 67.2 and 67.7, for year 3 between 66.6 and 66.9, for year 5 between 66.4 and 66.7. These ranges either do not overlap or

TABLE 10.5   *Percentage allocations to industry relative to total allocations to industry, agriculture and transport and communications*

Year serial no.	From budget only (forecast)							From all sources (forecast)				
	(a) FYP serial no.							(a) FYP serial no.				
	4	5	6	7	8	9	10	6	7	8	9	10
1	73.2							65.5				68.0
2	73.1				70.9				68.7	67.2	67.4	67.7
3	73.5								67.0	66.9	66.6	66.2
4			72.4									67.0
5		58.9		65.7				72.1		66.7	66.4	67.2

SOURCE (From budget only) Table 7.1; (from all sources) Table 7.2.

TABLE 10.6   *Percentage allocations to industry only relative to total FNE*

Year serial no.	From budget only (forecast)							From all sources (forecast)				
	(b)							(b)				
	4	5	6	7	8	9	10	6	7	8	9	10
1	62.4			47.5	51.1	38.4	41.9			52.3	50.9	53.0
2	60.6		48.4	45.6	46.7	38.7		53.6	54.0	52.8	51.2	
3	63.0	42.9	50.2		47.6	39.2	42.7		53.3		51.8	52.7
4			47.0		38.1	38.6	42.5	52.1		51.3	51.7	52.4
5	51.9		46.2	48.6	37.7	41.2	45.7	53.4	52.9	50.0	52.5	54.0

SOURCE (From budget only) Table 7.1; (from all sources) Table 7.2.

scarcely overlap with those of other years, so that apparently year 2, year 3 etc. each has its distinct ranking – although the actual differences between years are in proportionate terms very small. Similarly, the single reading in the series for a year 4 (67.0) lies between year 2 and year 3, while the single reading for year 1 (68.0) is above all the other years. Thus it would appear that the industrial proportion tends to be highest in year 1, and then declines continuously except that in year 4 it recovers to a level betwen that of years 2 and 3.

When industry is related to *total* allocations, a partly different assortment of years comes into play. Summing up what emerges from all sections of Table 10.5, we obtain the results shown in Table 10.6, while Table 10.7 shows how these ratios changed within successive five-year periods.

Thus, all post-war FYPs except the 5th (about which nothing can be deduced) exhibit either concave, partly concave or falling sequences, except the 6th which emerges as convex as regards allocations from the budget but as concave as regards allocations from all sources.

The dissimilarity relates to the second half of the plan period as originally forecast. However, it is possible that this budget sequence actually consists of two concave cycles, which meet each other in 1958. In that case, the 6th FYP within its truncated span could not be an exception to a most frequently concave or partly concave sequence of allocations to industry.

Approaching the same subject from another angle: in four post-war five-year plan periods (the 6th, 8th, 9th and 10th) annual percentage changes in allocations to industry (from the budget or from all sources) are available for all years of the plan (Table 7.5). Listing in order of size the year-to-year transitions when the largest percentage increases were forecast, we will produce Table 10.8.

Within a five-year matrix, these results show little consistency. Even the years chosen for priority increases from the budget and from all sources within a given five-year plan rarely coincide.

Allocations to industry from the budget only tend to be de-emphasised in the second year of a five-year plan, by comparison with its first year. In 1962 and 1967, the forecast budget allocations to

TABLE 10.7 *Nature of change within Five-Year Plan period of ratios exhibited in Tables 10.5 and 10.6*

FYP serial no.	Budget only		All sources	
	(a)	(b)	(a)	(b)
4th	concave 1–3	concave 1–3	n.a.	n.a.
5th	n.a.	n.a.	n.a.	n.a.
6th	n.a.	convex	n.a.	concave
7th (notional)	n.a.	concave	n.a.	falling
8th	n.a.	concave 1–3, falling 3–5	falling	n.a.
9th	n.a.	rising 1–3, concave 3–5	falling	rising 1–3, concave 3–5
10th	n.a.	concave 3–5	concave	concave

TABLE 10.8 *Proportionate increases in year-to-year transitions in order of size Year-serial-number to year-serial-number*

FYP	Budget only					All sources				
	1st	2nd	3rd	4th	5th	1st	2nd	3rd	4th	5th
6th	3–4	2–3	5–1	1–2	4–5					
8th	5–1	2–3	4–5	1–2	3–4	5–1	3–4	2–3	1–2	4–5
9th	4–5	5–1	3–4	1–2	2–3	1–2	3–4	5–1	4–5	2–3
10th						3–4	4–5	1–2	2–3	5–1

industry were actually lower than in the immediately preceding years. The growth of allocations to industry from the final year of a previous FYP to the first year of a new plan was much lower in 1956 — the initial year of the 6th FYP — than in the initial year of any subsequent five-year plan. Presumably this comparative lack of emphasis on industry in the first year of the 6th FYP was a major factor in that Plan's non-viability; consequently, such lack of emphasis would have been seen as a dreadful warning by those responsible for drawing up subsequent plans. The first year of the 9th FYP (1971) even seems to have flown to the other extreme, following which more modest increases were scheduled in both 1976 and 1981.

There is some tendency to favour the transition 3–4 (third year to fourth year): this increase is in the first place in the 6th FYP from the budget only and in the 10th FYP from all sources, and in the second place in the 8th and 9th FYPs in allocations from all sources. This seems quite reasonable, as this would be the last effective opportunity to spend money with the aim of achieving any sizeable rise in output before expiry of the plan period. A year which could claim to be both fourth and (especially post-1956) first, should be in an unusually strong position for claiming funds for industry. This seems an impossible condition, yet may have applied in some degree to 1959 — which was both the fourth year in the (now superseded) 6th FYP, and the first year in the Seven-Year Plan. The jump in allocations to industry in 1959 was actually quite marked.

To the extent they are known, actual expenditures on industry from all sources are also compatible with the favouring of the fourth year — 1969 even registering an increase of as much as 17.4 per cent (see column (c) in Table 7.5). This unusually large increase approximately matches an abnormally large rise in capital investments from the budget in the same year (see immediately following section).

INVESTMENT AND NON-INVESTMENT

The sums devoted in the budget to investment can be compared with the amounts of FNE, irrespective of whether or not the former are entirely included within the latter. Except for three years (1953, 1955, 1964) the ratio of budget allocations to capital investments to budget allocations to FNE generally can be calculated for the period 1952–72 inclusive, and also for 1975. The result is an undulating sequence, shown in the left-hand side of Table 10.9. There is no evident regularity

TABLE 10.9 *Budget allocations to capital investments as a percentage of budget allocations to FNE*

FYP	1	2	3	4	5		1–2	2–3	3–4	4–5	5–1 (next)
5th		54.4		56.0		6th	11.1	14.1	13.4	13.3	12.6 u d d d d
6th	49.9	52.9	55.5	52.5	54.9	7th	5.1	9.0	8.0	6.0	4.9 u d d d d
7th	57.5	60.7	59.1		55.5	8th	1.7	5.6	20.4	3.6	14.3 u u d u d
8th	52.0	47.3	48.0	43.7	40.6	9th	7.7	5.2		d	
9th	38.3	38.1			39.0			3.6*	9.7	9.1	4.0 u*d d u
10th						10th	4.1	3.7	5.3	2.2	4.2 d u d u

* Changeover to different series.

here: therefore whatever forces generate concavity or convexity in spending within vertical sub-divisions apparently do not extend to the relationship between capital and non-capital expenditure. However, if attention is focused on changes in amounts allocated to capital investments *irrespective of* their relationship to total FNE, as is done in the right-hand half of this table, some regularity does emerge or more exactly, elements of *two* regularities, one of which is common to the 6th and 7th FYPs and the other (much less uniform) to the 9th and 10th FYPs. By contrast, the chronologically intermediate 8th FYP, which recorded a very big (20 per cent) rise in investments in 1969, exhibits still another sequence.

CYCLICAL PATTERNS OF FULFILMENT OF EXPENDITURE FORECASTS

The budget participates not only in cycles of expenditure in absolute terms but in cycles relating to the extent of fulfilment of forecast spending. This, of course, is a dimension where the Soviet economy offers opportunities for detecting cycles which are *not* offered by an unplanned type of economy.

In this connection, fulfilment by FNE shows a very interesting picture. Post-war, up to and including the last full year before Stalin's death, there was seemingly a random pattern: over- and underspending alternated. But in 1955–60 inclusive the forecast was invariably exceeded. While 1961 fell short, from 1962 onwards the forecast has again been exceeded every single year, as shown in 10.10 (left-hand side).

From the 6th Five-Year Plan onwards, an approximately regular pattern can be distinguished; the degree of overspending falls in the

TABLE 10.10   *Overspending or underspending of FNE*

FYP	Year					Year-to-year transitions				
	1	2	3	4	5	1–2	2–3	3–4	4–5	5–1 (next)
4th	−6.4	+0.7	−1.0	+6.2	−4.0	u	d	u	d	u
5th	+0.5	−0.9	−6.0	−1.4	+4.9	d	d	u	u	d
6th	+3.4	+9.1	+12.9	+4.8	+3.8	u	u	d	d	d
7th	−3.8	+11.5	+12.3	+4.8	+6.0	u	u	d	u	d
8th	+3.0	+12.4	+17.0	+7.0	+17.4	u	u	d	u	d
9th	+9.6	+2.7	+5.5	+4.8	+7.9	d	u	d	u	d
10th	+3.5	+5.2	+12.4			u	u			

+ = overspending; − = underspending

first year of a five-year plan, rises (usually) in its second year, rises in its third year, falls in its fourth year, rises (usually) in its final year, and falls again in the first year of the next five-year plan period. Clearly, this timetable is related to the timetable of five-year plans. The 'normal' sequence is evidently u–u–d–u–d. Any exceptions to that sequence can then be pinpointed, and since 1956 there has been only a single one (1972).

In view of this result, it is most difficult to understand how anyone who has paid serious attention to the subject can claim that the Soviet economy exhibits no record of systematic fluctuation.

The *extent* of overspending has been less regular, but frequently has been greatest in the plan's middle year. In 4 out of the 5 most recent middle years, the overspending was 12 per cent or more. In 1978 it was even as much as 17 per cent. Reckoning by individual five-year plan periods, by far the largest overspending in proportionate terms was during the 8th FYP (on average, 11.4 per cent).

HEAVY INDUSTRY AND LIGHT INDUSTRY

Concerning allocations to light industry there is no proven plan-cycle, but the sequence is possibly convex, with the proportions allocated to light industry within the total industry allocation rising in the second and third years of a five-year plan up to a peak in its third or fourth years, as shown in Table 10.11. Table 7.6 also registered actual spending on light industry from all sources in certain years (1964, 1966, 1967, 1969, 1973, 1975). Direct comparisons with forecasts are possible only in 1967, 1969 and 1975, in which years the forecasts were overspent by the following percentages: 1967, 38.7; 1969, 15.9; 1975, 30.6 (from Table 7.6). Certain other results can be inferred. The forecast was

TABLE 10.11 *Allocations to light industry from all sources (percentage of allocations to all industry)*

FYP	Year 1	2	3	4	5
5th	14.1				13.7
6th	14.1				
7th					14.7
8th		11.4	15.6	12.5	13.0
9th	16.6	17.8		15.6	11.5
10th	14.5	16.2	16.7	18.1	17.9
11th	17.6				

SOURCE Table 7.6.

almost certainly overspent in 1970 as well, given the jump from 1970 to 1971 in forecast expenditure, while actual spending in 1965 probably exceeded forecast spending in 1966. Thus clearly there is a tendency for light industry to be favoured in practice in, or approaching, the final year of a five-year plan. This seems quite reasonable, though the degree of overspending in 1975 (almost one-third) seems remarkably large, especially as it was achieved marginally at the expense of heavy industry. By contrast, overspending on light industry in 1967 (proportionately even bigger) would not fit such a rhythm, and is perhaps to be ascribed to the price revision in 1967. If so, the proportion devoted to light industry in later years may need to be lowered to make it comparable with the proportion in earlier years. It is also possible that popular welfare was to be specially favoured in a year that commemorated the fiftieth anniversary of the Bolshevik Revolution; analogously, publication policy in regard to economic statistics was greatly affected, almost certainly to mark this anniversary (Hutchings, 1982, p. 5).

If spending on light industry was planned to be convex, relative to total allocations to industry, spending on heavy industry must have been planned to be concave.

CYCLES WITHIN SCM

For expositional symmetry, one should construct the same matrix for SCM as for FNE, though it can be foretold that the results will be less positive (Table 10.12). Here the deviations are almost always very small.

TABLE 10.12 *Overspending or underspending of SCM*

FYP	Year 1	2	3	4	5	Year-to-year transitions 1–2	2–3	3–4	4–5	5–1 (N)
4th	−3.4	−0.6	−9.2	−2.7	−3.2	u	d	u	d	u
5th	−1.6	−1.6	−0.8	0.5	0.1	l	u	u	d	u
6th	1.8	5.2	0.9	−0.4	0.6	u	d	d	u	d
7th	−0.0	0.8	−0.1	1.6	1.9	u	d	u	u	d
8th	0.9	1.3	5.5	1.4	2.0	u	u	d	u	d
9th	1.6	0.9	−0.3	1.5	2.9	d	d	u	u	l
10th	2.9	0.5	1.6			d	u			

The direction of movements in extent of fulfilment is sometimes the same in SCM as in FNE, for example in the 4th and 8th FYPs — reflecting perhaps a general budgetary stringency, or the lack of it — but on the whole the sequences of SCM are much less regular, and in fact barely diverge from a random movement. One may therefore see SCM as a neutral 'control', which thereby shows up more clearly cyclical movements in the other two principal expenditure components.

Although SCM as a whole exhibits no cyclical pattern, the same does not necessarily apply to all its components. One of these is science, to the extent that this is included in budgetary rather than non-budgetary spending. Spending on science on the whole exhibits no cyclical pattern, or at most a weak convexity, the convexity being more marked than usual in the 6th FYP due probably to special circumstances at that time: the launching of the first Sputnik (on 4 October 1957), and the large repercussions of that event on scientific spending within, as well as outside, the USSR. However, further sub-division of the total should show expenditure on innovations to be concave; this at least is the chronological pattern both of the innovations themselves and of other innovation-linked series. At a slightly greater remove, the 'technical sciences' group of scientific workers in proportion to the total number of 'scientific workers' exhibits no consistent convex or concave sequence, but possibly changed over from a concave sequence in the 6th FYP to a convex one in the 7th (notional) and 9th (the 8th exhibiting neither concavity nor convexity). A main element in the convexity in the 7th FYP is a jump in the proportion from 37.6 per cent in 1961 to 41.4 per cent in 1962, which apparently reflected a re-classification involving a substantial transfer of personnel from the chemical sciences to the technical sciences divisions within the statistical records, as there could hardly have been an actual change of that magnitude in personnel allocation (Hutchings, 1976, p. 264). The rather striking coincidence of this reclassification with the jump in DEF relative to total spending in 1962 raises a question whether any of the personnel so reclassified might have been involved in defence activities − for instance with chemical warfare. About 10 000 scientists were affected by the reclassification.

CYCLES IN FULFILMENT OF EXPENDITURES ON DEFENCE AND ADMINISTRATION

As regards DEF, from 1963 onwards the same total is always reported for actual as for forecast spending, which precludes any analysis of differences between them. For earlier post-war years, the sequence of under- or overspending had been as in Table 10.13.

TABLE 10.13   *Overspending or underspending of DEF*

FYP	Year					Year-to-year transitions				
	1	*2*	*3*	*4*	*5*	*1–2*	*2–3*	*3–4*	*4–5*	*5–1 (next)*
4th	0.6	−0.9	0.3	0.1	4.4	d	u	d	u	d
5th	−3.1	−4.6	−2.2	n.a.	−4.2	d	u			d
6th	−3.1	−6.7	−2.8	−2.5	−3.2	d	u	u	d	u
7th	25.4	−6.0				d				

Of course, there are far too few entries here to show any pattern convincingly, while special factors closely related to the international situation are liable to (and did) impinge on DEF more directly than on other expenditure clauses. In particular, one may have in mind Khrushchev's announcement in July 1961 of a rise of about one-third in defence spending (1961 was year 1 in our notional 7th FYP). Yet possibly traces of a quinquennial rhythm were then starting to emerge. In undisturbed international circumstances a 'normal' sequence of changes in degrees of overspending or underspending of forecast spending on defence which also was not obscured by the censorship would perhaps be d−u−u−d−d. Trying out this hypothesis for 1954, the only post-war year for which actual spending on defence is not available: on an assumption that

$$E(A) - \{DEF(A) + FNE(A) + SCM(A)\} =$$
$$E(P) - \{DEF(P) + FNE(P) + SCM(P)\},$$

(where E = DEF + FNE + SCM, P stands for forecast and A for actual)

actual DEF in 1954 would have been 10.55 bn roubles, which also fits reasonably well with DEF(A) 1953 and DEF(A) 1955; forecast DEF in 1954 would in that case have been exceeded by 5.2 per cent, while in the 5th FYP the sequence would become d−u−u−d−d, as suggested above. Although almost certainly 10.55 bn is not exact, it is very likely that in 1954 actual DEF did exceed the forecast, which would generate the same d−u−u−d−d sequence. The suppression from 1963 onwards of any deviation of actual from forecast DEF also tends to suggest that a regular pattern was emerging, in that information may have begun to be suppressed with the aim of concealing such a regularity.

Setting opposite each other the 'normal' sequences for FNE and DEF, we obtain:

> FNE (fairly clearly)   u−u−d−u−d
> DEF (much more tentatively) d−u−u−d−d

which expresses a sequence of over- or underfulfilment of forecasts for these two expenditure items which partly coincides but mainly accents the different items at different times within the plan timetable. In this combined series FNE peaks twice (in the second to the third and then in the fifth year), DEF only once (in the third to the fourth years). No cycles are detectable from the minimum amount of available data about expenditure on administration.

BUDGET RESIDUE AND SURPLUS AND BUDGET REVENUE GENERALLY

The sequence of the residue during the course of a five-year plan has tended to be concave: the most perfect illustration of this is the 7th (notional) FYP. Although the 6th, 8th and 9th FYPs show concavity there is a decline in the final year of the plan; such a decline *may* also be exhibited in the 5th FYP when, however, the sequence is obscured by the abnormally large residues in 1953 and 1954, due to the method of recording price reductions in those years (see above, pp. 13, 88, 90). The residue usually rises in the fourth year of a five-year plan, as compared with its third. Likewise, although there is little regularity in the ratio of the actual to the forecast residue, since 1959 this ratio has always risen in the fourth year of a plan relative to its third year. On the whole, concavity but with a reduced residue in the final year of the plan can be regarded as the most normal sequence, but since 1970 the

TABLE 10.14   *Percentages of combined total of TT and PP in total revenues (actual)*

FYP	1	2	3	4	5
4th	63.5	68.0	66.8	65.6	65.2
5th	63.9		58.1		61.2
6th	61.4	62.7	65.4	63.6	65.0
7th	66.7	67.3	67.2	69.3	68.0
8th	70.6	69.9	68.0	65.9	66.1
9th	66.3	66.1	63.4	63.5	62.3
10th	60.8	61.7	61.2	61.3	
Nos. of movements	*1–2*	*2–3*	*3–4*	*4–5*	*5–1 (next)*
Upwards	4	1	3	2	4
Downwards	2	5	3	3	2

SOURCE Appendices 1 and 2.

plan-cycle is less regular and its amplitude is smaller. The evidence thus suggests a further modification in the status of the residue from about that date.

There is no cyclical pattern of fulfilment of TT or of dfp. While the extent of fulfilment of dfp varies within much wider limits than that of TT, the *frequency* of underfulfilment of both is about the same. *Total* revenues also do not show any cycle.[1]

However, the combined total of TT and PP does show some tendency to fluctuate in relation to total revenue. The actual combined totals relative to actual total revenues are shown in Table 10.14. It will be seen that the combined proportion tends to rise in the first and second years of a plan period, to fall in most other years (especially in the third). This matches a trend for production and investment to rise especially in the first half of a five-year plan, consumption especially in its second half.

A link between this rhythm and that of arms exports can be imagined: for example, revenues other than TT and PP could possibly be correlated with revenues from such exports. The rank correlation by Spearman's formula (over 1950–75, reckoning this without any time-lags) actually is positive, but far below the level of significance ($R = 0.119$). Any closer relationship could hardly be expected, given that (a) the valuation of arms exports may not correspond to profit levels, (b) only a fraction of total arms exports are claimed to be included in the SIPRI series, (c) that series does not specify whether the arms are paid for or not, or if so, over what period, and finally (d) some profits from those sales may be channelled into the budget via payments out of profits. However, these obstacles to calculation of a meaningful coefficient of correlation also leave open the possibility of a closer connection between the two rhythms than is suggested by the above-stated rank correlation.

The absence of any plan cycle in total revenues, in conjunction with the presence of such a cycle in expenditure, naturally affects the chronological balance of revenues and expenditure. The budget surplus (the difference between total revenues and total expenditures, whenever this is positive — which it has been since 1944), also shows marked traces of a cyclical sequence which is related to the timetable of the five-year plans. Focusing on the actual sequence: its sequence is often convex, with a peak being reached in the third year of the plan in half of the examined series; the 4th and 7th (notional) five-year plans display the most regular convexity, with an identical ordering in each case of the proportionate size of the surplus in the five successive years (4–2–1–3–5). Convexity is also well shown in the 8th FYP, though here the surplus rose in the final year. The series in the 5th Five-Year Plan was cut into in 1953 by 'expenditures' for reducing prices, as previously explained. Without this abnormality, the sequence in the 5th FYP would also have been cyclical. The 6th and 9th FYPs record less regular fluctuations; in the 6th FYP the surplus was in fact concave, due to the big jump in the size of the republic section of the budget in 1957 which resulted from the reorganisation in that year of the system of industrial administration and planning. This moulded a large 'step' in the sequence. In the 9th FYP the sequence was again stepwise, but this time it reached a summit in the Plan's middle year.

The forecast budget surplus is about as convex as the actual surplus. The forecast surplus is almost always exceeded in practice; since 1946, only 1948, 1949, 1955 and 1956 have not conformed to this rule. Revenues exceed expectation probably owing to an exaggerated tendency for new plants to come on stream towards the end of the plan-period; naturally, units try to perform their best before the plan-period ends, although it might have been thought that the authorities could now reckon this more accurately, whereas it seems that their capacity to predict actually is falling rather than rising.

The residue tending to be concave but the surplus convex, naturally the ratio residue:surplus has tended to be markedly concave, as is perfectly exhibited in the 4th and 7th (notional) FYPs. As an extreme instance of contrast, this ratio was 0.917 in 1963 but 9.629 in 1965. In the 6th, 8th and 9th FYPs this ratio was mainly concave but it declined in the final year of each plan, due to the already-noticed tendency of the residue to fall in the plan's final year.

Their plan-sequences during a five-year plan being approximately opposite, simultaneous movements of the residue and the surplus are – not surprisingly – usually in different directions. However, on a broad view both over a long period have declined considerably in importance, though at present they are showing a modest revival. As compared with the 1940s and 1950s the importance of both within the total budgetary scene has greatly diminished, which implies a correspondingly reduced scope of the alternation mentioned in the previous paragraph.

REPUBLIC SECTION OF THE BUDGET

Since 1961 the chronological pattern of over- or underspending of the republic budget has shown some traces of a cyclical sequence, relative to the five-year plans, of u–u–d–u–d (which is common to the 7th (notional) and 8th FYPs and as reported so far of the 10th FYP); by contrast, the union budget does not exhibit any plan-cycle. The republics, in other words, accent overspending in the middle and final years of a FYP, which is understandable in series which include above all FNE. As shown already, u–u–d–u–d is the 'normal' rhythm of overspending of FNE generally; again, this rhythm is exhibited in the 7th (notional) and 8th FYPs. It seems to be becoming more marked, which may reflect the rising share of FNE in total republic budget expenditure (from 23.5 per cent in 1950 to 55.3 per cent in 1960 (*Gosudarstvennyy* . . ., 1962, p. 74). The absence of any plan-cycle in the union budget is not surprising in a series that includes both FNE and DEF (as well as SCM which, as already shown, does not take part in any plan-cycle), as FNE and DEF would dovetail rather than reinforce each other; however, this absence in conjunction with the rising share of the union budget is tending to weaken the intensity of the budgetary plan-cycle.

BUDGET AND NATIONAL INCOME

Soviet economists have paid little attention to fluctuations within their own economy, which are supposed to be banished by the type of economic system; this of course is nonsense, or rather is almost the opposite of the truth, since the finite duration of economic plans is one of the circumstances that instigates economic cycles. However, the relationship of the budget to the national income is traced by Ya. G. Liberman over the period 1959 to 1965 and is illustrated by him diagrammatically: the rate of growth of the budget, relative to that of the national income, declined from 1959 to 1961–2, rose to a higher level in 1963–4, then declined again (Liberman, 1966, p. 240). Liberman does not draw attention to the fluctuation, but within the period of the Seven-Year Plan this is conspicuous. However, a comparison of these series over longer periods does not uncover any systematic variation.

CONCLUSIONS

To sum up this chapter: both expenditures from the budget alone and expenditures from all sources exhibit fairly clear signs of cyclical behaviour, the periodicity of the cycle approximately matching that of the five-year plans.

This applies to some, but not all, spending components. While SCM shows very few traces of any cycle, FNE is clearly concave and DEF probably convex – the former in conceptually normal circumstances being the independent variable and the latter the dependent one. Within FNE, spending on industry is mildly concave, whereas spending on agriculture or on transport and communications does not exhibit any plan-cycle. Spending on heavy industry is forecast as concave and on light industry as convex, but in actuality the latter tends to rise sharply in the plan's final year. There are certain other chronological regularities, such as that industry is likely to receive specially augmented allocations in the fourth year of a five-year plan, while capital investments are likely to receive augmented allocations in the plan's third or fourth year. On the whole, a cycle is less apparent in capital investment than in allocations to industry. These rhythms are understandable as aspects of behaviour, rational from their viewpoints, or organisations which are subject to plans that are confined within a rigid time-frame; nevertheless, recognition that this is how the system as a whole tends to behave amounts to an addition to our knowledge which, apparently, could have been obtained in no other way than through direct study of the Soviet budget.

As regards non-budgetary cycles, Soviet exports of major arms to the Third World have displayed a marked fluctuation which may well have been connected with budgetary movements, although here both the connection and the causation remain up to now unclear.

The relationship between forecast and actual allocations also shows clear traces of a plan-cycle. Here again, SCM must be excepted from that rule. FNE exhibits the clear sequence u–u–d–u–d, DEF perhaps approximately the opposite. The republic section of the budget exhibits the same sequence of overspending as FNE. The extent of overspending of FNE is often considerable, especially in the middle year of a plan-period. As regards allocations to industry, and perhaps in particular to light industry, here overspending is most noticeable in the final year of a plan. The residue is concave but the surplus convex, which makes the ratio residue/surplus markedly concave. Turnover tax and payments from profits do not show any plan-cycle, but their combined total tends to be convex.

It could be anticipated that the chronological sequences of certain budgetary quantities would be affected by the periodicity of the five-year plans, but the precise form of those sequences emerges as new knowledge.

NOTE

1. There appear to be traces of a quinquennial cycle in the 'gaps' in budget revenues from the population, as reckoned by Birman (1981, Table I–3 and p. 17, footnote 5).

11　The Budget and Savings

GROWTH OF SAVINGS DEPOSITS

Savings bank deposits in the Soviet Union have risen from 1.853 bn roubles in 1950 to 156.514 bn in 1980 − an astonishing increase of more than 80-fold (see Table 11.1 and, as regards annual increments, Figure 11.1). The rate of growth has been declining, but rather slowly. From 1950 to 1960 the increase was 5.9 times; from 1960 to 1970, 4.3 times; from 1970 to 1980, 3.4 times. While the trend hardly permits reliable extrapolation, a further decline in the rate of growth, combined with further increases in absolute terms, seems probable.

TABLE 11.1　*Total amounts of savings on deposit in savings banks (bn roubles) (end years)*

1950	1.853	1965	18.727
1951	2.192	1966	22.915
1952	2.644	1967	26.869
1953	3.865	1968	32.360
1954	4.835	1969	38.397
1955	5.366	1970	46.600
1956	6.375	1971	53.215
1957	8.058	1972	60.732
1958	8.719	1973	68.660
1959	10.056	1974	78.905
1960	10.909	1975	90.985
1961	11.671	1976	103.000
1962	12.745	1977	116.660
1963	13.992	1978	131.100
1964	15.707	1979	142.600
		1980	156.514

SOURCE　Annual statistical handbooks.

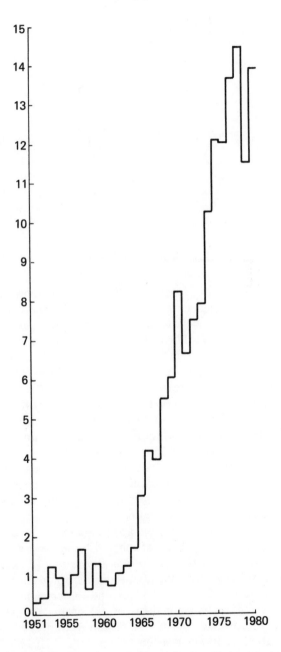

FIGURE 11.1 *Annual increments in savings deposited in savings banks (bn roubles)*

T<small>ABLE</small> 11.2   *Amounts of deposits in Gosbank (m. Roubles)*

1950	181	1965	129
1951	n.a.	1966	131
1952	101	1967	128
1953	n.a.	1968	140
1954	n.a.	1969	140
1955	n.a.	1970	143
1956	n.a.	1971	154
1957	n.a.	1972	157
1958	120	1973	156
1959	124	1974	179
1960	127	1975	169
1961	147	1976	174
1962	135	1977	179
1963	133	1978	167
1964	128		

S<small>OURCE</small> Annual statistical handbooks.

Soviet statistics also (continuously from 1958 onwards) report popular deposits in the Gosbank (see Table 11.2). These, by contrast, show no long-term increase: total deposits in 1950 amounted to 181 m. roubles, in 1977 to only 179 m. In some years there have been fairly marked increases or decreases, notably in 1961 (+20 m.), 1962 (−12 m.), 1968 (+12 m.), 1971 (+11 m.), 1974 (+13 m.) and 1978 (−12 m.). Pronounced increases occur especially in the first year of a five-year plan, while in its second or third year there is often a decrease. On the whole, a relationship to the timetable of the five-year plans is suggested, but its origins and meaning are unclear. Possibly, certain individuals have been able to boost their personal bank holdings at the start of five-year plans by diverting into those accounts some fraction of the extra funds then allocated; or the other hand, any such diversions are minute by comparison with total savings bank deposits. We may therefore focus on the latter.

The growth of savings follows approximately a linear path (see Figure 11.1), which reveals an affinity with the growth of the total budget, as reported in Chapter 6 (see above, p. 81). According to Keese, the best linear fit by the least-squares method for savings over the period 1961–5 is $2280.6 + 626.75X$, the unit being m. roubles and X the number of years elapsed (+ or −) since 1964 (Keese, 1968, p. 143);[1] if 1961 is made the date to reckon from, this translates into $400.35 + 626.75X$. It was previously found that $31094.7 + 2820.0X$ was the best linear fit (reckoned by the same method and unit and in each case from the initial year of the series) for total budget expenditures over the period 1946–60 (Hutchings, 1962a, p. 2). Comparing 400.35 + 626.75X and 31094.7 + 2820.0X, the second term divided by the first emerges as 17.262 times higher for savings over the later period than for total budget expenditures over the earlier. While spending has been accelerated, the growth of savings is much faster.

The USSR used to be characterised by very low rates of personal saving, as indeed seems natural in an environment where the state provides some safeguards against many of life's emergencies, while against others, such as arrest or internal exile, savings would offer no protection; where except for housebuilding (almost entirely for personal occupation) there is no legal outlet for private investment, while average living standards are fairly low. Even to the extent it is now conditioned by higher living standards, better personal security, and higher and more sophisticated expectations, the current phenomenon of mountainous savings appears an aberration.

From the welfare angle – not this book's primary concern – it is an ambiguous development. To an individual saver it may be preferable for him/her to have money which cannot be spent on what would ideally be preferred than not to have it at all, as the money is there in case of need or for taking advantage of a sudden opportunity. On the other hand, the amassing on a national scale of a huge total of purchasing power precludes any possibility of its being spent in significant amounts by more than a small proportion of deposit holders, the others being in effect, for the time being, disfranchised.

The deposits have created a vast overhang of purchasing power. The end-1980 total of 156.5 bn roubles can be compared with a total retail trade turnover in 1980 of 268.5 bn roubles (*Pravda*, 24 January 1981). In theory, the public merely by drawing out its savings could buy goods and services corresponding to almost three-fifths of the entire annual turnover. This also takes no account of monetary holdings not in savings deposits, which also are probably large, and surely exert an inflationary effect (Birman, 1980, pp. 85–6; Wimberley, 1981, pp. 444–5). However, the amount of monetary holdings not in savings deposits is unknown even to the Soviet authorities, though proportions of one-third or even one-half (relative to the amount of savings deposits) have been suggested.

The accumulation of savings is one of the major elements in what Birman has called a 'financial crisis' in the USSR (Birman, 1980, pp. 84–105). 'Crisis' is probably not the most accurate term as it suggests a sudden and acute emergency facing a system which is ill-prepared to meet it, whereas the financial excess has been building up over decades and it confronts a system which incorporates many defences. Nevertheless, there can be no doubt that the problem is serious: there is suppressed inflation, work incentives are weakened, there is fertile soil for a black market, and the planning system may be hindered.

Amounts of net deposits from year to year (that is to say, differences between the successive annual totals) tend to stand still or decline at, or just before or after, the terminal year of a five-year plan; this interrupts an otherwise steeply rising sequence. In the only completed Five-Year Plan (the 5th) which did not share in the very marked upward movement, a cyclical trend rising to a peak in the middle year but then declining again is delineated. The abortive 6th Five-Year Plan and the ensuing Seven-Year Plan exhibit confused pictures. In 1957 deposits mounted on schedule, but the following year they plunged.

The sequence also traces two long cycles, each lasting 9–10 years and ending in 1971 and 1980 respectively. A cycle of about five years shows through, delimited by lesser dips in 1967 and 1976. Yearly additions to deposits reached a peak in 1979, whereas in 1980 they fell back to about the 1974 level. The rather sharp fall in annual additions to deposits in 1980 suggests the possible arrival of a new or partly new phase.

The 'normal' five-yearly sequence can perhaps be explained as follows. Towards the mid-point of a five-year plan the Soviet economy is concentrating on investment, most of which has not yet borne fruit. Thus payments to constructors and engineering workers during this phase are large, while the output of consumer goods has not yet grown commensurately. Savings are perhaps swollen also by enlarged payments to employees in the defence branches. Towards the end of the five-year period investment activity declines, thus curbing the growth of incomes derived directly from it, while new production lines for consumer goods completed during the plan period start to come on stream, raising consumer goods output. These converging trends tend to close the scissors of purchasing power and of goods available for purchase. In 1980, this convergence reached the point of contraction of new additions to savings deposits, although the total sum on deposit was still expanding.

The apparent exception of 1958 is not in fact an exception, as that year was in effect outside the five-year plan sequence, which could have led to a tailing-off of construction and so to reduced cash earnings and savings deposits.

A tendency to concentrate on reaching the targets for consumer goods production especially towards the end of the five-year period is consistent with evidence, exhibited elsewhere, about trends in the seasonality of Soviet industrial output, and it recalls the habit of political democracies of seeking to offer concessions to consumers especially when these are on the point of becoming electors (Hutchings, 1979, p. 255).

REASONS FOR LONG-TERM GROWTH OF SAVINGS

If the amount of new savings deposits is some indicator of inflation — obviously others would also be needed[2] — then the reduced accretion to savings in 1980 suggests that inflation was then being brought under better control. But by the same token, there would have been fairly pronounced inflation, reckoning by this indicator alone, between 1961 and 1979. What triggered this off? Several origins may be suggested.

(1) The post-war recovery, and subsequent rise, of living standards became fairly marked from 1950 onwards, though due to the total absence of consumer sovereignty this could not be a sufficient reason.

(2) On the monetary plane, in 1961 a new rouble was introduced, worth ten of the old — all wages and prices being divided by ten. Thus in a formal sense their relationship did not alter, so there should have been no impact on savings deposits. However, every currency reform, even one as apparently innocuous as this, also has a psychological impact. Some Soviet citizens may have drawn the conclusion that it was safer to keep money in savings banks than in domestic hoards. Indeed, Garvy's view is that 'forcing concealed currency hoards into the open' was a major purpose of the reform (Garvy, 1977, p. 41).

(3) The announced one-third enlargement of defence spending from mid-1961 onwards provoked imbalance between the goods supply and the money supply, with the result that more cash lingered in savings banks.

This does not mean that one can subscribe to any simple equation 'higher defence spending equals inflation'. Periods when the rate of inflation was highest in the USSR are only moderately well correlated with those when defence spending was rising the most rapidly. For the Soviet state can and does spend heavily on many other projects that do not immediately alleviate the money/goods imbalance. The primary alternative to defence spend in the USSR is spending on economic development, especially capital investment. If as a result of spending more on defence less could be spent on developing the economy, there might be no instant boost to inflation. There would be a prompt alteration in the structure of demand for particular types of materials, equipment and manpower, but without more information one cannot assert which types would be in the shortest supply; conceivably, items required for defence might be in more elastic supply in the short-run than those required for economic development. In addition, there is the export market to consider. The Soviet Union has become a large-scale exporter of arms, which according to the US Defense Intelligence Agency financed about half the expansion in Soviet trade with developing countries during the 1970s (JEC, 1981, p. 56). It is extremely unlikely that arms exports figure directly within *oborona* totals, yet the two series exhibit some resemblance to each other; perhaps a need for foreign exchange is most acute at particular times within five-year plan periods, more exactly in their second or third year, judging by what seems to be the characteristic rhythm of Soviet exports to the Third World in general (see Chapter 10).

With these qualifications, it will probably be correct to ascribe to heavier military spending part of the impetus behind the post-1961 growth of savings.

(4) However, a rise in annual deposits sustained over nearly two decades requires even stronger and more pervasive forces. Short-comings in the planning and distribution systems should figure prominently here. Output per head and productivity have not risen as fast as had been hoped. From 1958 onwards the Soviet capital-output ratio has generally been rising (Gregory and Stuart, 1974, p. 340). Underlying factors such as these, operating over a long period, would have fomented imbalance.

(5) Consumers had become more critical of poor quality and assort-ment, and less ready to accept inferior substitutes for the products they really wanted. The revival of interest in design of consumer goods was partly a response to a 'shoppers' strike' against badly designed goods (Hutchings, 1976, p. 231). A growth of annual savings deposits over two decades, combined with an aversion from spending money on what was not really wanted, implies nevertheless a degree of faith that the preferred items *would* come on sale reasonably soon.

(6) The style of enrichment in the Soviet economy probably contri-buted. Typically, production of food has lagged while that of durable goods has forged ahead; heaping up personal savings will help in-dividuals to purchase the latter, but scarcely the former. Another major development in recent decades has been condominiums (the co-operative financing of the construction of an apartment block, by its future residents), which also must have stimulated long-term savings.

(7) A rather important direct lever in generating extra savings seems to have been budgetary overspending. There is a common approximate starting point in 1962–5 both of overspending of FNE and of the upsurge of savings. Whereas from 1950 to 1956 total budget forecast expenditure was usually underfulfilled, since 1956 it has usually been overfulfilled (that is, overspent). From 1965 onwards, except in individual years, the overspending has become sizeable (see Chapter 6). As a general rule the overspending has occurred predominantly in FNE. The quantitative relationship is by no means stable, but in the great majority of years total expenditure and FNE were either both overspent or both underspent (the two deviations therefore being probably connected), while more commonly than not when total forecast expenditure was overspent, all or more than all of the excess was accounted for by overspending of FNE. This is true of 1962–8 inclusive. From about 1965 onwards overspending of total forecast expenditure has become normal, and in this overspending FNE has been the chief component.

Linear regressions of columns (a) and (b) and of columns (b) and (c) in Table 11.3 are indicated in Table 11.4. Over the whole period, both (a) and (c) are correlated positively with (b), the correlation of (b) with (a) being slightly the higher. It can, of course, be expected that over time all quantities would increase, so part of the correlation may be due

TABLE 11.3 *Deviations from forecast total expenditures (a) and from forecast FNE (c), and annual net additions to savings bank deposits (b) (bn roubles)*

	(a)	(b)	(c)		(a)	(b)	(c)
1951	−0.85	0.339	+0.09	1966	+0.19	4.188	+1.35
1952	−1.68	0.452	−0.16	1967	+5.22	3.954	+5.88
1953	−1.59	1.221	−1.15	1968	+4.96	5.491	+8.51
1954	−0.89	0.970	−0.30	1969	+4.63	6.037	+4.08
1955	−2.40	0.531	+1.08	1970	+9.94	8.203	+11.12
1956	−0.61	1.009	+0.80	1971	+3.38	6.615	+3.37
1957	+0.28	1.683	+2.23	1972	−0.39	7.517	+2.27
1958	+1.50	0.661	+3.31	1973	+2.37	7.928	+4.77
1959	−0.36	1.337	+1.48	1974	+3.29	10.245	+4.59
1960	−1.48	0.853	+1.25	1975	+6.11	12.080	+8.07
1961	−1.29	0.762	−1.30	1976	+3.27	12.015	+4.05
1962	+1.78	1.074	+3.73	1977	+4.06	13.660	+6.41
1963	+0.80	1.247	+4.26	1978	+14.09	14.440	+15.64
1964	+0.84	1.715	+1.85	1979	+7.44	11.500	+7.01
1965	+2.08	3.020	+2.54				

+ = overspending; − = underspending.

SOURCE Budget laws and annual statistical handbooks.

TABLE 11.4   *Directions of change of excess total expenditures and FNE and of savings increments and linear regressions of these quantities*

Period	Similar directions of change		Linear regressions	
	(a) and (b)	*(b) and (c)*	*(a) and (b)*	*(b) and (c)*
1951–59	4	1	0.302	0.167
1959–69	4	6	0.789	0.601
1969–79	9	8	0.744	0.546
1951–79	17	15	0.771	0.750

SOURCE Table 11.3.

to this cause alone. But also in many cases (for example, 1967, 1978) rather similar absolute amounts are facing one another in columns (a) and (b) and/or (b) and (c). Totalling up the figures at five-yearly intervals, that is for 1955, 1960, 1965, 1970 and 1975, we obtain: net excess of total expenditures 14.25 bn, savings deposits 24.687 bn, net excess of FNE 24.06 bn. Thus, for these five years 58 per cent of savings deposits might have been accounted for by overspending of total expenditures, whereas 97 per cent of the growth of savings deposits could have been accounted for by above-forecast FNE. For individual years the scatter is not too wide (see Figure 11.2). Moreover, considering directions of movement of excess total expenditures or excess FNE and of savings deposits from year to year, between 1951 and 1979 there are 28 transitions and directions of movement of above-forecast expenditure and of savings deposits are the same in only 17 instances in respect of total expenditures or 15 instances in respect of FNE – almost random results. But if this long period is split up into decades, the following trend emerges in respect of both comparisons: the frequency of 'same' directions of movement becomes much higher for both series in the 1970s than in the 1950s, and for the FNE excess (only) is also much higher in the 1960s than in the 1950s. The linear regressions for these sub-periods confirm a much closer relationship between budgetary overspending and savings in the 1960s and 1970s than in the 1950s, though by this measure the relationship was also slightly closer in the 1960s than in the 1970s. In the latest decade, savings deposits are related to excess FNE almost as closely as to total overspending.

One might imagine that whether roubles tumbling into the hands of the public come from above or below the forecast target would be irrelevant to the choice of their next destination. However, the overspill must go somewhere. More exactly, the explanation may well be

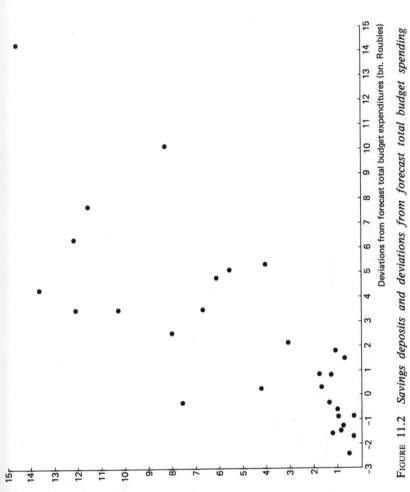

FIGURE 11.2   *Savings deposits and deviations from forecast total budget spending*

found in an approximately accurate *ex ante* estimate by the Budgetary Directorate of consumer spending and saving, as based on an anticipated exact fulfilment of the FNE forecast. If it still seems puzzling that the expenditure target is overshot so substantially and so frequently, some conjunction of forces is demanded which at the relevant moment is strong enough to bend actual FNE to its will, or at any rate can bend to its will what is reported as FNE. These forces must be exerted within an annual time-span, yet must have been invisible to the finance minister at the time when the budget was confirmed; or if visible, he must have been confident of overcoming them; or if not confident of overcoming them, he cannot have seen any prospective course of action that looked superior; or finally, if part of what is reported as FNE actually is not, he must have acquiesced in the impersonation. The continual pressures to overfulfil the plan and to overinvest, in conjunction with the budget's 'republic bias' and with pressures to spend more heavily on defence, would meet these specifications.

If budgetary overspending, especially of FNE, has become an important determinant of the volume and chronology of savings deposits, savings should vary approximately in step with general budgetary behaviour. In particular, the tendency for FNE to rise at the start and end of five-year plans should be reflected in the amounts of savings deposits. In fact, whereas during the 5th and 6th Five-Year Plans these rose to a peak near the middle of the plan-period, from then onwards (except in 1980) they have tended to reach a peak in the final year of the plan, that is to say when FNE also reaches a peak as a proportion of total budget spending, according to the mechanism set out in Chapter 10. Thus, the previous chronological pattern of savings bank deposits relative to the plan timetable has been overlaid by a new one. As it seems unlikely that this would result from any autonomous rescheduling of popular preferences, the cause needs to be sought in objective circumstances, which might well be found in the behaviour of FNE. If – as appears likely – this is in fact the connection, the behaviour of savings deposits is linked to that of budget spending generally.

While additions to savings deposits are comparable in magnitude with the excess of actual over forecast FNE they are, of course, much smaller than total FNE. However, these additions rose from 1.9 per cent of total actual FNE in 1951 to a peak of 11.0 per cent in 1970, since when the proportion has not declined appreciably: 1977 being 10.5 per cent. These are not negligible fractions. From the Seven-Year Plan

(1959–65) onwards, this proportion has been reaching a peak in the final year of the long-term economic plans: either falling initially and then continuously rising, or rising continuously throughout the plan period.

Changes in this proportion exhibit also the effects of changes in policy at strategic moments in the leadership succession. Post-Stalin (1953) it shot up from 2.5 to 6.7 per cent. It was evidently the intention at this time of the new government to favour consumers who, however, found themselves with little collective alternative to expand their savings deposits as the quantity of goods on sale did not keep pace with the growth of monetary demand. Post-Khrushchev (1965) the proportion again reached 6.7 per cent, though from the higher starting-point of 4.2 per cent the year before. While the equality of the proportions in 1953 and 1965 may have been coincidental, the coincidence is not without interest. The intention at both epochs to show greater favour to consumers was surely the same.

(8) Over the same widely dispersed five years SCM too was overspent, by a total of 2.32 bn. If that total could simply be added to the total of overspending of FNE, and their aggregate then related to the growth of savings deposits, the percentage growth of such deposits which might thereby be accounted for rises to 107 – a little more than we need.

(9) Considering now budgetary spending on defence: here higher than forecast outlays might generate additional savings by servicemen or anyone else whose emolument came from the *oborona* appropriation. But given that since 1963 neither over- nor underspending of defence is admitted in official statistics, the last three out of five final years of five-year plans (1965, 1970 and 1975) report no shortfall or excess. At face values, then, these statistics do not show defence as participating in any cycle that has as one of its eventual results the enlarging of credit investments. However, the implied perfect coincidence of planned and actual spending is not believable, as noted in Chapter 9 which alluded also to evidence for unequal degrees of visibility of budget spending on defence in successive post-war phases. Most likely the forecast defence vote has sometimes been exceeded in the third phase (1964 onwards), just as it sometimes was in the first. In that case, some fraction of the overspending now included under FNE in official statistics might be more accurately included within actual DEF. Such a re-sorting would shrink the large above-forecast outlays in FNE especially in 1970 and 1975, though with some damage to the theorem that FNE rises towards the end of a five-year plan, and

without altering the fraction of changes in savings deposits that can be attributed to total overspending within *all* the three main spending clauses.

(10) If budget expenditures are involved in the growth of savings deposits, it is extremely likely that the involvement extends back to budget revenues. The changeover from 1966 onwards to payments out of profits, divided threeways, replacing deductions from profits, represented a switch to a more complicated in-payment system, the total revenue from which not surprisingly proved harder for budget managers to predict. Thus, in the seven years preceding this change (1959–65 inclusive) the average deviation from planned deductions from profits (either excess or shortfall) was 3.1 per cent, whereas in the seven years immediately afterwards (1966–72 inclusive) it rose to 4.9 per cent. Over the same two periods the average deviation from planned turnover tax declined from 3.2 to 2.6 per cent. The divergent trends suggest that reliance to a smaller extent on TT made total budget revenue less predictable.

Overspending on FNE since 1965 has been accompanied by above-forecast receipts of PP, in a moderately close relationship: over 1966–72 by Spearman's rank correlation $R = 0.685$. The correlation between deviations in FNE and in TT over the same span is much weaker: $R = 0.335$. To the extent that revenues govern expenditures, a reason for massive growth of savings deposits may then be found in the changeover to a new division of budget revenues. This, of course, can be only a partial reason: the growth of deposits antedated the threefold split, and in absolute terms overspending of FNE has considerably exceeded above-forecast receipts of PP, and even of PP and TT put together. For instance, in 1970 overspending of FNE amounted to 11.1 bn roubles but above-plan receipts of PP and TT together to only 6.7 bn; moreover, in 1972 FNE was overspent by 2.3 bn, whereas receipts from PP and TT together were 2.5 bn *below* forecast. Above-plan receipts in these established revenue sources have generally fallen short of the amounts overspent by the FNE clause. How then was this overspending financed? Part of the answer may be found in above-forecast receipts from taxes outside TT and PP or from non-tax revenues. To the extent that the increase represents real values, another part of the explanation may be found in inflationary emission, as suggested by Birman (1980, pp. 96–7). The extent of such emission could be reduced by exclusion from the budget total of any portion which consisted merely of funds which were flowing in a circle between the budget and state enterprises.

REPUBLIC BUDGETS AND SAVINGS

Comparative savings deposits per person in the various republics must correspond at any rate fairly closely to their comparative living standards. (Their *ranking* should be shown correctly by the comparative levels of deposits, apart from any inter-republic differences in the average propensity to save; on the other hand, comparative differences in deposits should magnify differences in living standards, the deposits representing surpluses after making needed purchases.) Reckoning then by savings deposits *per capita*, the title of most prosperous republic has shifted away from the RSFSR to certain of the smaller republics. Between 1950 and 1960 Georgia gained a lead which it held throughout the 1960s, but in 1971 (rather surprisingly) the lead was claimed by Lithuania, which has held it ever since. Since 1972 the front-runners have been Lithuania, Armenia and Georgia (in that order), while − as in all previous years since 1950 − Moldavia has come last.

The distribution of savings bank deposits per head among republics has not become either much less or much more uneven. Judging by ratios of average deposits per head in the 15 republics since 1950, the distribution at first became more equal, then less equal, and most recently has become more equal again. (The ratios of highest to lowest per head deposits were: 1950, 1.947; 1960, 1.679; 1965, 1.804; 1970, 2.199; 1975, 1.989; 1977, 1.941). Thus according to this scale the end-result was almost the same as the starting point.

While this distribution by itself is of limited interest from the viewpoint of this book, there is an intriguingly close relationship between it and the size of republic budgets per head of the populations of the respective republics. A comparison of the 1965 forecast republic budgets with their per head budgets, based on their populations at 1 January 1966, yields by Spearman's ranking correlation 0.657, but if Kazakhstan and Georgia are excluded the correlation rises to 0.901, and if Belorussia is excluded as well, even to 0.965. The two main exceptions, Kazakhstan and Georgia, diverge from the norm in opposite directions: while in Kazakhstan savings deposits per head compare unfavourably with the size of the republic budget, in Georgia they compare favourably. In 1965, for example, Kazakhstan was first in per head budget but eleventh in per head savings deposits, whereas Georgia was eighth in its budget but first in its deposits. Belorussia too did well in its savings bank deposits relative to its budget, though not as markedly as Georgia. In all other republics the correlation between savings bank deposits and the size of the republic budget is strikingly close.

Does this generally near relationship occur because savings bank deposits depend on the size of the budget, or − on the contrary − does the budget depend on the size of savings bank deposits? Or do both depend on some third set of circumstances?

Kazakhstan's relatively big budget is largely due to federal subsidies. Although these apparently have not benefited the population of the republic proportionately, *some* benefit can be inferred from the republic's rise in the league table of savings bank deposits *per capita* from thirteenth place in 1940 and 1960 to eighth in 1970; though by 1977 the republic had fallen back to eleventh place. The Georgian divergence in the opposite direction is evidently the product of its own efforts, without federal assistance. For other years the picture is rather similar. In 1975 the rank correlation was 0.590; again Georgia had above-normal deposits, but so too and even more markedly had Azerbaydzhan and Turkmenia, while Kazakhstan again had below-normal deposits.

Since republics apart from Kazakhstan, and in some years certain others, have not received subsidies from the federal budget, their budgets must have depended primarily on the size of their own revenues. These in turn depend on the level of prosperity, which also governs the level of savings bank deposits. The broadest answer to our question is, therefore, that both the size of the budget and the size of savings bank deposits in a given republic are governed by the prosperity of that republic. But then why does the budget of Georgia not reflect that republic's relatively high level of prosperity? Apparently, private revenues are unusually high there relative to public revenues. A large part of the explanation may well lie in an unusually flourishing 'second economy', although the fact that Armenia apparently does not have at its disposal independent sources of savings whereas its circumstances should resemble those of Georgia sounds a warning note here. Another part of the explanation Georgia may share with Armenia. Since 1965, the second highest level of savings deposits per capita is found in Armenia, though this is only slightly better than its per head budget rating. Evidence for a booming non-public sector is therefore not so strong in Armenia as in Georgia. The two republics share a greatly above-average level of participation in scientific research (Hutchings, 1976, p. 32). Soviet scientists being well paid, the savings of Armenian and Georgian scientists doubtless help to swell total bank deposits in those republics.

GENERALISED INTERRELATION OF SAVINGS BANK
DEPOSITS WITH BUDGET AND EXTRA-BUDGET
EXPENDITURE

Neglecting minor influences and side-effects, the typical sequence is
apparently the following. Especially towards the end of the five-year
plan period, in their pursuit of plan fulfilment in terms of physical or
sold production even at the cost of overspending, business ministries
spend appreciably more than the sums forecast for them. Most of this
excess rather quickly winds up in the form of additions to citizens'
savings bank deposits. Since these amounts are not collectively spend-
able, the plan is in effect being fulfilled through a monetary confidence
trick – though, of course, this is normally true as regards inflationary
situations in general. However, this does not yet complete the cycle.
Additions to savings bank deposits then form the basis for increases in
credit from the Gosbank. Since 1963, the budget has been released
from the obligation to finance such loans. The timing seems to have
been very convenient for the Gosbank, since from about that time total
deposits in savings banks began to show such a dramatic rise. Through
this mechanism, a portion of budget expenditure in effect does double
duty: having helped at first to fund plan-implementation especially in
the final stages of a five-year plan, via consumer incomes it reappears
as savings bank deposits which, as the second stage in the process,
finance credit investments. These investments will in turn generate
earnings, production and retail turnover, and consequently payments
of turnover tax to the exchequer at a later stage, which still later will
contribute towards financing a further cycle of budget expenditure.

This generalised explanation – like all generalisations – can no
doubt be regarded as somewhat oversimplified and overdrawn. With
that reservation, we can give a rough answer to what happens to a
fraction of budgetary, especially FNE, expenditure: it winds up as
long-term popular savings. In effect, savings deposits are caught up in
a second cycle, which is analogous to the cycle of payments between the
budget and state enterprises, except that in this case the circulation is
arrested due to the combination of an institutional blockage and an
imbalance of demand and supply.

It could therefore be arguable that if – as already suggested – by
1980 savings deposits were entering a new phase, that may also have
been true of certain expenditures which those revenues directly or indirectly financed. As there is no single-line track leading from specific
revenues to specific expenditures, the evidence for that would have to

be deduced from comparable shifts of the right magnitude and occurring at the appropriate time.

The link between budget expenditure and savings extends to most of the individual republics, so far as total budget expenditure of those republics is concerned.

NOTES

1. Keese uses a series that is not quite the same as that quoted in statistical handbooks which are available to the present writer: for instance, he gives savings deposits in 1965 as 18.856 bn whereas Table 11.1 in this book gives 18.727 bn. However, any necessary correction would make scarcely any difference to the trend of deposits.

2. Relatively ambitious attempts have been made to measure Soviet inflation. In principle, one might construct price indices based on observation, to supplement and perhaps supersede the official retail price index, which excludes several relevant kinds of alteration. The present writer has at times set out to make such compilations, but the practical difficulties are great and while their results may be suggestive they cannot lead to scientifically based conclusions. David E. Howard and Steven Rosefielde have discussed this theme: the former advancing what he claimed to be a novel method, the latter rejecting it (Howard, 1976, pp. 599–608; Rosefielde, 1980, pp. 423–7). See in particular National Foreign Assessment Center (1979, pp. 1–9).

   The presence of repressed inflation has been strongly questioned by Portes: queues should be getting longer, and the gap between fixed and free marked prices should be getting wider, whereas in fact neither of these trends is observable (Portes, 1976). On the other hand, Dyker suggests that just raising the price for vodka may have had a considerable effect in mopping up excess demand (Dyker, 1981, p. 66). Moreover: (1) if people balance the benefit to themselves of being able to purchase a commodity against the disservice of having to queue for it, there will be a limit to the length of queues, especially given that shops are not open 24 hours a day and that people considering whether to join a long queue would be aware that supplies would be likely to run out before their turn came, (2) parallel markets exist for only certain commodities, and primarily for food, the demand for which has been satisfied to a much greater degree than for various kinds of durable goods, such as automobiles, where there is no parallel market. One returns here essentially to one (no. 6) of the reasons cited below for the growth of savings – that this has been contributed to by the style of enrichment. True, most recent reports suggest a sharp rise in the degree of relative dissatisfaction with the supply of food products, reversing (at least partially) point (2) above; one would then expect the price differential between fixed and free prices to widen, and if it did not, that would be rather persuasive evidence against repressed inflation. (The present writer, not having seen the original paper by Portes, relies in this case on the allusions to it in

Dyker, op. cit. The similarly named article by Portes in *Economica*, May 1977, seems to provide a more sophisticated argument.) According to Pickersgill (1976, pp. 142–3), rates of saving are not unusually high, but this seems to neglect the fact that in Soviet circumstances they ought actually to be unusually low. Her savings data go only up to 1971; since then, between 1971 and 1980, the total sum deposited in savings banks has almost trebled, whereas travellers' reports suggest no even remotely comparable jump in real incomes. Over the same period there has been a reduction in the number of days' stocks of goods carried by the retail trade network from 88 days to 76, due to 'inadequate balancing of supply and demand' (Lebedev and Lokshin, 1981, p. 117).

In sum, the arguments swirling around the fact or (less probably) non-fact of repressed inflation do not all point one way; however, they are being overtaken by evidence not so much of repressed as of actual inflation. Thus, according to Komin, to avoid losses in those industries it was necessary to raise coal prices by 42 per cent, that of commercial timber by 40 per cent, of ferrous metals by 20 and of non-ferrous metals by 14 per cent. Obviously there would be repercussions in many other areas of the economy (Komin, 1980, p. 35). A rise in the wages of coal-miners in the Ukraine by 27 per cent with miners in other areas due to receive similar increases (*Daily Telegraph*, 11 February 1982) apparently comprises in this industry the wages side of the package, which in every other country would be regarded as quite clearly inflationary.

However, the USSR is not 'every other country', and although if one were obliged to respond to a question 'Is there or is there not inflation in the USSR?', the answer would have to be affirmative, it is preferable to suggest more concretely what is happening. This is attempted in Chapter 12.

12 Summing-Up and Final Remarks

When assessing the degree of success, or of failure, of the Soviet budget it is important to distinguish between what might be called the achievements of the budget proper (or its failures), on the one hand, and those of the entire society and politico-economic system on the other. An economic evaluation of Soviet socialism is not the objective of this book. The consensus view among Sovietologists is that the USSR has enormously increased her military and industrial strength, and also has raised living standards very substantially but not as sharply as her military and industrial strength. What fraction of these achievements may rightly be attributed to the budget?

First, areas where Soviet successes are most manifest – military strength, building up the economy (in particular, industry) and social-ised aspects of the economy – are precisely those which have been the budget's direct concern. Personal consumption, which is not in the budget except where it is funded by payrolls of the military or of civil servants, has not grown so markedly or successfully. The coincidence makes out a good *prima facie* case for budgetary effectiveness.

The budget is structured so as to facilitate holding down revenues and expenditures rather than to expand them, which argues against ascribing to the budget the main responsibility for these achievements. But again, had it not been structured to exert a damping down effect on competing expenditures, the Soviet Union would not have found it possible to concentrate spending in what were seen as strategically vital areas. Thus, here too the budget's structure can claim at any rate an oblique responsibility.

A conglomeration of budgets of very different size and importance, the budget has exerted a centralised influence as regards revenue-gathering and thence on the authorisation of expenditure, although actual disbursement has been decentralised. Against this, the budget embodies a 'republic bias', which is borne out in the rather dissimilar behaviour of its union and republic sections.

Turning to the budget's role as repository and reservoir of state funds, one must be conscious of its huge scale and the tremendous intricacy of its contents. Only a collaborative and exactly regulated effort by a large number of people can ensure any adequate degree of control. Besides the difficulties of scale and complexity there are problems in principle of discovering what actual benefits can be expected from particular kinds of expenditures, and also procedural problems consisting in the fact that categories of financing become routine, and are consequently not subject to strict investigation. Education and science can be cited as illustrations in either case.

Even if to only a limited degree rational, the redistributive effect of the budget among branches of expenditure has been powerful, although it must be noted that the budget is not the only redistributive instrument. Since production takes place in a spatial dimension, and to the extent that individual districts or regions of the USSR have specialised on particular branches of output, the budget's impact on certain districts or regions has also been considerable. Redistribution does not appear to have had a comparably great impact on the economic status of whole republics, which has to be seen in the context of their very uneven size. The budgets of the different republics have grown at rates which are mainly governed by their particular circumstances. To the extent that redistribution has taken place, it is evidently for purposes of economic development rather than with the aim of equalising living standards. At the same time, the trend towards territorial rather than hierarchical subsidisation is noteworthy.

Analysis reveals not only what we may claim to know about the budget, but the considerable extent of our ignorance. Substantial residues are discovered at many points. The larger relative volume of unitemised forecast allocations to FNE from the budget alone than from all sources is especially noteworthy, together with the small proportion (about one-third) of FNE that consists of capital investment.

Division of the whole post-war period into three approximately equal parts proves helpful in the characterisation of budgetary trends: in particular, FNE was growing relative to total budget expenditure in the first and third sub-periods, declining in the second. The information flow changed following Zverev's replacement by Garbuzov.

Chronologically, the predominant feature of the budget is its rapid and persistent growth. This has not been at constant rates, but more nearly has been linear, however with one major discontinuity: the jump from 1962–5 onwards to larger annual increments. This two-stage upwards movement tends to swamp shorter-term fluctuations.

There seems to be little connection between the events recorded in budget legislative history and the course of quantitative series. If anything, the more stable has been the legislative procedure, the more rapid has been the expansion. The bias towards raising, as against lowering, initial forecasts of expenditure may find reflection in the overall growth of the budget. Dates of adoption of the budget law apparently affect forecast-fulfilment, and a part of the faster growth of the budget since about 1956 to 1958 can apparently be assigned to earlier adoption of the annual budget law.

A number of phenomena (the total budget, FNE, overspending, savings) exhibit expansionary trends. Over time, the budget is able to grow (or, of course, it might remain stable or decline). In practice the Soviet budget has exhibited an enormous expansion. This has been partly due to growth of an internal circular flow, but partly also to the price revision of 1967 and to an upward drift of prices resulting from replacement of lower-priced items by higher-priced ones. The primary source of budget growth is naturally to be found in expansion of the whole economy, with which the total budget has, on the whole, kept pace. However, the difficulty of accounting both for total revenue and for total expenditure increases the likelihood that both are inflated by currency emission or by some undisclosed unorthodox process. The budget grows also owing to the natural reluctance of enterprises to cease to avail themselves of budgetary grants, and owing to the continuing importance of types of expenditure with which the budget is exclusively associated.

Trends relating to the proportionate size of main expenditure categories are in several respects unexpected. One might imagine that a series of amounts of spending from all sources, rather than from the budget alone, would outline developments differently, or would make the reported trends and their interrelations more convincing. Yet so far as published figures are concerned, on the whole this is not the case. Defence being funded only from the budget, as a proportion of total expenditure from all sources this sum would look even smaller than it does already − and it already looked too small. Allocations to FNE from both budget and non-budget sources have risen at least as fast as budget allocations to FNE. Only as regards SCM does the inclusion of other sources modify the picture in a more understandable direction, but as the budget supplies much the larger fraction of allocations to SCM, the inclusion here of expenditure financed from other sources does not change the picture fundamentally. While SCM has been focused especially on education, the chief deliberate movement within SCM has been the expansion of spending on science, which most recently has been augmented also by large contributions from outside the budget.

Besides growth another chronological pattern is present, and is related to the sequence and timetable of the five-year plans. (The 6th FYP is assumed to have run its full course and to have been followed by a '7th' FYP.) The coincidence confirms the officially claimed relationship of dependence of the budget on the plan. The nature of the most prominent variation in budgetary series also confirms that dependence: FNE tends to peak at the beginning and end of five-year plans while the other main item of expenditure which has this periodicity of fluctuation, DEF, adopts a dovetailing sequence. This periodicity provides fresh confirmation of the ascendancy of the plan over the budget, and suggests also that in normal circumstances FNE, rather than DEF, is the independent variable. The same periodicity does not apply to SCM, which to a greater degree is governed by longer-term policies (scientific development) and influences (for example, demographic). The fact that FNE and DEF peak usually at different times reflects the restricted elasticity of budget funds at any given time. This cyclical sequence has become much less marked, but this is probably due at least in part to intentional obscuring or falsification of the total amount of defence spending. One consequence has been a reversal of the total budget's quinquennial rhythm.

A more striking dependence on the plan timetable has been shown in certain other series both inside and outside the budget: notably among the latter, Soviet exports of major arms to Third World countries in 1955–70. While the connections between these fluctuations have not been established reliably, the similarities suggest that these were potent.

Numerous other traces can be seen of cyclical behaviour, affecting ir particular elements of FNE: the investment sequence and the extent of overspending of FNE may be especially noted, and the cyclical behaviour of the republic section of the budget rather than of the all-union budget. The generalisation may be ventured that convexity is frequently associated with military expenditure, concavity always or almost always with expenditure on the economy.

There are also some traces of a biennial cycle, which suggests dependence on the procedures of budgetary composition rather than on the plan timetable.

As regards monetary circulation, savings and price changes: the budget does not appear to bear primary responsibility either for the marked inflation of the 1930s or for its virtual elimination after the Second World War, but here problems still remain of understanding exactly what happened. Overspending of forecast budget expenditures, especially relating to FNE, does seem to have contributed to the steep rise in savings bank deposits after 1961 − a rise which in turn enables larger loans to be made by the Gosbank.

The budget continues to be divided into three main expenditure clauses: FNE, SCM and DEF. Over time the first two of these, in particular FNE, have grown in relative importance. FNE, above all, has become so large that this alone, even if no other circumstances generated uncertainty, would shed doubt on the veracity of certain budget data. But while one cannot believe in the literal correctness of all the figures − such as the virtual coincidence since 1963 of forecast and actual DEF − nevertheless the key position of the budget within the national financial system and structurally close relationship to other political and economic arrangements preclude any supposition that the budget as a whole is falsified. When allowance is made for what is obviously unplausible, the budget behaves in ways which can be integrated with other aspects of the behaviour of the economy. Moreover, the characteristic features of budget behaviour shed light on the working of the economy which could be obtained in no other way.

In particular, the budget fills out the evidence for the existence at many points of a plan-cycle, which is related to the chronology of the five-year plans. Whoever has long been convinced of the prevalence in the Soviet economy of fluctuations which are related to the duration of the five-year plans will find here little to evoke surprise. However, the evidence of cyclical behaviour may come as a surprise to some students of the system. They will be welcome to rework any of the analyses.

On the other hand, if we may judge by the fact that Sovietologists have not noticed these fluctuations, they evidently are not derived automatically from motivations or mechanisms which are external to the budget. They reflect an interaction between these motivations and mechanisms, on the one hand, and the budget's inherent structure and nature on the other hand: above all, the unequal elasticity of its parts and the restricted elasticity of total budgetary expenditures and revenues within an annual time-span. The key to deciphering how the budget behaves, and how this behaviour will influence what decisions are taken to expand or contract its scope, to alter the proportions of its internal structure, or to make other changes, is to be found in the manner in which it responds to internal and external tensions.

While the periodicity of the quinquennial fluctuations is clearly determined by the duration of the five-year plans, the fact they are present at all implies the existence of a financial mechanism for re-distributing funds within a relatively short time-span and in step with current priorities, and therefore also of a good system of control and communication.

The behaviour of the budget also sheds considerable light on trends which lead up to, or which follow, major announced decisions in the management and structure of the economy. It can be likened to a sensitive gauge which registers incipient changes or their aftermath, and which therefore, if watched attentively, can give advance warning of such changes. This is true, for example, of the run-up to the *sovnarkoz* reform of 1957; a major change, even if not necessarily that precise one, was clearly foreshadowed in such phenomena as the greatly increased degree of overspending of republic budgets from 1953 onwards.

However, external evidence points to incorrect, in fact grossly understated, totals of defence spending, especially before 1961 and during the Brezhnev era. While if only budgetary evidence had been available this might not have been discovered, in fact, the behaviour of certain budget series lends to it additional support. This behaviour embraces both the behaviour of the defence series considered by itself and the relationship between that series and other budgetary series.

The principal source of caricature in the configuration of the budget relates to DEF. Whereas other elements, more properly includable within DEF, apparently formerly lurked within the residue, they are now more likely to be contained with FNE.

Two basic regularities can be distinguished, and are of assistance in suggesting directions in which the published figures need to be cor-rected. Firstly, there have been changes in the visibility of defence spending: a threefold phasing which is fairly closely related to changes in the leadership, and consequently to broader policy changes. In the most recent period, secretiveness in regard to defence spending has been intensified. Secondly, the plan-cycle – since it affects DEF – suggests at any rate probable directions of change at different moments in the plan timetable. While its total at least in recent years is unacceptable, the earlier behaviour of DEF relative to FNE within the time-frame of five-year plans does not appear irrational. The deliberate curtailment from 1963 onwards of the possibility of meaningful comparisons may be seen as confirmation that previous comparabilities were too revealing. The post-war upsurges of defence spending at intervals of 9–11 years must also be noticed. If that pattern is to be repeated, another peak or plateau will be reached in 1980–3. As up to the time of writing (November 1981) no increase has been announced, if the same pattern is to be repeated (despite the current phase of enhanced secretiveness) such an announcement cannot be long delayed.

The mysteries that still remain are ranging themselves in a pattern which suggests a way in which they may be generalised, and in some degree explained. The accelerated growth of budget totals after 1962–5 sets a problem in interpretation which is compounded by the later more rapid growth of FNE and by the earlier substitution of a trend dovetailing DEF and FNE for one dovetailing DEF and SCM. As regards major subdivisions of the expenditure totals, our problems of comprehension are distributed rather unevenly: in FNE and DEF, more than in SCM; in the union section of the budget rather than in its republic section; but also in revenues as well as in expenditures; and also outside the budget, in the heaping up of savings. However, it would seem that a consistent distortion has taken place: of the whole budget upwards; of FNE upwards; of savings upwards; of revealed DEF downwards. While this might be called an 'inflationary' trend, a more meaningful assessment would be that there has occurred a selective expansion, in which only certain components have shared – but they in an enhanced degree. The mechanism that produced this result has surely included: a rigid ceiling upon revealed DEF; the inclusion of some portion of actual defence spending within FNE; over time, a further enlargement of budgetary, in particular FNE, expenditure, generated by an undue rotation of funds; the re-emergence of sums overspent relative to budget forecasts under the aspect of excess popular savings; and very possibly too, an unitemised source of revenue, including perhaps credits received from the Gosbank (Birman, 1981, e.g. p. 199).

While it cannot be gainsaid that problems of comprehension remain in this entire sphere, there seems to be enough coherence in the published budget to justify its detailed analysis, especially as a uniquely wide range of elements is surveyed; so that such analysis can make an indispensable contribution towards improving understanding of the Soviet economy. Excessive claims in this direction must, of course, be avoided; in particular, deduced explanations which, although apparently consistent with the available evidence, are not confirmed in original sources, must be regarded as probable rather than absolutely certain.

Appendices

Appendix I

TABLE A.1 *Soviet budget revenues and expenditures, 1940–81 (billions of post-1961 roubles)*

Years		Total revenues	Total expenditures	Budget surplus	Union section of budget (expenditures)	Republic section of budget (revenues and expenditures)
1940	Forecast	18.40	17.99	0.41	13.71	4.29
	Actual	18.02	17.43	0.59	13.22	4.21
1941		21.68	21.61	0.08	16.97	4.64
		19.14	19.14	0.00	16.02	3.12
1942						
		18.28	18.28	0.00	16.07	2.21
1943						
		21.00	21.00	0.00	18.35	2.65
1944		24.96	24.96	0.00	21.47	3.62
		26.87	26.40	0.47	22.58	3.82
1945		30.77	30.77	0.00	25.92	5.23
		30.20	29.86	0.34	25.04	4.82
1946		33.35	31.94	1.41	25.40	6.54
		32.54	30.75	1.79	24.40	6.31
1947		39.42	37.41	2.01	29.18	8.23
		38.62	36.15	2.47	27.85	8.30
1948		42.91	38.80	4.11	30.00	8.80
		41.05	37.09	3.96	28.41	8.68
1949		44.60	41.54	3.06	32.29	9.24
		43.70	41.23	2.47	31.85	9.38
1950		43.32	42.79	0.52	33.13	9.66
		42.28	41.32	0.96	31.73	9.59
1951		45.87	45.15	0.72	35.40	9.75
		47.03	44.30	2.73	34.59	9.71
1952		50.89	47.70	3.19	37.82	9.88
		49.77	46.02	3.75	36.25	9.77
1953		54.34	53.06	1.28	42.79	10.26
		53.98	51.47	2.51	40.80	10.67
1954		57.25	56.28	0.97	44.32	11.96
		56.86	55.39	1.47	42.66	12.73
1955		59.02	56.35	2.67	43.61	12.73
		56.43	53.95	2.48	39.84	14.11

TABLE A.1 *(cont.)*

Years		Total revenues	Total expenditures	Budget surplus	Union section of budget (expenditures)	Republic section of budget (revenues and expenditures)
1956	Forecast	59.28	56.96	2.31	43.00	13.96
	Actual	58.59	56.35	2.24	38.76	17.59
1957		61.72	60.45	1.26	41.05	19.40
		62.69	60.73	1.96	32.19	28.54
1958		64.30	62.77	1.52	31.11	31.97
		67.24	64.27	2.97	30.22	34.05
1959		72.34	70.76	1.57	36.66	34.35
		74.01	70.40	3.61	31.56	38.84
1960		77.30	74.58	2.72	36.30	38.79
		77.10	73.10	4.00	30.10	43.00
1961		78.99	77.59	1.40	35.72	42.86
		78.00	76.30	1.70	30.70	45.60
1962		81.92	80.37	1.50	36.68	44.78
		84.31	82.15	2.15	34.2	48.0
1963		87.72	86.20	1.52	39.98	47.35
		89.54	87.0	2.54	36.0	51.0
1964		91.93	91.39	0.54	42.64	50.08
		94.41	92.23	2.18	38.8	53.4
1965		99.70	99.54	0.16	46.23	54.53
		102.32	101.62	0.70	43.2	58.4
1966		105.54	105.39	0.15	49.25	57.32
		106.30	105.58	0.72	51.8	53.8
1967		110.25	110.02	0.23	58.45	52.80
		117.16	115.24	1.92	59.3	55.9
1968		123.91	123.60	0.31	69.59	55.21
		130.84	128.56	2.28	69.9	61.7
1969		134.10	133.90	0.20	73.31	60.59
		140.03	138.53	1.50	72.0	66.5
1970		144.93	144.66	0.27	80.65	64.01
		156.70	154.60	2.10	80.6	74.0
1971		160.97	160.77	0.20	88.73	72.04
		165.96	164.15	1.81	84.9	79.3
1972		173.81	173.61	0.20	95.55	78.06
		175.11	173.22	1.89	89.6	83.6
1973		181.84	181.61	0.23	99.60	82.01
		187.78	183.98	3.80	96.1	87.9
1974		194.30	194.09	0.21	105.79	88.30
		201.32	197.38	3.94	101.7	95.7
1975		208.60	208.41	0.19	112.44	95.97
		218.77	214.52	4.25	109.7	104.8
1976		223.67	223.47	0.20	123.83	99.64
		232.23	226.74	5.49	119.8	106.9
1977		238.94	238.73	0.21	133.13	105.61
		247.82	242.79	5.03	126.2	116.6
1978		246.37	246.13	0.24	136.32	109.8
		265.81	260.22	5.59	132.4	127.8

TABLE A.1 *(cont.)*

Years	Total revenues	Total expenditures	Budget surplus	Union section of budget (expenditures)	Republic section of budget (revenues and expenditures)
1979	269.21	268.93	0.28	151.73	117.20
	281.53	276.37	5.16	144.1	132.3
1980	284.77	284.51	0.26	162.06	122.46
1981	298.36	298.16	0.20	167.49	130.87

SOURCES Soviet budget laws and statistical handbooks.

Appendix II

TABLE A.2 *Elements of Soviet budget revenues and expenditures, 1945–81 (billions of post-1961 roubles)*

	Revenues		Expenditures		
Years	Turnover tax	Deductions from profits	Defence	Finance of national economy	Social and cultural measures
1945 Forecast			13.79	6.47	6.61
Actual	12.31	1.69	12.82	7.43	6.27
1946			7.22	10.22	8.32
	19.02	1.62	7.26	9.57	8.04
1947			6.70	13.18	10.71
	23.99	2.26	6.64	13.27	10.65
1948			6.61	14.90	11.63
	24.75	2.65	6.63	14.75	10.56
1949			7.91	15.25	11.92
	24.55	4.10	7.92	16.19	11.60
1950			7.94	16.44	12.07
	23.61	4.04	8.29	15.79	11.68
1951			9.64	17.85	12.08
	24.78	4.78	9.34	17.94	11.89
1952			11.38	18.04	12.48
		5.84	10.86	17.88	12.28
1953			11.02	19.25	12.98
	24.36	7.03	10.78	18.10	12.88
1954			10.03	21.63	14.13
			n.a.	21.33	14.20
1955			11.21	22.23	14.70
	24.24	10.28	10.74	23.31	14.72
1956			10.25	23.72	16.15
	25.81	10.12	9.73	24.52	16.44
1957			9.77	24.47	18.84
	27.47	11.84	9.12	26.70	19.82
1958			9.63	25.72	21.22
	30.45	13.54	9.36	29.03	21.42
1959			9.61	30.89	23.22
	31.07	15.96	9.37	32.37	23.12
1960			9.61	32.85	24.78
	31.30	19.00	9.30	34.10	24.94

TABLE A.2 *(cont.)*

Years	Revenues		Expenditures		
	Turnover tax	Deductions from profits	Defence	Finance of national economy	Social and cultural measures
1961 Forecast			9.25	33.91	27.20
Actual	30.9	21.10	11.59	32.61	27.19
1962			13.41	32.47	28.75
	32.9	23.9	12.64	36.22	28.97
1963			13.89	34.54	31.00
	34.5	25.7	13.87	38.80	30.97
1964			13.29	38.75	32.80
	36.7	28.7	13.28	40.60	33.31
1965			12.79	42.36	37.45
	38.7	30.9	12.78	44.91	38.16
1966			13.43	43.85	40.38
	39.3	35.7	13.40	45.17	40.76
1967			14.50	46.92	42.92
	40.1	41.8	14.50	52.76	43.48
1968			16.70	50.19	45.81
	40.8	48.2	16.70	58.73	48.31
1969			17.70	58.32	51.12
	44.3	48.0	17.70	62.38	51.86
1970			17.85	63.48	54.85
	49.4	54.2	17.9	74.55	55.94
1971			17.85	77.03	58.52
	54.5	55.6	17.9	80.4	59.44
1972			17.90	82.63	62.94
	55.6	60.0	17.9	84.9	63.48
1973			17.90	86.53	67.51
	59.1	60.0	17.9	91.3	67.34
1974			17.65	95.11	70.28
	63.5	64.4	17.7	99.7	71.30
1975			17.43	102.63	76.82
	66.6	69.7	17.4	110.7	77.04
1976			17.43	114.45	80.51
	70.7	70.6	17.4	118.5	80.74
1977			17.23	123.39	83.85
	74.6	78.4	17.2	129.8	84.27
1978			17.23	125.66	87.63
	84.1	78.6	17.2	141.3	89.05
1979			17.23	144.39	91.27
	88.3	84.2	17.2	151.4	92.82
1980			17.12	149.39	97.22
1981			17.05	159.90	101.93

Note In some years the forecasts must have been revised. The table shows only the initial forecasts.

SOURCES Soviet budget laws and statistical handbooks.

Appendix III

TABLE A.3 *Elements of expenditures on finance of national economy, 1955–70 (actual) (billions of post-1961 roubles)*

Years	(1)	(2)	(3)	(4)	(5)	(6)	(7)
1955	10.95	2.52	3.32	1.07	1.85	0.09	0.90
1956	12.75	1.65	3.26	1.22	2.04	0.12	1.13
1957	13.08	2.36	2.83	1.73	2.13	0.13	1.52
1958	13.67	2.59	1.41	2.03	2.26	0.15	1.90
1959	14.88	3.41	0.11	3.21	2.54	0.15	2.75
1960	15.59	4.35	0.07	3.59	2.64	0.17	3.21
1961	15.81	6.10	–	1.77	2.48	0.19	3.65
1962	15.36	7.53	–	1.75	2.54	0.21	3.85
1963	17.29	7.80	–	2.16	2.51	0.21	0.97
1964	18.87	8.67	–	1.79	2.55	0.22	3.79
1965	20.99	6.77	–	2.27	2.59	0.24	4.23
1966	21.06	6.30	–	2.84	2.36	0.26	4.53
1967	23.53	6.96	–	4.92	2.35	0.27	5.05
1968	24.15	9.27	–	6.09	2.38	0.28	5.25
1969	24.68	10.85	–	6.43	2.56	0.32	5.89
1970	30.53	12.37	–	6.26	2.84	0.26	6.46

Legend (1) Industry and Construction; (2) Agriculture and Procurements; (3) Machine-Tractor Stations and Specialised Repair Stations; (4) Trade; (5) Transport; (6) Communications; (7) Housing and Communal Economy.

SOURCE *Gosudarstvennyy byudzhet SSSR i byudzhety soyuznykh respublik* (1962), p. 18.
Gosudarstvennyy byudzhet SSSR i byudzhety soyuznykh respublik (1966), p. 20.
Gosudarstvennyy byudzhet SSSR i byudzhety soyuznykh respublik 1966–70 gg.
(1972), p. 25.

Bibliography

Abouchar, Alan (1981) 'A Statistical Test of the Cyclical Soviet Arms Export Hypothesis', *Osteuropa-Wirtschaft*, June 1981.

Agursky, Mikhail and Hannes Adomeit (1979) 'The Soviet Military-Industrial Complex', *Survey*, Spring.

Aleksandrov, A. M. (ed.) (1965) *Gosudarstvennyy byudzhet SSSR* (Moscow).

Allakhverdyan, D. A. (1951) *Nekotoryye voprosy teorii sovetskikh finansov* (Moscow).

Allakhverdyan, D. A. (1961) *Finansy sotsialisticheskogo gosudarstva* (Moscow).

Ames, Edward (1965) *Soviet Economic Processes* (Homewood, Illinois: Richard D. Irwin).

Aspin, Les (1975) 'The Defense Budget and Foreign Policy: The Role of Congress', *Daedalus*, Summer.

Bahry, Donna (1980) 'Measuring Communist Priorities: Budgets, Investments, and the Problem of Equivalence', *Comparative Political Studies*, October.

Barkovskiy, N. D. and K. S. Kartashova (1966) *Kreditnoye planirovaniye v SSSR* (Moscow).

Becker, Abraham (1969) *Soviet National Income 1958–1964* (Berkeley: The Rand Corporation).

Bescherevynkh, V. V. (1976) *Kompetentsiya Soyuza SSSR v oblasti byudzheta* (Moscow).

Birman, Igor (1978) 'From the Achieved Level', *Soviet Studies*, April.

Birman, Igor (1980) 'The Financial Crisis in the USSR', *Soviet Studies*, January.

Birman, Igor (1982) *Secret Incomes of the Soviet State Budget* (Martinus Nijhoff).

Bobrovnikov, A. A. (1977) *Gosudarstvennyy byudzhet Rossiyskoy federatsii* (Moscow).

Bogdanova, Ye. (1970) *Ekonomicheskaya rabota v uchrezhdeniyakh gosudarstvennogo banka* (Moscow).

Bogolepov, M. I. (1935) 'Finansy na perevale vtoroy pyatiletkei', *Planovoye khozyaystvo*, no. 4.

Burt, Richard (1975) *Defence Budgeting: The British and American Cases*, Adelphi Paper no. 112 (London: The International Institute for Strategic Studies).

Chernomordik, D. I. (1936) *Ekonomicheskaya politika SSSR* (Moscow).

Clarke, Roger A. (1972) *Soviet Economic Facts* (London: Macmillan).

Davies, R. W. (1958) *The Development of the Soviet Budgetary System* (London: CUP).

Dyker, David A. (1981) 'Planning and the Worker', in L. Schapiro and J. Godson (eds), *The Soviet Worker* (London: Macmillan).

Dyskin, V. (1954) 'Bankovskiy kontrol' za proyektirovaniyem v stroitel'stve', *Finansy i kredit SSSR*, no. 2.

Ekonomicheskaya gazeta (1966) no. 23.

Ellman, Michael (1978) *Soviet Studies*, October.

Fitzlyon, Kyril (1969) 'Plan and Prediction', *Soviet Studies*, October.

Garbuzov, V. F. (1961) *Pravda*, 30 September.

Garbuzov, V. F. (1979) *Pravda*, 29 November.

Garbuzov, V. F. (1981) 'Osnovnyye napravleniya razvitiya sotsialisticheskoy ekonomiki i finansov v odinatsatoy pyatiletke', *Finansy SSSR*, no. 4.

Garetovskiy, N. V. (1978) *Finansy i kredit v desyatoy pyatilekto* (Moscow).

Garvy, George (1977) *Money, Financial Flows, and Credit in the Soviet Union* (New York: National Bureau of Economic Research Inc.).

Glushkov, N. (1977) *Pravda*, 5 January.

Glushkov, N. (1980) 'O dal'neyshem sovershenstvovanii planovogo tsenoobrazovaniya i ego vozdeystviya na povysheniye effektivnosti proizvodstva i kachestva raboty', *Planovoye khozyaystvo*, no. 6.

Gosudarstvennyy byudzhet SSSR i byudzhety soyuznykh respublik (1962 and 1966) (Moscow).

Gosudarstvennyy byudzhet SSSR i byudzhety soyuznykh respublik 1966–70 gg. (1972) (Moscow).

Gozulov, A. I. (1953) *Ekonomicheskaya statistika* (Moscow).

Green, Donald W. and Christopher I. Higgins (1977) *SOVMOD I. A Macroeconomic Model of the Soviet Union* (New York and London: Academic Press).

Gregory, Paul R. (1974) 'Economic Growth, US Defence Expenditures and the Soviet Defence Budget: A Suggested Model', *Soviet Studies*, January.

Gregory, Paul R. and Robert C. Stuart (1974) *Soviet Economic Structure and Performance* (New York: Harper and Row).

Gumpel, Werner *et al.* (1967) *Die Sowjetwirtschaft an der Wende zum Fünfjahresplan* (München – Wien: Günter Olzog).

Gusakov, A. D. (1974) *Planirovaniye denezhnogo obrashcheniya v SSSR* (Moscow).

Hedtkamp, Gunter (1974) *Das sowjetische Finanzsystem* (Berlin: Duncker and Humblot).

Holzman, Franklyn D. (1955) *Soviet Taxation* (Cambridge, Mass: Harvard University Press).

Holzman, Franklyn D. (1975) *Financial Checks on Soviet Defense Expenditures* (Lexington: D.C. Heath).

Howard, David H. (1976) 'A Note on Hidden Inflation in the Soviet Union', *Soviet Studies*, October.

Howe, Sir Geoffrey, *Daily Telegraph*, 11 March.

Hutchings, Raymond (1958) Studies in Soviet Industrial Development (Ph.D. thesis, University of London, unpublished).

Hutchings, Raymond (1961) 'The Origins of the Soviet Industrial Price System', *Soviet Studies*, July.

Hutchings, Raymond (1962a) 'Some Behavior Patterns of the Soviet Post-War Budget', *The ASTE Bulletin*, Fall.

Hutchings, Raymond (1962b) *Soviet Budget Defense Expenditures since 1940* (unpublished).

Hutchings, Raymond (1971a) *Soviet Economic Development* (Oxford: Basil Blackwell).

Hutchings, Raymond (1971b) *Seasonal Influences in Soviet Industry* (London: OUP for RIIA).

Hutchings, Raymond (1973a) 'Fluctuation and Interaction in Estimates of Soviet Budget Expenditures', *Osteuropa-Wirtschaft*, no. 1.

Hutchings, Raymond (1973b) 'Plan, Prediction and Fluctuation', in Werner Gumpel and Dietmar Keese (eds) *Probleme des Industrialismus in Ost und West* (Munich – Vienna: Gunter Olzog).

Hutchings, Raymond (1976) *Soviet Science, Technology, Design* (London: OUP for RIIA).

Hutchings, Raymond (1978a) 'Soviet arms exports to the Third World: a pattern and its implications', *The World Today*, October.

Hutchings, Raymond (1978b) 'Regular Trends in Soviet Arms Exports to the Third World', *Osteuropa-Wirtschaft*, June.

Hutchings, Raymond (1979) 'Recent Trends of Seasonality in Soviet Industry and Foreign Trade', in Franz-Lothar Altmann (ed.), *Jahrbuch der Wirtschaft Osteuropas*, Band 8 (Munich: Osteuropa-Institut).

Hutchings, Raymond (1981) 'Soviet Defense Spending: Towards a Reconciliation of Different Approaches', in Franz-Lothar Altmann (ed.), *Jahrbuch der Wirtschaft Osteuropas*, Band 9 (Munich: Osteuropa-Institut).

Hutchings, Raymond (1982) *Chronological Patterns in the Presentation of Soviet Economic Statistics* (Köln: Berichte des Bundesinstituts für ostwissenschaftliche und internationale Studien, No. 20–1982).

JEC (1980) *Allocation of Resources in the Soviet Union and China – 1979* (Hearings before the Subcommittee on Priorities and Economy in Government of the Joint Economic Committee Congress of the United States, Ninety-Sixth Congress, First Session) (Washington: US Government Printing Office).

JEC (1981) *Allocation of Resources in the Soviet Union and China – 1980* (Hearings before the Subcommittee on Priorities and Economy in Government of the Joint Economic Committee Congress of the United States, Ninety-Sixth Congress, Second Session) (Washington: US Government Printing Office).

Kaser, Michael (1970) *Soviet Economics* (London: Weidenfeld & Nicolson).

Keese, Dietmar (1968) 'Freiwillige Esparnis in der Sowjetunion', *Osteuropa-Wirtschaft*, no. 2.

Kennedy, P. M. (1977) 'British Defence Policy Part II: An Historian's View', *Journal of the Royal United Services Institute for Defence Studies*, December.

Komin, A. (1980) 'Zadacha soversheustvovaniya optovykh tsen i tarifov v promyshlennosti', *Planovoye khozyaystvo*, no. 5.

Kondrashev, D. (1952) 'Tsenoobrazovaniya v SSSR,' *Finansy i kredit*, no. 4.

Khrushchev, N. S. (1961) *Pravda*, 9 July.

Lavrov, V. (1955) 'Zadachi uluchsheniya finansovo-khozyaystvennoy deya-tel'nosti predpriyatiy' *Planovoye khozyaystvo*, no. 6.

Lavrov, V., R. Kudryashov and A. Shuvalov (1961) *Gosudarstvennyy byudzhet* (Moscow).

Lebedev, V. and Lokshin, R. (1981) 'Analiz tovarno-denezhnykh otnosheniy' (*Planovoye khozyaystvo*, no. 1).

Lee, William T. (1975) *The Credibility of the USSR 'Defense' Budget* (Santa Barbara: General Electric – TEMPO).

Lee, William T. (1976) 'Soviet Defense Expenditures', *Osteuropa-Wirtschaft*, June.

Lee, William T. (1977) *The Estimation of Soviet Defense Expenditures, 1955–75* (New York: Praeger).

Liberman, Ya. G. (1966) *Gosudarstvennyy byudzhet i problemy sotsialisti-cheskogo vosproizvodstva* (Moscow).

Liberman, Ya. G. (1970) *Gosudarstvennyy byudzhet SSSR v novykh usloviyakh khozyaystvovaniya* (Moscow).

Massarygin, F. S. (1968) *Finansovaya sistema SSSR* (Moscow).

Melnyk, Z. L. (1965) *Soviet Capital Formation – Ukraine 1928/29–1932* (Munich: Ukrainian Free University Press).

Mestnyye byudzhety SSSR (1960) (Moscow).

Millar, James A. (1980) 'Financing the Soviet Effort in World War II', *Soviet Studies*, January.

Narodnoye khozyaystvo SSSR v 1977 g. and for other years.

National Foreign Assessment Center (1977) *The Soviet State Budget since 1965* (Washington DC).

National Foreign Assessment Center (1979) *An Analysis of the Behavior of Soviet Machinery Prices, 1960–1973* (Washington DC).

Nove, Alec (1980) *The Soviet Economic System*, 2nd edn (London: Allen & Unwin).

Ostrovityanov, K. V. *et al.* (1955) *Politicheskaya ekonomiya* (Moscow).

Pallot, Judith and Denis J. B. Shaw (1981) *Planning in the Soviet Union* (London: Croom Helm).

Pickersgill, J. (1976) 'Soviet Household Savings Behaviour', *Review of Economics and Statistics*, May.

Piskotin, M. I. (1971) *Sovetskoye byudzhetnoye pravo* (Moscow).

Plotnikov, K. N. (1954) *Ocherki istorii byudzheta sovetskogo gosudarstva* (Moscow).

Portes, Richard D. (1977) 'The Control of Inflation: Lessons from East European Experience', *Economica*, May.

Rosefielde, Steven (1980) 'A Comment on David Howard's Estimate of Hidden Inflation in the Soviet Retail Sales Sector', *Soviet Studies*, July.

Rudolph, Vladimir (1953) in Robert Slusser (ed.) *Soviet Economic Policy in Postwar Germany* (New York: Research Program on the USSR).

Safronov, A. M. (1957), *Izvestiya*, 7 February.

Schroeder, Gertrude (1976) 'A Critique of Official Statistics on Public Administration in the USSR', *The ACES Bulletin*, Spring.

Sharlet, Robert (1978) *The New Soviet Constitution of 1977* (Brunswick, Ohio: King's Court Communications).

Shvedskiy, A. (1946) 'Ukrepit' platezhnuyu distsiplinu khozorganov,

Sovetskoye finansy, nos 7–8.

Sitaryan, S. A. (1968) *Khozyaystvennaya reforma i byudzhet* (Moscow).

Stec, George (1955) *The Local Budget System of the USSR* (New York City: Research Program on the USSR, Mimeographed Series no. 75).

Suchkov, A. K. (1945) *Dokhody gosudarstvennogo byudzheta SSSR* (Moscow).

Tsypkin, S. D. (1973) *Dokhody gosudarstvennogo byudzheta SSSR* (Moscow).

Tul'chinskiy, Ye. (1945) 'O dopol'nitel'nykh istochnikov finansirovaniya kapital'nogo stroitel'stva', *Sovetskiye finansy*, nos. 1–2.

Turetskiy, Sh. Ya. (1936) *Plan*, no. 18.

Turetskiy, Sh. Ya. (1948) *Vnutripromyshlennoye nakopleniye v SSSR* (Moscow).

US Defense Intelligence Agency (1981) *Soviet Weapons Production* (US Embassy, London: International Communication Agency).

Vaynshteyn, E. (1957) *Razvitiye bankovskoy sistemy kassovogo ispolneniya gosudarstvennogo byudzheta* (Moscow).

Vladimirov, L. (1971) *The Russian Space Bluff* (London: Tom Stacey).

Voluyskiy, N. M. (1970) *Svodnyy finansovyy plan* (Moscow).

Voznesenskiy, N. A. (1946) *Voyennaya ekonomika SSSR* (Moscow).

Wagener, Hans-Jürgen (1969) 'Die RSFSR und die Nichtrussischen Republiken: ein Ökonomischer Vergleich', *Osteuropa-Wirtschaft*, no. 2.

White, Stephen (1982) 'The Supreme Soviet and Budgetary Politics in the USSR', *British Journal of Political Science*, January.

Wimberley, J. (1981) 'The Soviet Financial Crisis? A Comment', *Soviet Studies*, July.

Yevdokimov, V. A. (1974) *Kontrol' za ispolneniyem gosudarstvennogo byudzheta SSSR* (Moscow).

Yezhov, A. I. (1965) *Sistema i metodologiya pokazateley sovetskoy statistiki* (Moscow).

Zlobin, I. D. (1971) *Finansy SSSR* (Moscow).

Zverev, A. G. (1946) *Gosudarstvennyy byudzhety Soyuza SSSR 1938–1945 gg.* (Moscow).

Zverev, A. G. (1966) *Problemy tsenoobrazovaniya i finansy* (Moscow).

Zverev, A. G. (1970) *Natsional'nyy dokhod i finansy SSSR* (Moscow).

Zverev, A. G. (1973) *Zapiski ministra* (Moscow).

Zwick, Peter R. (1979) 'Ethnoregional Socio-Economic Fragmentation and Soviet Budgetary Policy', *Soviet Studies*, July.

Index